K2
The Savage
Mountain

CHARLES S. HOUSTON, M.D.
ROBERT H. BATES

and Members of the Third American
Karakoram Expedition

Foreword by Jim Wickwire

Additional art by Dee Molenaar

The Mountaineers
Seattle

THE MOUNTAINEERS: Organized 1906 ". . . To encourage a spirit of good fellowship among all lovers of outdoor life."

Published by
The Mountaineers
719 Pike Street
Seattle, Washington 98101

Published simultaneously in Canada by
Douglas & McIntyre Ltd.
1875 Welch Street
North Vancouver, British Columbia

Published simultaneously in Great Britain by
Diadem Books Ltd.
85 Ballards Lane
London N3

Manufactured in the United States of America

Library of Congress Catalog Card Number 78-71666
ISBN 0-916890-73-2

Foreword

IN THE ANNALS of Himalayan mountaineering, the American expedition to K2 in 1953 stands out as one of the most gripping sagas of man's thrust to reach the highest summits. Displaying an abundance of courage, tenacity, and strength in the face of almost overwhelming odds against their safe return, the Charles Houston-led team survived a severe 10-day storm high on K2 and an accident that almost ended in disaster when virtually the entire team was injured in a fall down the mountain's steep upper slopes while attempting to evacuate Art Gilkey, who had developed thrombophlebitis. Hillary and Tenzing's climb to the top of Everest that same summer provided the world with electrifying news; but the events on K2 are the stuff of legends and seem even more compelling with the passage of time. Somehow, the K2 climbers' struggle with wind, storm, sickness, and high altitude seems more poignant than other climbs that achieved success.

With the reissue of *K2, The Savage Mountain*, The Mountaineers continue a program of bringing out-of-print mountaineering classics to the public. *K2, The Savage Mountain,* by Charles Houston, Robert Bates, and other members of the third American Karakoram Expedition, chronicles the 1953 expedition's valiant attempt to reach the summit of the world's second highest peak. A common bond of brotherhood enabled these men to survive one of the epic experiences of Himalayan mountaineering history.

The 1953 expedition, like its predecessors in 1938 and 1939, was carried off in the finest style. Lightweight by contrast with other Himalayan expeditions of the same period, these American attempts on K2 came very close to success. This new edition of *K2, The Savage Mountain* is enhanced by the addition of a never-before-published transcript of a tape recording made at base camp of the climbers' account of their final climb and ordeal, new material from each team member on his experiences in the 25 years following the expedition, and Dee Molenaar's excellent sketches of the mountain and surrounding environs. Except for Art Gilkey, who perished on the descent, and the late Col. M. Ata-Ullah, the entire team celebrated a 25-year reunion in the Wind River range last summer, where the reminiscences developed that led to this edition.

K2 was finally climbed in 1954. An Italian team under the leadership of Professor Ardito Desio, who had explored the area around K2 in 1929 with the Duke of Spoleto, came not merely to climb K2, but in Desio's words, "to conquer the mountain." Taking the same route that the three previous American expeditions had pioneered, Achille Compagnoni and Lino Lacedelli walked onto the summit at 6:00 p.m. on July 31, oxygen-starved from having their bottles run out a few hundred feet below the summit.

Six years later, an American-German expedition, led by Bill Hackett, attempted the Abruzzi Ridge, but did not get above 24,000 feet. For 14 years thereafter, the contested border between Pakistan and China made K2 and other Baltoro peaks off-limits to mountaineering expeditions and trekkers. Finally, with the thawing of relations between the two countries and a desire on the part of the Pakistani government to promote tourism to its country's mountainous regions, the Baltoro was reopened in 1974.

A Polish team was given permission to attempt K2 that summer but could not field an expedition in time to take advantage of the permit. Bob Bates, a veteran of the 1938 and 1953 expeditions, and Adams Carter and their wives Gail and Ann were able to walk to the base of K2 during the summer and reconnoitered the Savoia Glacier on the mountain's west side. In 1975 another American expedition, this time led by Jim Whittaker, tried a new route.

Plagued by porter difficulties, storms while on the mountain, and sickness among the small team of eight climbers, the expedition gave up its attempt to reach the summit via the unexplored Northwest Ridge in early July. At the 22,000-foot high point, a series of sharp towers blocked further progress. A year later, a strong Polish expedition, led by Janusz Kurczab, made a magnificent try along the lengthy and difficult Northeast Ridge. After a series of storms delayed the expedition's upward movement, two climbers, Eugeniusz Chrobak and Wojciech Wroz, succeeded in climbing through the major difficulties of the headwall on the summit pyramid. At 27,550 feet, they turned back at 7:00 p.m. on August 15, halted by a sudden storm that greatly complicated their descent. Of all the unsuccessful expeditions to challenge K2, the Poles came the closest to victory.

In 1977 a massive Japanese expedition, composed of 50 climbers and 10 Hunza high-altitude porters, assaulted the well-traveled Abruzzi Ridge. The Japanese succeeded in two of four summit attempts, with six Japanese and one Pakistani, Ashraf Aman, reaching the summit. Oxygen and fixed ropes were used above the highest camp at 26,500 feet. Despite its success, this expedition represented a substantial departure from the smaller-size expeditions of the past. Some question whether *any* Himalayan peak merits the size of climbing party that the Japanese employed.

The Americans returned in 1978 for a sixth attempt. Fourteen climbers led by Jim Whittaker were able to complete the difficult Northeast Ridge route. Deep snow conditions and avalanche hazards on the summit pyramid prevented the team from completing the Polish route to the summit. Instead, a risky traverse was made beneath the summit icecliff to a high camp at 25,800 feet near the upper Abruzzi route. From there, Lou Reichardt and I climbed to the summit on September 6, 1978. John Roskelley and Rick Ridgeway repeated the climb a day later.

* * * * *

As I neared the summit in the fading light of late afternoon, I was filled with a sense of history and admiration for what had gone on before. I could look down to where Charlie Houston's team had withstood the storm 25 years before. The site of the accident was clear. I could see the famous Abruzzi Ridge, which dropped off at nearly right angles to the Godwin-Austen Glacier far below. As Lou Reichardt and I walked those last few steps to the summit, I could feel the presence of Charlie Houston, Bob Bates, Fritz Wiessner, Pete Schoening, and the others who, but for the vagaries of storm and circumstance, would have been there ahead of us. Somehow, reaching the summit of K2 seemed less important than the magnificent efforts of all who had preceded us.

JIM WICKWIRE

Seattle, Washington
December 1978

Aerial view
from southwest

——— American, 1953
——— Italian, 1954; Japanese, 1977
– – – American, 1975
– · – · British, 1978
· · · · · American, 1978

28,250

Savoia
Pass

NW Ridge

Skyang
Kangri

Windy
Gap

Abruzzi Ridge

NE Ridge

Godwin-Austen GI

S Ridge

W Ridge

Avalanche

The Angelus

1953
Base Camp

Base Camp
Savoia GI

Gilkey-Puchoz
Memorial

CHARLES S. HOUSTON, M.D.
ROBERT H. BATES

and Members of the Third American
Karakoram Expedition

COL. M. ATA-ULLAH
ROBERT H. BATES
GEORGE I. BELL
ROBERT W. CRAIG
ARTHUR K GILKEY
CHARLES S. HOUSTON, M.D.
DEE MOLENAAR
PETER SCHOENING
CAPT. H. R. A. STREATHER

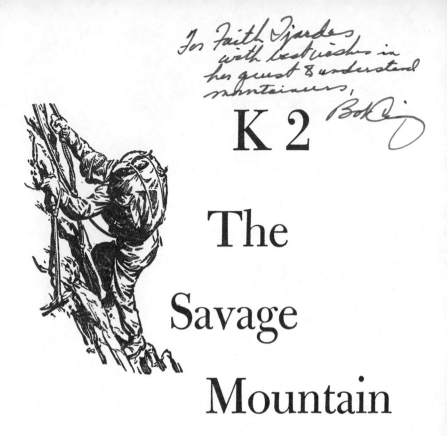

For Faith Fjardes
with best wishes in
her quest 8 understand
mountaineers,
Bob ...

K 2

The

Savage

Mountain

Maps and line drawings by Clarence Doore

Illustrations from photographs taken by
Members of the Expedition

McGRAW-HILL BOOK COMPANY, INC.
New York   Toronto   London

To Art Gilkey

WILLIAM P. HOUSE

Member, First American Karakoram Expedition (1938)
Treasurer, Third American Karakoram Expedition (1953)

Preface

Himalayan mountaineering is a type of exploration which must be conducted within very exacting limitations, both physical and human. They are so exacting that there is little margin for error or bad luck. With the best of planning and expedition management they make the chances for success so slim that only a very fortunate combination of events can bring the summit within reach. It is not surprising, therefore, that many years of determined efforts by strong parties can go by with a major summit still unattained.

Only rarely have the Himalayan giants been overcome on the first major attempt. Generally they have resisted attacks through several generations of climbers and have required a slow, painful build-up of information and experience over many years of effort. This gradually produces a clearer picture of the obstacles that must be overcome, and at the same time skills and techniques to cope with them are developed and perfected. Finally the stage is set, the right combination of party, mountain condition, weather, and luck come together—and the mountain is climbed.

The importance of the achievement is primarily in the skill, judgment, and courage of the team. Beyond that, however, and of even more lasting significance, is the fact that the final success is built on the past efforts of many others—often of different nationalities and races. They have known the bitter disappointment of defeat, tempered only slightly by the realization that they had exerted their best efforts. Only when the mountain is climbed can their struggles be seen in true perspective as positive, hard-won steps toward a common goal. Then the pioneers can justly share in the victor's accomplishment and be truly happy that their summit has at last been reached.

My thoughts were hardly so objective as my friends and I retreated from the upper slopes of K2 on the First American Karakoram Expedition sixteen years ago. We realized then on that earlier expedition that the summit was not to be ours and that problems of supply and approaching bad weather demanded immediate descent. It softened our disappointment to know that we had unlocked some of the mountain's major secrets, and that a practical route had been established to within striking distance of the summit. We thought we had a clear picture of the mountain, and there was little doubt in our minds that another strong party —perhaps including some of us—given reasonable luck with weather, would make the summit.

However, in 1938 we were never able fully to assess the weather hazard, although we had plenty of respect for it, or to comprehend clearly the problems of evacuating a sick or injured member of the party from high on the mountain, let alone a combination of both. The experience of the next two expeditions showed that the picture was fainter than we thought and that we had only partially understood the mountain's defenses. The 1953 expedition, whose heroic story is told in this book, brought the picture into sharper focus. Its members brought back a truer picture of weather problems which will be invaluable to future expeditions to K2. More important, they demonstrated that a strong, well organized and equipped party could survive prolonged exposure to severe weather and still retreat in good order over an extremely difficult route.

Though defeated in its attempt, the 1953 expedition's success in overcoming almost impossible problems of survival will continue to give strength and encouragement to mountaineers in peril on the high peaks.

Contents

CONTENTS

Illustrations

ILLUSTRATIONS

CHARLES S. HOUSTON

Introduction

As this book goes to press, word has been received of Professor Desio's magnificent success on K2. Plagued by weather as bad as or worse than we encountered, facing other obstacles which we were spared, this gallant party laid siege to the mountain for two and a half long months. Thanks to brilliant leadership and meticulous planning, a pair of climbers were able to take full advantage of a brief clearing in the weather, and the summit fell. It is fitting that these successors of Luigi Amedeo, Duke of the Abruzzi, should have won the prize, and those of us who had the good fortune to visit this great mountain, to run our brief race in 1938 and 1953, applaud our Italian friends.

Like Everest, K2 was climbed by a large party equipped with every aid. Nothing was spared to ensure success. Oxygen was used, though apparently not to the very summit, and thousands of feet of nylon rope were employed to make a literally continuous handrail up the ever-steepening ridge. The spearhead pair were repeatedly replaced by fresh teams recuperated at Base Camp. It is sad that their success is shadowed by the death of Mario Puchez, who died suddenly of pneumonia at Camp III.

No mountain is climbed by one man or two. Behind them stand the shadows of dozens of others who tried, hoped, and failed. In their failure they gained much, and they look with pride, respect, but with sadness too at those who won.

K 2—The Savage Mountain

1. The call to climb

CHARLES S. HOUSTON

1. The call to climb

During the terrible days of storm at Camp VIII we thought seldom of the reasons which had brought us to the mountain; all our energy was focused on survival. We were trapped in three small mountain tents near the summit of the highest unclimbed mountain on earth, trapped by an endless storm of wind and snow which made impossible advance or retreat. All eight of us had been working for two months to establish this high camp and another one still higher from which two men might reach the top. All eight of us and many others had been planning for a year to make the expedition possible. During the ten days of hardship and disappointment, of pain and tragedy, which climaxed our venture, we spoke of the summit and of home, we remembered other storms and other critical times. No one tried to answer the question then, "Why? Why climb mountains?"

In the year that has passed since our ordeal we have been asked that question many times and have answered it in many ways. No answer is complete or satisfactory. Perhaps there is no single answer; perhaps each climber must have his own reasons for such an effort. The answer cannot be simple; it is compounded of such elements as the great beauty of clear cold air, of colors beyond the ordinary, of the lure of unknown regions beyond the rim of experience. The pleasure of physical fitness, the pride of conquering a steep and difficult rock pitch, the thrill of danger—but danger controlled by skill—are also there. How can I phrase what seems to me the most important reason of all? It is the chance to be briefly free of the small concerns of our common lives, to strip off nonessentials, to come down to the core of life itself. Food, shelter, friends—these are the essentials, these plus faith and purpose and a deep and unrelenting determination. On great mountains all purpose is concentrated on the single job at hand, yet the summit is but a token of success, and the attempt is worthy in itself. It is for these reasons that we climb, and in climbing find something greater than accomplishment.

This is the story of an expedition that failed to reach its summit. It is the story of a venture made for sport and not for gain, of a small, compact expedition rather than a large and organized campaign. But more than that, it is the story of a team of men from three nations, a team that tried and tried again, that faced privation and danger, that suffered much but gained more. In a tiny way ours is the story of other ventures, bigger, older, braver, but ventures which have made and will make man great. As Maurice Herzog said, speaking of his ordeal on another great Himalayan peak, "There are other Annapurnas in the lives of men."

2. Historical and geographical

ROBERT H. BATES

2. Historical and geographical

In Central Asia, 5 miles higher than all the oceans, thousands of tons of ice and snow hang from the precipitous south side of K2, the second highest mountain in the world. Here for a few days in the summer of 1939 a tiny tent with one American in it clung to a small shelf of snow, which projected out above thousands of feet of empty space. In this tent, remote from civilization, lay Dudley Wolfe of Boston, cut off completely from his closest companions, who were thousands of feet below him. Then, on July 28, 1939, two Sherpa porters, Pasang Kikuli and Tsering, made one of the most amazing climbs in mountaineering history. In one day they ascended nearly 7,000 feet of dangerous rock and snow to reach Camp VI at 23,300 feet on K2. On the way they were joined by two other Sherpas, who had previously climbed to Camp IV. These four men spent that night on a narrow ledge of rock 1,500 feet below the snow shelf where Dudley Wolfe lay trapped in his tent without communication with those below. He could not descend alone. His rescuers had food and fuel for only two days. They were risking their own necks in going so high with such a slender food supply, but another man's life was at stake.

Next day three of the Sherpas climbed up a dangerous gully above Camp VI and across steps previously cut in a great ice slope that drops off 7,000 feet in one precipitous swoop to the base of K2. Beyond, on a relatively flat and protected space, they found Dudley Wolfe. Exposure to altitude had weakened him, so that when the Sherpas reached his tent he was almost too feeble to stand. He was too weak to climb down the mountain but too heavy for the porters to carry. The Sherpas cooked him a meal and explained that they had little food at the camp below but would come back for him. The next day, when they climbed up to him again across the dangerous slabs, he was to come with them or give them a note saying that he was done for, too far gone to make the descent. The weather, they told him, would almost certainly prevent any further rescue attempt.

Weather was stormy next morning, but on July 31, the same three Sherpas said good-by to Tsering at Camp VI and set out on their last trip to Camp VII, where Dudley Wolfe was awaiting them. They were never seen again! Nor has any trace been found of the brave man they sought to rescue.

From that month until June, 1953, nobody set foot on K2, although the challenge of this stupendous mountain was not diminished by the tragedy. Instead, the mystery of what had happened to the four men of the Second American Karakoram Expedition in 1939 increased the challenge of the mountain; for K2 has long been a lodestone pulling men to the unknown magnificence of the Karakoram Range, to the "mountaineer's mountain." But few people know the geographic position or history of exploration in this remote area.

Among the great mountain ranges of the world, none is so famous for giant peaks and untrodden passes as the mighty Himalayas, which for 1,500 miles separate the dry plateaus of Central Asia from the moist and fertile regions to the south. But the Himalayas do not form the continental divide. Instead, the height of land is formed by lower ranges, even more remote from centers of population, that run east and west across Tibet and join to the west with the jagged backbone of the Karakoram Range.

The Karakoram, a massif of wild, forbidding peaks, is located north and slightly west of the Himalayas, and extends for 300 miles from the Shyok River to the Hindu Kush Range. Within this 300-mile sweep, one-fifth the extent of the Himalayas, the Karakoram has the longest high rampart in the world, a continuous crest of high peaks 104 miles long. The Karakoram has thirty-three peaks over 24,000 feet compared to the forty-two in the entire system of the Himalayas, while within 18 miles of K2 eight peaks rise to over 25,000 feet, and others of equal height are not far away. The Karakoram Range consists of several smaller groups, called *muztaghs* (*muz* meaning ice and *tagh*, mountain), the highest of which, the Baltoro Muztagh, forms the continental divide and has as its dominant point 28,250-foot K2. Probably nowhere in the world do so many giant peaks rise from so small an area as in the Baltoro Muztagh.

The name Karakoram, which means black rock, sometimes deceives people, for it was also the name of a prosperous city in Chinese Turkestan north of the mountains. This was the Mongol capital under the great emperor Genghiz Khan, but after Kublai Khan moved the capital to Peking in 1267, this great city began to decline and eventually was so completely swallowed up by the desert that its remains were not rediscovered until 1889. Although the Karakoram Pass, some 75 miles to the east of K2, is still used, and the Karakoram Range is known to mountain climbers across the world, the man-made city of Karakoram has disappeared beneath the sands of Central Asia.

The name K2 was one of a number of provisional designations given by the Survey of India. K stood for Karakoram, and the peaks of the area were numbered in rough order. K1 was later called Masherbrum, and K3, K4, and

K5 became known officially as the Gasherbrum peaks. To add to the confusion, at one time it was decided to renumber the peaks to produce continuity from west to east, and accordingly, in some early publications *K2 was renamed K13!* The symbol K2 had already become widely known around the world, however, and this confusing duplication of symbols was quickly eliminated and K2 became again K2. That is still its official name.

To complicate matters still further, however, K2 on many maps is called Godwin-Austen, for Maj. Gen. H. H. Godwin-Austen, a well-known English geographer and surveyor of the mid-nineteenth century. Among other names suggested have been Mount Waugh, Mount Albert, Mount Akbar, and Mount Baber, but none has been adopted. Nor has the name of Godwin-Austen been accepted, even though it adorns many maps, and though the man so honored has carved on his tombstone the words "He surveyed the Karakoram." Explorers and topographers have tried to discover an established native name for the giant rock and ice mountain. Although Chogori, Lamba Pahar, Dapsang, and Lanfafahad have been mentioned, today natives in adjacent areas appear most likely to call it Kechu (K2) or Cheku or even Kechu Kangri (K2 Ice Mountain).

The exact altitude of K2 was also a source of controversy for a number of years, but as the Survey of India has pointed out, the height of K2 has probably been measured as accurately as the height of any of the world's highest

33

mountains. The height first given by the survey was 28,278 feet, but "the value now accepted is 28,250 feet." Mount Everest is officially listed as being 752 feet higher and Kangchenjunga 104 feet lower; but such accurate judgments are of course impossible.

Everest and the other great Nepalese peaks rise about 900 miles to the east of K2. Between these giants stretch Buddhist Ladakh and Tibet, while north and northwest lie the uncharted wastes of Chinese Turkestan and Russian Turkestan and, even farther to the west, Afghanistan. K2 obviously has a fascinating geographical position. Almost exactly on the opposite side of the Northern Hemisphere from Denver, Colorado, K2 has approximately the same latitude as North Carolina and Tokyo. Like Mount Everest, the country to the north of K2 is at present Communist-dominated but, unlike Everest, the international boundary appears to lie well north of the mountain. Fortunately, too, the least accessible side to reach from Pakistan is the north side—the side that appears to be the most difficult to climb. This side was seen by Younghusband in 1887 and later by Shipton and Tilman of the Shaksgam Expedition in 1939, but they made no careful examination of the precipitous north wall. The other thirty-three expeditions to visit the Karakoram apparently never saw this side.

The first European to see K2 was probably the surveyor Montgomerie in 1858, but Godwin-Austen and others of Montgomerie's party apparently saw it while surveying the

lower Baltoro Glacier in 1861. This group did not get to the base of K2, nor did Sir Martin Conway, who in 1892 explored the Baltoro Glacier to Concordia. Just as Conway profited by the experience of his predecessors in the Karakoram, so Eckenstein, who had been with Conway, used Conway's map in 1902 when his party explored the Godwin-Austen Glacier and found at its head Windy Gap, a possible pass into Chinese Turkestan. This party made the first attempt to climb K2. It consisted of three Englishmen (Eckenstein, Crowley, and Knowles), two Austrians (Drs. Wesseley and Pfannl), and the Swiss Dr. Guillarmod. On July 10, 1902, they attempted to climb to the crest of the long Northeast Ridge, but were turned back about 150 feet below the crest at a height of approximately 21,400 feet. Steep snow with hard ice under it defeated them, but bad weather was also a severe handicap. On July 21, 1902, Eckenstein wrote, "We established our Camp X, height about 18,600 feet, just 49 days ago. Since then we've had 8 partially fine days (no 3 consecutive) and the rest of the time continuous snowstorms. Never anywhere in the world have I experienced such bad weather. Our present snow storm has gone on for over 96 hours, and shows as yet no sign of abatement. At our camp here there are over 5 feet of fresh snow."

On the expedition's return, Guillarmod stated in his book *Six Mois dans l'Himalaya* the belief that K2 could be climbed by the Northeast Ridge. This statement intrigued the famous Italian explorer Prince Luigi Amedeo of Savoy,

Duke of the Abruzzi, who in 1909 led the next expedition to K2. With him were Dr. Filippo de Filippi, and the renowned photographer Vittorio Sella, as well as seven guides and porters from Courmayeur. The party reached Base Camp below the tremendous south wall of K2 on May 26, and four days later the duke attempted to climb the Southeast Ridge. He established a camp at 18,245 feet, and from there the guides climbed upward 1,000 feet to leave loads on a narrow saddle. Next day the guides returned to the saddle and went on to a height of "certainly 20,000 feet." Here they gave up the climb "not because they had encountered insurmountable obstacles, but because it was hopeless to think of bringing so long and formidable an ascent to a successful issue, when from the very first steps they had met with such difficulties as made the climb barely possible to guides not hampered by loads, and put out of the question the conveying of luggage necessary to keep one from perishing from cold and exhaustion."

Next the duke entered the Savoia Glacier and went up it along the west side of K2. Here on June 7, after four hours of climbing, he reached the West Ridge at an elevation of 21,870 feet. Unfortunately the cornice was a big one and blocked the view of the north side of K2, but he could tell that the slope below must drop off very steeply on the far side. "As a reward for his labors," Dr. de Filippi wrote, "the duke thus saw utterly annihilated the hopes with which he had begun the ascent." Three weeks later a view

37

of K2 from Skyang Kangri convinced the duke of the futility of attempting to climb the Northeast Ridge of K2 or indeed of making any other attempt to climb the world's second highest mountain.

This lavish expedition established the reputation of K2 as a mountain that would never be climbed. On the duke's return to Europe Sir Martin Conway's remark was significant of the opinion of the day: "Every foot of a route may be climbable, and yet if it cannot all be climbed in one day and there is nowhere to spend a night, what can you do?"

Such was the opinion of many climbers as late as 1929, when Aimone di Savoia-Aosta, Duke of Spoleto, led another Italian expedition to K2, but for the purpose of cartography only. Spoleto's expedition was scientific, but the next party to reach the upper Baltoro went to secure motion pictures. After a brief examination of Hidden Peak (Gasherbrum I), this group, led by Dr. and Mrs. Dyhrenfurth, a well-known Swiss team, climbed two of the lower mountains to the east: the Golden Throne (23,990 feet) and Queen Mary Peak (24,350 feet).

The upper Baltoro was visited next by the first French expedition to try to climb an 8,000-meter peak. This party, led by Henry de Segogne and consisting of nine carefully selected French mountaineers, took thirty-five Sherpas. The party did not visit K2, but instead made a serious attempt on Hidden Peak (26,470 feet), where they were turned back by bad weather after reaching an altitude of 22,960 feet.

Two Sherpas were hurt in a 2,000-foot fall during the expedition and had to be carried 360 miles back to Srinagar. Most remarkable of all perhaps was the fact that this prodigious expedition required *650 porters* to transport it from the last village, Askole, to the foot of Hidden Peak.

Such was the record in the Baltoro Muztagh until 1938, when the American Alpine Club sent out a "reconnaissance party" to examine K2 and scout out if possible a potential route to the summit. Number one objective was to make as thorough an examination of K2 as possible, for though an Italian, a Swiss, and a French expedition had seen K2 since the Duke of the Abruzzi attempted to climb it in 1909, twenty-nine years before, none of these men had set foot on the mountain or returned to the Karakoram to try to climb it. K2's reputation was not inviting.

The First American Karakoram Expedition (1938) was led by Dr. Charles S. Houston, then of New York City, who had been a member of the British-American Himalayan Expedition, which in 1936 had reached the summit of Nanda Devi (25,600 feet) in Garhwal, the highest mountain then climbed. With him was Richard L. Burdsall,* who had climbed Minya Konka (24,900 feet) during one of the most successful high-mountain expeditions of our generation. Other members of the party were William P. House, a bril-

* Burdsall died on Mount Aconcagua in Argentina (22,835 feet) on February 20, 1953, after climbing the mountain and making a futile effort to descend to help rescue two Italians exhausted near the summit.

liant young rock climber, who with Fritz Wiessner had first ascended Mount Waddington in British Columbia in 1936, after sixteen previous parties had been unsuccessful. Next was Paul K. Petzoldt, rancher and guide from Jackson Hole, Wyoming, well known for his climbs in the Tetons and Wind Rivers in Wyoming, and for a double traverse of the Matterhorn made in one day. Capt. N. R. Streatfield, who had been transport officer of the French expedition to Hidden Peak in 1936, directed porter operations; and the writer, who had climbed Mount Lucania (17,150 feet) and other peaks in Alaska and the Yukon, completed the climbing party. Six Sherpa porters were taken.

After being turned back from reaching Savoia Pass by steep ice, the 1938 party, reconnoitering in several teams, was also stopped on two routes leading to the West Ridge of K2, and again on the Northeast Ridge, before making a determined bid on the southeast rib where the Duke of the Abruzzi three decades before had pressed his attack. House and Petzoldt's good reconnaissance work over fretted ribs of rotten rock interspersed with snow gullies brought them eventually to a campsite, later known as Camp II, at 19,300 feet. House and Houston continued the reconnaissance and Camp III was set up at 20,700 feet. This camp proved very dangerous, however, for falling stones struck two of the three tents there, one of them while all three high-altitude Sherpa porters were in it. Petzoldt and Houston led up over a short but difficult overhang to place Camp IV at 21,500

feet, below a cliff. Here, while I belayed him, House made
the most important "lead" of the expedition. He ascended
a steep, 100-foot gash that has become known to more re-
cent expeditions as House's Chimney. More camps were
pushed higher until the food supply, depleted by the long
reconnaissance, was nearly exhausted. House and I, with
the famous porter Pasang Kikuli, helped Houston and
Petzoldt to establish Camp VII at 24,700 feet. From there
they had food enough to push their way to the foot of the
summit pyramid, and Petzoldt reached a height of approximately 26,000 feet before starting down. A more extensive
food supply might have permitted this expedition to reach
the summit, but a large amount would have been needed,
for stormy weather was coming in as the party descended
the mountain. The 1938 team, however, had found a route
up K2 and brought back the strong hope that the world's
second highest mountain could be climbed.

The Second American Karakoram Expedition, consisting
of six climbers and a transport officer under the leadership
of Fritz Wiessner, reached the foot of K2 on May 31, 1939.
Wiessner, a brilliant rock climber, was best known for his
attempt on Nanga Parbat with the Dyhrenfurth Expedition
in 1932. With him were Jack Durrance, who had made dar-
ing ascents in Wyoming; the experienced veteran Eaton
Cromwell; forty-two-year-old Dudley Wolfe; and two young
climbers from Dartmouth College, Chappel Cranmer and
George Sheldon. With Lieutenant Trench as transport officer,

41

and nine picked Sherpas under Pasang Kikuli, the party reached Base Camp on schedule, and after a brief look at the Northeast Ridge decided to try the route of the 1938 party, known as the Abruzzi Ridge. Eventually eleven loads were moved up to Camp VII, and two days later Wiessner and Wolfe pitched Camp VIII five and a half hours higher. On July 17 Wiessner with Pasang Lama pushed forward to set up Camp IX at 26,050 feet, but deep snow caused Wolfe to return to Camp VIII.

On July 18, in good weather, Wiessner and Pasang Lama made a bid for the summit, but difficult climbing slowed them, and finally at 6:30 P.M., when they were well over 27,000 feet—perhaps to 27,500—Pasang Lama anchored the rope and would not let the indomitable Wiessner continue. Wiessner had been planning an all-night climb! During the dangerous night descent that followed, the Sherpa lost his crampons (ice creepers). Back in camp at two-thirty in the morning, the two men were too tired to make another attempt next day. On July 21 they tried a different route, but without crampons 400 to 500 steps must be cut— too many for one day. If Lama had not lost his crampons! It was now too late to try the first route again. The chance was gone.

Next day the two went down to Camp VIII, added Wolfe to the rope, and descended to Camp VII to bring up more supplies, but on the way Wolfe slipped, and though Wiessner stopped the fall, Wolfe lost his sleeping bag. When the group reached Camp VII, they found to their horror that the camp had been largely evacuated during their long absence. The reserve sleeping bags had been taken, with the result that they spent the night with only one sleeping bag and one air mattress for the three! Luckily the weather was still good, and next day while Wolfe remained at VII, the others went down to VI to bring up additional food and sleeping bags so that the summit attempt could be continued. But Camp VI had also been evacuated, and so were the other camps as their descent continued. To save their lives, Wiessner and Lama continued to go down. After a dreadful night at Camp II, the two climbers next day, completely broken physically, reached Base Camp.

The explanation of the stripped camps was that the Sherpas had thought the climbers long overdue and apparently dead. Trying to salvage something, unfortunately they had packed down the precious sleeping bags so painfully carried up.

This was the tragic story of the nearly successful fourth expedition to K2, but their experiences did not discourage the world's mountaineers. Instead, the challenge that had drawn Dudley Wolfe to the mountain had become even greater, and if World War II had not begun, it is certain that the fifth attempt to climb the Karakoram giant would have come much sooner.

3. Preparations

ROBERT H. BATES

3. Preparations

Grim, stark, dangerous, each time K2 has defeated a team of climbers, it has strengthened the desire of others to take up its challenge. After the Wiessner expedition to K2 was turned back within 1,000 feet of the summit in 1939, Houston, House, and I of the 1938 party began to plan another assault.

During World War II, of course, our return was impossible, but soon after the war ended, House and I called on the Indian ambassador to discuss applying for permission to go to K2 in 1947. We were dissuaded. Then came partition of the subcontinent into India and Pakistan, followed by a struggle of these countries for Kashmir, until eventually a cease-fire line that absolutely nobody could pass was set up across this divided country. The political division of Kashmir seemed to block completely any hope of expeditions to K2, for the southern half of the route was under India's control and the northern part, known as Baltistan, was held by Pakistan.

But Dr. Houston, who had already done more mountain climbing in Asia than any other American, should not be underestimated, for after House and I had given up hope of returning to K2, he became more determined than ever to go. Realizing that to reach K2 without crossing the cease-fire line might be possible, he wrote to a distinguished diplomat and friend of long standing, the Honorable Avra Warren, who in 1951 was the American ambassador to Pakistan. The right man in the right place can do wonders, and despite earlier indications of failure, in the spring of 1952 permission was granted to Dr. Houston to lead an expedition to K2 in 1953.

From then on, we were caught up in a whirlwind. We were disappointed at first when Bill House of the 1938 party decided that his business would not permit him to make such a lengthy trip, but others were eager to go. That spring we talked to George Bell, who was preparing to go to Salcantay in Peru; wrote to Peter Schoening, leader of the King Peak Expedition; and saw or corresponded with a host of others. Selecting personnel was critical and difficult. Who could tell whether candidate X, who had climbed so well in British Columbia, was potentially a better man for the K2 expedition than candidate Y, famous for his rock acrobatics among the Dolomites and his ice work in Bolivia.

Finally we decided to wait until after the summer climbing season of 1952–1953 to select the party; and we agreed on the characteristics we wanted most in members of the K2 "team," for a mountain expedition above all else is just that: a team. It must act cohesively, and there is no place for the brilliant climber who thinks only in terms of personal success. Anyone selected for such an adventure must be a *good all-around mountaineer,* but even more important, he must have that indefinable quality *good personality,* and be able to keep his good nature and add to the humor of the party when bad weather, danger, or hardships strain the nerves. (High-altitude dispositions are notoriously bad.) Next in importance we placed *expedition experience,* for no number of daily climbs from a hut give the practice in living and working together under trying conditions that one gets from being on an expedition—especially one where the members carry their own loads. Third in importance we put *technical ability* on rock and snow. Probably no major Himalayan peak yet climbed requires such diversity of mountaineering skills as K2. Therefore we could not take brilliant rock climbers if they were inexperienced on snow or men whose climbing background was in any way one-sided. K2 is no mountain for the specialist. Unlike Everest, which is almost entirely a snow mountain on the side by which it was climbed, K2 on the south side is a rock and

49

snow mountain with a wide range of technical mountaineering problems.

These were the main criteria for selecting the team. We discovered that many of the candidates were overly modest, and in the end we found ourselves with more suitable men than places. Initially we had thought of a six-man party, which had worked well in 1938, but when we learned that we could not take Sherpas, we increased the number to eight. Sherpas had been a help to us in 1938 and have been employed with great success on Everest, Annapurna, and other great Asiatic mountains. Feeling against India ran so strong in northern Kashmir at that time, however, that it seemed unwise to take with us any of these sturdy little men. In their place we should have Hunzas, bigger men, who come from a small, mountainous border state in northern Pakistan. Hunzas have not had the years of expedition training that many Sherpas have had, and therefore we thought it unlikely that they could climb on the Abruzzi Ridge of K2 above Camp II. To compensate for the fact that we should be doing all our own load carrying on the upper part of the mountain, we decided to enlarge the climbing party to eight, with the idea that the carrying capacity of at least eight men would be needed.

If eight men would be better than six, why wouldn't ten or twelve be better than eight? In some ways they would, but campsites on precipitous K2 are scarce. It would be very dangerous, even if possible, to move a group of seventeen porters up to 26,580 feet on K2 as was done on Mount Everest in 1953. Steepness, lack of campsites, and loose rock limit the size of the party. Houston and I agreed on a party of eight and at once began exhaustive letter writing and interviews to help us to decide who the other six would be.

Selecting the party from the numbers of strong and experienced men who wished to go was especially difficult, but the choice was finally made. Our biggest member physically was 6-foot-5-inch, twenty-seven-year-old George F. Bell, assistant professor of physics at Cornell University. Bell has climbed widely, but is best known in the mountain world for his part in the successful expeditions to Yerupaja and Salcantay in Peru. Also tall and a veteran climber is twenty-eight-year-old Robert Craig of Aspen, Colorado, philosopher and ski instructor, whose first ascents of Kate's Needle and Devil's Thumb in British Columbia brought him national prominence in 1947. The Middle West was represented by Arthur K. Gilkey of Iowa, a geologist who was finishing his work for the Ph.D. at Columbia University. Gilkey in the summer of 1952 had directed with great skill the Juneau Icefield Research Project in Alaska, basic glaciological research by the United States government, and was known for his youthful climb of Devil's Tower in Wyoming, and subsequent brilliant ascents in the Grand Tetons.

A climbing companion of Bob Craig of many years' standing was thirty-four-year-old Dee Molenaar, artist, ski

51

instructor, and geologist, who had been an outstanding member of the Mount St. Elias Expedition to Alaska in 1946. Like Craig and Peter K. Schoening, a chemical engineer, Molenaar came from Seattle, but twenty-six-year-old Schoening is the only one of the three still living there. Schoening's climbs on extremely difficult rock were well known before his leadership of the highly successful King Peak Expedition to the Yukon in the summer of 1952. Our transport officer, Capt. H. R. A. Streather of Warminster, England, and our Pakistani member, Col. M. Ata-Ullah, were to join us later.

While personnel problems were being solved, we worried about finances. At least $25,000 needed to be raised, and only part of that sum could be expected to come from the members of the expedition. To assist in solving this major problem, Richard L. Burdsall of Port Chester, New York, a member of the First American Karakoram Expedition, accepted the arduous job of expedition treasurer; then after Burdsall's tragic death on Mount Aconcagua in Argentina, William P. House, another member of the 1938 party, took on the financial burden with great skill. (Eventually, about one-quarter of the money was put up by members of the expedition, one-quarter came from advances on television rights and articles, one-quarter came from loans, and one-quarter from gifts.) Unlike most European expeditions, we were not subsidized by our government, nor were funds given us by any organization. Although the American Alpine

Club sponsored our expedition, we used none of the club's funds. Mountaineers and friends helped us out individually, but we did most of our own deficit financing.

While money was being raised and selection of the expedition team was going on, first steps had already been taken in the selection of food and equipment, and as each member was added, he took over some phase of the work. Through Pete Schoening, some fine down jackets, made to the expedition's specifications, were donated by a Seattle firm. Gilkey worked on stoves and Molenaar on some lightweight nylon parkas. Boxes began to pile up in the garage and front hallway of the Houston residence in Exeter, New Hampshire.

Hundreds of decisions had to be made. What type of mountain boots should we use? Should they have rubber cleated soles, or leather soles with metal boot nails, or rubber cleated soles with metal nails? (Each man finally used the type of sole he thought best.) Some boots were made to our measure free of charge by a French firm; others came from England and from Canada; while still others were the rubber, vapor-barrier boots developed by the United States Army. Similar problems concerned gloves, underwear, and even socks. Pete Schoening for instance had socks and mittens made for the whole party by Indians in the Pacific Northwest, but their ideas of size must have been based on ancient legend, for some of them had heroic proportions.

Each man showed some special preferences in clothing.

53

Schoening kept snow out by tying his outer trousers to a tab sewn around the upper part of his boots, while Art Gilkey used puttees for the same purpose. George Bell sported Peruvian hats, while Bob Craig had several colorful head-pieces, one with a long red tassel down the back. But perhaps the most treasured items of clothing were a wool helmet and some lightweight underwear made in the Hebrides and saved by Charlie Houston since his first expedition to K2 in 1938.

Food was one of the most important of all problems. Mrs. Houston became accustomed to experimental dinners of dried vegetables, strange soups, and special compounds, some of which were finished by the dog. We tried Antarctic pemmican and honey biscuits, special chocolate beverages from the Rocky Mountains, dried meat bars from Chicago, and several varieties of baby food. The baby-food cereal seemed a good idea, for we needed food that required little or no cooking to simplify life and save fuel at high altitudes. Baby food had simplicity, all right, as we were later to agree, but the simplicity applied to the taste, too, so that we later unanimously agreed that babies have been cheated for years. Once let them taste something with flavor and they will be through with baby food forever.

Finally, after days of experiment with prepacked, light-weight foods and delicacies that had been favored on former expeditions, we settled on the foods we wanted, added one-quarter extra to most quantities to make sure that Pete Schoening would have enough, and started to order. Almost at once the Houston residence began to look like a grocery store. Cases of meat bars—each bar a pound of steak dehydrated to 4 ounces—began piling up at the foot of the stairs, and dried apricots and dehydrated toasted onion soup blocked the route to the garbage can. Mrs. Houston fortunately is blessed with patience, for the Houston children celebrated each new arrival with delight and curiosity, as if a new Christmas were being arranged especially for them.

Finally, when the Houston home had been turned almost completely into a workhouse and the family were considering a sleeping-bag existence in a tent in the yard, the big "packing week end" came. Senior members of the Exeter Mountaineering Club and the Harvard Mountaineering Club and other friends foregathered with some "heat sealers" and large quantities of plastic tubing, for we planned to eliminate weight of packaging and increase efficiency by packing all the individual items of high-camp food into units for two men for one day. The small packets were placed in larger plastic bags, and these in turn in cloth bags, weighing about 28 pounds each, which would nourish eight men for three days.

The "packing week end" was sensational. Assembly lines were set up in the Houston kitchen and dining room. A visiting scholar from India and a visiting educator from Pakistan worked together vigorously and cooperatively, and as the empty cartons piled high, amazing progress was made. In one corner Mrs. Houston's best bread knife was in service cutting twenty-four wheels of Italian *pan forte* (fruitcake) into eight sections each. The knife has never been the same since. In another area, dehydrated potatoes were measured into plastic bags, the air was squeezed out, and the plastic was sealed together by a heat sealer. It was important that these seals be firm, so an inspection service was set up to test the bags for defective sealing or for too much air, which might cause the bags to explode at high altitude. Sample testing grounds were established in the living room, only to be removed in haste to the kitchen when Mrs. Houston witnessed the damage wrought by a few defective bags of powdered potato and flaky baby-food oatmeal. The linoleum of the kitchen floor also suffered, especially from a gummy combination of excelsior and sticky raisins that clung as if cemented in place.

For two days this group worked at furious speed, making plastic containers, heat-sealing them, and packing them in specially made plywood boxes which were to go all the way to Base Camp unopened. Lids were nailed on the boxes and a Harvard–M.I.T. team strapped them with metal bands; then they were numbered, printed labels were stapled on, and the containers were ready for their voyage halfway around the world. During these vigorous days, vast quantities of excess chocolate and sugar-coated peanuts were consumed, and somehow Mrs. Houston provided meals for the whole hungry crew. At one sitting, a 24-pound turkey, roasted in front of the living-room fire, completely disappeared.

Along with the boxes of food, we packed climbing equipment: 960 feet of nylon climbing rope, crampons (ice creepers with spikes 2 inches long), snap links, rock *pitons*, and ice *pitons*. Pitons are spikes which can be driven into rock or ice. A snap link or *karabiner* (a large snaffle) can then be snapped into a hole at the end of the spike, and the rope secured to it. Our snap links were very light ones, developed by the U. S. Army Quartermaster Corps for the use of mountain troops during the war. The ice pitons, of a new design and very strong, had been carefully made for us under the most modern engineering principles by David Bernays, a student at M.I.T. Perhaps the most unusual piece of climbing equipment was a light aluminum A-frame with pulleys, which was to be used in hauling loads past one of the steepest parts of the route.

We also packed two containers of oxygen, which Dr. Houston had obtained from Dr. Ulrich Luft of the Army Air Force for use in case of emergency or frostbite, or perhaps for a needed boost near the top if the summit party could not acclimatize properly. We did not plan to use artificial oxygen as the Everest parties have recently done, not because we considered its use unsporting, but because it is expensive, cumbersome, and introduces many complex problems. A large number of load carriers are needed if oxygen is to be used regularly, and as already described, K2 is not a peak which can support many men at once. Also, if oxygen fails to work when an unacclimatized climber is high, he may even die on the spot. But we knew that at least half a dozen climbers on Everest had reached over 28,000 feet without oxygen in the past and believed that we could go as high. We would rely on acclimatization to train our bodies to live in thin air.

Exposure to high altitude is often uncomfortable. Anoxia seems to drain the body of energy and will, but severe illness on mountain expeditions is a rare thing. Naturally, however, Houston as expedition doctor selected his medical kit with great care, and it was packed and sent out with the rest of the 4,500 pounds of supplies which were to go by freighter to Karachi, Pakistan.

Finally, after weeks of struggle, some sixty-three packing cases were loaded on a truck which would take them to the New York piers, and the Houston garage was freed for normal use for the first time in months. I saw the whole consignment loaded on the *City of Carlisle* in New York on April 23 and returned to Exeter to get ready to fly to Karachi to meet the freighter when she steamed into that busy roadstead of the Indian Ocean.

4. To the mountain

ROBERT W. CRAIG

4. To the mountain

On the night of May 23 a magnificent farewell party was given by members of the American Alpine Club in honor of our expedition. Older members of the club, on whose shoulders we had in a sense stood in order to gain our own reputation and ability, gathered about us and imparted a warmth of feeling and a spirit of unity that none of us were to forget throughout our whole adventure. Next day a few last-minute dashes from one end of Manhattan to the other netted the expedition such items as half a dozen extra hand warmers, more photographic film, and a tape recorder. At last we all assembled at Idlewild International Airport on the afternoon of Monday, May 25.

Morning found us in London, wishing we could leave the

airport to touch elbows with the Coronation crowds, but our stop was hardly long enough for lunch. In the late afternoon we were trying vainly to buy a quick beer in Frankfurt. We then discovered that we could satisfy our thirst adequately on the plane, and even managed to round up a few bottles of an excellent airline vintage for "cold nights in Base Camp." Some weeks later we were to think enviously of those bottles so easy to buy on the plane.

Through the second night we traversed the eastern Mediterranean, and morning brought us a brief but impressive glimpse of Beirut, Lebanon. During the rest of the morning we flew across the northeastern part of the Arabian peninsula and over much of the area where history was being made two millenniums ago.

In midafternoon of the second day of flight we dropped down onto the sun-baked airport of the young city of Karachi, capital of Pakistan. We stepped from the air-conditioned aircraft into a vise of heat which was to haunt us in varying degrees until we reached the cool, dry land of Baltistan far to the north. High-ranking officials of Pakistan and the press greeted us as we alighted. Bill Crockett, administrative assistant to Ambassador Hildreth, was there to help too, and several of his aides. Most important of all there was Bob Bates, who had flown to Karachi ahead of us to convoy more than 2 tons of food and clothing and equipment through customs. Since his arrival he had arranged to have the supplies shipped by rail to Rawalpindi, where they would be flown the last 190 miles to Skardu, the capital of Baltistan. It was wonderful to be together again, and we felt more and more like a team. We now lacked only Tony Streather and Colonel Ata-Ullah. Thanks to our many friends, we were quickly passed through customs, and were soon en route to the American embassy, where we were to spend the night through the kindness of the American ambassador. The air-conditioned bedrooms were most welcome, but even more so were quick baths, in which we removed the dust of half the world. After this we walked through the sticky, humid evening air along mysterious lanes to Bill Crockett's garden, where a party was given in our honor. We found an amazing amount of interest in our expedition, and much of the conversation in the garden that hot, muggy evening concerned mountains. We talked to many Pakistanis who had traveled there, and saw a superb moving picture of the area.

We slept for a few hours, and were up next morning at four to fly via Orient Airways to Rawalpindi, 900 miles to the north. The flight was hardly a scenic one, for much of it lay across the baking Sind Desert, a wasteland of sand uninhabited for thousands of miles, and visibility was limited by a misty layer of dust which formed in the great heat. We landed at noon in Rawalpindi, a city which saw a lot of action in Kipling's day and which has long been a gateway to the Northwest Frontier Province and the western Himalayas.

We were hardly down the ramp of the aircraft when we became aware of the presence of Colonel Ata-Ullah, the

Pakistani who was to be our friend and companion on the expedition. One of Houston's principal hopes for this expedition was that it should form friendship between Pakistan and America by showing that young country how similar its people are to our own in ambitions, ideals, and abilities. We wanted Pakistan to share in our attempt to climb its highest mountain, and we had looked for a climber and a companion. Thanks to Sir Zafrullah Khan, foreign minister of Pakistan, who had taken a great interest in the expedition from its beginning, the ideal man was found in the person of Colonel Ata-Ullah. Our first impression of him as we left the plane was that of a dynamic individual with great power, great ability, a sensitive intelligence—one who would become our warm friend.

Beside him, equally impressive though not so formidable, was smiling, alert Capt. Tony Streather. Tony is a twenty-seven-year-old officer in the British First Gloucestershire Regiment, who had reached the summit of Tirich Mir (a 25,260-foot peak several hundred miles west of K2) with a Norwegian expedition in 1951. Houston had corresponded with him, their letters had led to friendship, and he had been accepted sight unseen. Within a few days of our meeting in Pakistan, Streather was one of the most popular members. His disposition never changed, he told fabulous tales of Northwest Frontier country, and he always had a story about that part of the world. Best of all, he was not only an excellent transport officer, which was his primary responsi-

1. The expedition at Rawalpindi. From left to right: Craig, Bell, Houston, Molenaar, Schoening, Gilkey, White (expedition agent), Bates, Colonel Ata-Ullah. Captain Streather had already left for Skardu to hire porters.

2. The entire population at Skardu turned out to welcome us. Bates, Houston, and Molenaar are here accompanied by a governor and three rajahs.

3. About to cross the Indus on Alexander's Barge. This ancient craft is said locally to have been built by Alexander the Great.

4. The homespun trousers, jacket, and shoes of this Balti porter are in the best Askole tradition. The hat is probably a relic of a former expedition.

5. A skin raft being prepared for crossing the Braldu River. A large raft may contain as many as twenty-eight goat or sheep bladders and will support a half-dozen men and their loads.

6. The expedition crosses the Braldu to the village of Dassu. Big rapids made this crossing appear exceptionally hazardous.

7. Houston crossing a rope bridge. A few minutes after this picture was taken, the bridge turned over with a porter on it. The porter was saved.

8. Virgin rock and snow across the glacier from Urdukas. The golden age of climbing in this area has just begun.

9. Paiju Peak at sunrise. Its summit towers 12,000 feet above the Baltoro ice.

10. Captain Streather sought in vain for likely climbing routes up Masherbrum. It has never been attempted from this side.

11. A porter with a wooden "coolie crutch" passes in front of the Mitre. This wedge of stone, 18,930 feet high, looks down on Concordia, the great ice area into which four major glaciers flow.

12. K2 from Concordia. The summit of K2 rises some 12,000 feet above the rough ice of the Godwin-Austen Glacier.

13. At Camp I, the expedition saw big snowslides from the northeast slopes of Broad Peak in the background.

bility, but he soon became one of the party's strongest packers and climbers.

We were quickly taken in hand by these two efficient men,
both thoroughly familiar with Pakistan, and we and our baggage were transported to the home of Colonel Ata-Ullah,
where we were to stay. There we settled back and began for
the first time to see something of Pakistan and its culture.

In Karachi our stay had been so short, and so limited to
American surroundings, that we could not even begin to
feel the atmosphere of the country. In Rawalpindi all of this
changed, for we had as guides Ata-Ullah's two sons, Munir
and Shahid, as well as his nephew, Masood Ahmed. With
them we made excursions to all parts of the city and were
told of the age and importance of the various mosques,
bazaars, and the historical sites. We toured the oldest bazaars in a jeep, and visited parts of the city we would never
have seen on our own. Meanwhile we settled down in Ata's
house, and rapidly piled our equipment all over his lawn.

Many vital things had to be done, and we spent most of
our time opening crates shipped across the Atlantic, and repacking food and equipment into 60-pound porter loads.
Then, too, there were endless and inevitable check lists to go
over, and new lists to be made. Some equipment had been
damaged and must be replaced, and some new purchases
had to be made. The temperature was usually between 100°
and 120° in the sun, and the work came hard.

While our days were, if anything, too full, there was also

a considerable demand for our time in the evenings. Many of Ata's friends were anxious to meet the party, and many had a genuine desire to know more about the mountains which protect the northern frontiers of their country. Thus our evenings were spent in a round of wonderful dinner parties, where we met some of the most brilliant and capable of Pakistan's leaders. We ate enormous amounts of strange and delicious Pakistani dishes, and in the cool evenings on the lawn of the colonel's house we talked about mountains, men, and the world in general. We learned about the birth of Pakistan, formed in forty-six days as the result of the partition of western India (predominantly Moslem) and central India (predominantly Hindu) in 1947.

We talked about the problems faced by this the youngest of the world's great nations, and we came to admire deeply the courage, patience, and the energy with which the people are solving these problems.

Our stay in Rawalpindi was packed with excitement and new and interesting things. Houston visited several hospitals and was deeply impressed with the caliber of medical care given. We visited the Signal Corps training laboratories built up from nothing by Colonel Young, an English officer on duty with the Pakistan army. We made courtesy calls on the ranking officers of the Pakistan army, and were honored and pleased to be invited to return. All of this made our week in Rawalpindi an Arabian Nights adventure. But K2 was ever present in our minds, and we were drawn irresistibly by our future.

June 1 broke hot and clear, and in the earliest light of dawn we could see the blue Himalayan foothills shouldering above the misty plains. Trucks had carried our 2½ tons of equipment and food to the airport the night before, and all that remained was to say good-by to our kind hostess, Begum Ata-Ullah, collect our scattered possessions, and drive to the airport to begin one of the most exciting flights any of us had ever experienced. The flight to Skardu probably exacts more skill from a pilot than any other regular air route in the world. Capt. Henrik Franczak of Orient Airlines, who had been a pilot in the Polish Air Force and later in the British Air Force during World War II, told us about the flight which would take us through the foothills, over several 13,000-foot passes, flanked on either side by great mountains, and alongside such giants as Rakaposhi, Haramush, and Nanga Parbat, all of them over 25,000 feet high.

We left soon after six o'clock, with the heat of the day already beginning. It was a relief to ride above the baking plains, and fly over first the brown, arid fields which merged into gradually greener hills, steepening slopes, deeper gorges. Then appeared a little snow here and there, larger patches, glaciers, and then the great rock and ice kings themselves. Visibility was not always good, but we saw enough of certain peaks to be convinced that we were among mountains

75

that must be classed apart from all others. Our plane was joined by a second Orient Airlines plane which flew wing to wing with us through the rugged gorges, past mighty Nanga Parbat, which the Germans were so soon to climb.

All the time we flew among these fantastic hulks, the plane had painfully little clearance over ridges, summits, and between narrowing walls of the deep gorges. Abruptly we cleared one final ridge, saw the widening valley floor of the Indus, and in a sickening dive we seemed to plummet toward the ground. At the last moment the plane leveled off, skimmed some deep gullies, and touched down on the hard earth of the Skardu landing strip. We had arrived! In only an hour and a half we had reached Skardu, where the 1938 K2 party had arrived after a 220-mile trek, during which they had marched the equivalent of the distance from Boston to New York in two weeks.

We drove off to the village in jeeps, leaving our equipment to follow under the care of the Northern Scouts, a local levy of smart and capable mountain soldiers. To our astonishment we were met on the way about a mile from town by a huge delegation. Lined up along the sides of the road were all the school children of Skardu, cheering, throwing flowers, and waving banners to welcome us. There were speeches every few hundred yards, garlands of fresh and fragrant roses were placed about our necks, and the crowds cheered, *"Pakistan zindabad! America zindabad!"* (Long live Pakistan! Long live America!) Placards urged us to use our influence with the United Nations to see that a Kashmir plebiscite be held. Other banners thanked America for the gift of wheat. Still others welcomed us to the wonderful country of Pakistan. We felt that our welcome was a sincere demonstration of the hospitality of these people toward strangers, as well as a symbol of the affection felt by these people toward America, half the world away.

Changes had occurred since Houston and Bates had been in Skardu in 1938: then the 2,000 inhabitants had been cut off almost completely by distance from the outside world; now we heard that there were 7,000 people in Skardu, and as many more in the surrounding villages. Much of this increase can be attributed to the influx of refugees from Kashmir, and to the presence of the Pakistan army in Skardu. Also, the city had become more accessible because of the airlift, which supplies it completely with all its needs: jeeps, oil, food, equipment, as well as such luxuries as they have. Perhaps most significant for the future of all the changes in the orchard-fringed capital of Baltistan was the addition of a modern hospital, complete with a small electric-light plant and a movie theater. These developments were owing mainly to the work and patience of the chief surgeon, Major Khan, who had come back to Pakistan after twelve years of medical practice in London. He was to help us immeasurably in the months to come by his presence in Skardu.

In the few days we spent in Skardu, the final packing had to be done, and the porters had to be chosen, arrangements

77

made for forwarding mail, and schedules set for radio messages to us. We greeted our Hunza porters, who had marched fourteen days from the distant and famous valley of that name to serve as mountain porters for us. They had been selected by the Mir of Hunza, and we had no idea how much they were going to mean to us in the days which lay ahead. Between our preparations we were lavishly entertained by all the officials of Skardu, and managed to take in such sights as the ancient Skardu Fort (reputed to be 500 years old), and the lovely lake of Satpura. All of this activity took place in a setting of vast open plains of sand along the speedy, muddy Indus River. In the distance precipitous, multicolored rock peaks capped with snow looked down on irrigated fields and orchards lined by graceful Lombardy poplars. Here the Baltis grow barley, wheat, millet, apricots, mulberries, apples, and peaches. In the evenings we relaxed on the lawn of the summer house which was formerly used by the Maharajah of Kashmir, a beautiful garden on the edge of a steep cliff which falls sheer for hundreds of feet to the Indus River plain.

At last all of our preparations were completed, and early in the morning of June 5 as light faintly touched the highest peaks above the Indus Valley, our "bandobast" (porter caravan) started down the steep trail to the river. There we were ferried across the mile of muddy, rushing water in an ancient wooden craft not unlike our canal barges. This vessel is attributed to Alexander the Great, and is said to be the very barge in which the great Greek conqueror led his armies across the river. Whether or not this is the very vessel he used, it probably is a similar model, and uses the same means of propulsion. The shallow, rectangular barge is certainly primitive enough, and is moved across the river by water power with a minimum of paddling. Starting far upstream on the Skardu bank, where most of the townspeople had gathered to say good-by, each boatload of thirty or forty men and baggage pushed off into the current and was carried downstream at a terrifying rate. Only disorganized attempts to guide the barge were made by the four boatmen who wielded long oars in a style far removed from our regatta at Poughkeepsie, and yet we finally reached the far shore in safety, a third of a mile below our starting place on the opposite bank. The process of hauling the barge upstream and making the return journey took some time, and we were glad that most of our porters had crossed the night before. About a hundred and twenty-five porters stood back from the river with their loads arranged in a long line. Loads and men were checked, and then at a signal each man slung his 60 pounds on his back and we set off across the hot, dazzling sand of the old river bed. Our march had really begun; we were on our way to K2!

For the next fourteen days we plunged farther and farther into a land of fantasy. Beauty is not a term one generally can apply to Baltistan and the Karakoram, although certainly there are places where intense beauty confronts the traveler. Rather the land is one of harsh yet magnificent contrasts: immense rock spires soar thousands of feet to glistening ice summits, while below the stark brown monotony of parched earth and sand is broken only occasionally by roaring glacial torrents or emerald-green trees and fields of a village. These villages hang onto precipitous slopes and are made fruitful by painstaking irrigation. Wherever a small side stream falls from the mountain, generations of natives have built long ditches to bring the water to the terraced fields. The climate of Baltistan is pleasant: warm in summer, and not severe in winter. The mountain vistas are incomparable. The menaces of "civilization" seem far away. These people appear to have a heaven on earth, and perhaps they do, and yet for all of this they live in hovels of mud and straw like those used by their ancestors for the past 1,500 years. They are dirty, and their sanitation is nonexistent. Illness is common. Houston, as a doctor, could not help thinking aloud what wonderful changes could be made with even the simplest principles of cleanliness and public health.

There is a kind of magic which sometimes kindles when men are joined together in a common effort, and this seems particularly true in mountaineering. In the vast reaches of the Karakoram the experience is not restricted to the climbers but infects the whole expedition. The porters are not there for the money alone—it is hard and dangerous cash to earn—but because they too feel caught up in the spirit of the hills and the hunger for adventure. Particularly this is true of the mountain porters, in our case the Hunzas, who feel themselves set apart and above the baggage porters.

As day after day of hard marching passed, the porters began to form a solid group, and the whole expedition shook down together. Not only did the porters and the climbers come to know each other, but we climbers, most of whom had been strangers at the start, came closer together. Our various temperaments began to show, and we began to learn each other's good points and peculiarities. Only Bates and Houston, and Molenaar and I, had climbed with each other before. The others were comparative strangers. As we approached our mountain, the magic cement that binds men together, the qualities which make unbreakable friendships began to form. Unconsciously, and imperceptibly, we were forming a team. If we had not it is probable that most of us would not have survived the troubles that we were to face. Perhaps it is these bonds, formed of success and failure, that make mountaineering expeditions—like all ventures of man into the heart of nature—such a rich, emotional experience.

A typical day on the march to the mountain began when the Baltis began to murmur as the dawn chill pierced their blankets. Village sounds drifted through our camp (we were usually camped in an orchard near a village), and Vilyati (our cook, sirdar, and mountain porter) began preparing eggs and chicken bought from the villagers, or cereal, tea, and meat from our own stores. Try as we would to withdraw

81

deeper into our down bags, these noises soon woke us and we crawled out of our tents saturated with ten hours of sleep, to breakfast at four-thirty. Blisters and stiff muscles made the start painful, but first we had a long and complex period of load sorting and assigning. The daily consumption of sahib and porter food necessitated each morning a reshuffle of loads, and some crafty porters often tried to carry a bulky pack which looked as if it weighed a hundred pounds, but was in reality only twenty-five.

Unfortunately not all of the Balti porters felt "caught up in the spirit of the hills," and much of our time during the march was spent encouraging the laggards—giving a cigarette here and there, or shouting encouragingly a word which sounded like *"shabash"* (well done), which was usually sufficient to keep things rolling along.

Lunch was eaten along the trail at about eleven, and after this we usually marched until three-thirty or four to our campsite. From Skardu to the snout of the Baltoro Glacier is about 100 miles, and the days were blisteringly hot, the sun relentless. Soon after the porters straggled into camp our cook would produce what passed by the name of tea—several quarts of strong brew, crackers, jam, cheese, fruit, and a tin of sardines or kippers. We would barely have time to finish this feast before dinner was served, but there never seemed to be any difficulty in finishing this meal too. Dinner consisted of dried vegetables, soup, tinned meat or local chicken, pudding, and a hot drink. We sat around our tent or campfire until seven or eight o'clock, talking easily and happily on topics ranging from home and family to the day's march and the character of our new friends, or world politics and philosophies. In the middle of a learned discussion someone would break in with his thoughts on the subject dominant in all our minds—the mountain: "If we can't find a safe place for Camp III, protected from rockfall, will we be able to manage the long climb from II to IV in one day?"

Some of the days brought more dangerous tasks than plodding over boulder-strewn alluvial fans. There was, for example, the river crossing between Bahar and Niyil, about halfway from Skardu to Askole. The porters claimed that the old route on the right bank of the Braldu River had been destroyed by avalanches, and urged that we cross the turbulent river. At the place selected for crossing, the river is divided into two parts by a sand bar. The first and smaller part was forded through river water which rushed waisthigh. It was necessary to fix a handrail to help the lazy porters across, but even so a few preferred to return home. Once on the sand bar all porters and loads were collected in one place, while we watched the crossing of the larger half. This was done on a goatskin raft, a *zahk*, made of some thirty goatskins lashed together by a light flexible framework of split poplar poles. The resilience of these rafts, their seeming weakness, gives them strength, which was important in the turbulent water. Only four passengers and loads could be taken at a time, and all the porters prayed with great emotion before boarding the raft and tossing off into the high waves. Their fears were justified, too, for the icy river churned and boiled down through a narrow race with waves 4 or 5 feet high. The crossing was a tedious process, taking us a day and a half to get all the porters and their loads across.

Two more days' march up the valley we came to another river crossing, even more trying on the nerves. This was one of the infamous "rope" bridges of the Karakoram. These bridges are made by twisting pollarded willow shoots and twigs together into thick strands, two for handrails and one for a footwalk or treadway. The bridges sag deeply from the high banks on either side as they span the river at a narrowing point in its bed. Apparently they are placed in position during the winter when the river is either very narrow or frozen. They are replaced only when broken, and they sometimes turn upside down, pitching the traveler to certain death in the mauling, freezing waters below. One of these bridges actually did turn over with one of our porters on it, but he was so terrified that he did not let go, and the bridge was righted and he was saved. One other unpleasant characteristic of the bridge is for the two handrails to come together and squeeze the traveler like a vise, unless a man remains in the middle of the bridge to hold the cables apart. We had three of these miserable things to traverse, each seeming worse than the last, and many porters parted from us at each one. Fortunately, however, no one was lost, nor did even the most rickety bridge collapse.

Just below Askole, the last village we would pass, we enjoyed the long anticipated pleasure of a bath. Here a series of natural hot springs flowed out of the mountains, at precisely the perfect temperature for bathing. The natural pools have been only slightly improved by the local people, who seem to have no use for them. We enjoyed complete privacy as we soaked, up to our bearded chins, for several hours, with snow-capped mountains hanging almost over our heads.

In Askole we bought more flour, hired more porters, and enjoyed half a day of restful camp life. We were quartered in the village park, a shaded meadow surrounded by poplars and briar hedges. During the afternoon various members of our caravan and villagers broke into a spontaneous song and dance, much to our delight. Many hundreds of spectators watched and applauded as natives from different villages competed for the most impressive dance. The singing of Baltistan has a certain falsetto quality, and is mostly in half notes, but it is most pleasant and fascinating.

In the morning, our departure from Askole was signaled by a tremendous uproar as we collected porters and weighed out flour to feed them on the way into the mountain. Everyone wished to come, and every man wished to furnish his own flour. Much confusion resulted, and it seemed as though we would never get away; yet order was finally restored.

A short distance beyond Askole we left the path, no longer dignified by the name "beaten," and began the last five days of marching to the Baltoro Glacier. Our campsites were primitive, and lacking in firewood, which was a handicap to the porters. One day we were caught in a gigantic dust storm, which nearly blew away our tents; on another a sudden rainstorm overtook us and almost drenched our equipment. It was with mounting excitement that we rounded a great bluff and looked at the Baltoro Glacier, one of the largest in the temperate areas of the world. A great, ugly mass of ice, dirty and gray, covered with millions of tons of rock and gravel, filled the valley floor.

We had some trouble in climbing onto the glacier, and once on it no trail existed, for the rock, sand, and gravel which cover it are constantly shifting as the ice moves down the valley. The lower part of the glacier is occasionally visited by local people who seek wood along the side slope or who bring their goat herds to high pastures. Their visits are so infrequent as to leave few marks, but two recognized campsites have been developed on the shore. Our marches were slow and laborious, covering little more than 6 miles during eight hours of walking and climbing.

On the first day we reached Lilipru, a small, flat area on the shore, surrounded by vertical cliffs, where an ancient glacier had carved a channel. On the next day we walked an even longer march up the gully between the mountain and the glacier to Urdukas. This would be the last grass we would see for two months. It is a beautiful campsite, a series of grass-covered ledges, great boulders, and deep caves. It served as the Base Camp for the Duke of the Abruzzi, and also for the Duke of Spoleto, who camped here in 1929. Many mountain sheep and goats, snow leopards, bears, and wolves live here, the last game in the valley. We spent a happy afternoon in the grass and among the beautiful Alpine flowers, surrounded by incredible peaks above and about us. I wrote in my diary one day: "Scenery grows more fantastic as we progress—these are hardly mountains: they are fantasies of the imagination." At regular intervals along both sides of the valley blocks of rock, often capped with ice, rose vertically for 8,000 feet, for all the world like mammoth skyscrapers. Houston, who has been in three different areas of the Himalayas, stated that nowhere else had he seen peaks like this, and certainly none of us had seen their equal.

We then crossed the glacier, making two cold and uncomfortable camps on the ice before we reached the great open place called Concordia, where many glaciers flow together to form the Baltoro. Finally, about ten o'clock on the morning of June 19, we rounded the corner where the Godwin-Austen Glacier, flowing from the north, enters "Concordia." Here we expected to have our first glimpse of K2. Instead a great bank of clouds separated the high—the impossibly high— summit from its base, and gave us a tantalizingly brief view of the summit pyramid, high above the clouds. New snow covered most of the mountains above us, and a formidable wind spewed a long snow plume from all the summits. We could imagine the force of the wind that was lashing the upper slopes of K2, and we knew that before long we would be testing its might. Little was said at the moment, but we all realized that we were joining battle with a tremendous foe.

After this brief, imperfect, yet striking, view, clouds again covered the mountain as we marched up the last miles to Base Camp. Snow began to fall as the tired porters straggled into camp late that afternoon. Our long approach was at an end. The monarch of the Karakoram rose high above us, and the real work of the expedition was about to begin.

5. To the foot of
Abruzzi Ridge

CHARLES S. HOUSTON

5. To the foot of Abruzzi Ridge

Only a few inches of snow had fallen during the night, and we awoke on June 20, in Base Camp at last, to a perfect day. About us rose magnificent peaks sparkling in the clear, frosty air. Bride Peak was particularly lovely at the foot of the valley, her pure snow peak dyed by the sun with many colors. Directly above our heads, pile upon pile, towered the southern wall of K2, a series of precipices of rock and ice reaching to a white snow cone 12,000 feet above. Our porters, so miserable during the snowfall the night before, were all smiles and laughter as they woke, and buzzed around camp in their ragged brown cloaks, which resembled nothing so much as burlap Mother Hubbards. Two of the most exhausted and weak had been allowed to sleep in one of our mountain tents, and now to our surprise at least six men came out of that same tent. The independent Satpuras, who had built neat platforms of flat stones with a low surrounding wall to keep off wind, had fared well, and even had a surplus of wood to use for cooking breakfast.

Camp was soon humming with activity. Streather was anxious to pay off the porters as soon as possible, not only to start them early on their long march home, but also to clear camp of the confusion of the curious, itchy-fingered natives, so he and George Bell settled down at one end of camp to count out the amounts due the men. Each porter was called forward and asked for the metal tag given him upon "enlistment." His name was checked against our list, and our calculated amount was given him. Many of the porters had never before seen money, and their bewilderment was comical. They were obviously determined not to be cheated, but they had no conception of the value of the bank notes. An apparently fundamental rule of human conduct was not violated: however much you are given, ask for more. To pay off all 180 men, who came from a dozen different villages, each with a different amount due, took all morning, and then there were arguments and discussions about underpayments. Once paid they were reluctant to leave; they had been so long with the circus that they hated to miss any tricks.

In the meantime the rest of the team was not idle. Our small, two-man mountain tents were pitched in a neat military row along a flat stretch of glacier covered thinly with small stones. Behind and below the tents, a small brook flooded a gully during the day, but was reduced to a trickle during the cold of the night. Our tents faced the towering rock cliffs of Broad Peak across a waste of ice and rock, while down the valley we looked upon Bride Peak, grim Mitre Peak, and a score of lesser, unnamed summits. The kitchen tent was pitched on a platform in the gully near the brook. The Hunzas enthusiastically hacked out of the ice a neat footpath, complete with giant slabs of rock to bridge the stream. Our supplies, covered with tarpaulins, were stacked here and there about camp, while the Hunzas had their own tent off to one side. It was a wild and barren spot, with no blade of grass or even a patch of earth, only ice and rock about us. It would be our home for nearly seventy days.

Bates and Craig and Gilkey had set out in the early morning to reconnoiter the icefall between Base Camp and Camp I, while Schoening, Ata, and I unpacked supplies and organized camp. We had some shocks. Many of our 5-pound Cheddar cheeses were broken or crushed. Some of the chocolate had melted and mingled with other food. Tins of sardines had been punctured. Several tents were badly chafed, and the holes had to be patched. Two porter ice axes were "missing" and nowhere did we find the boots belonging to Tony and the porters, which had disappeared during the river crossing.

Soon after noon the reconnaissance party returned, freshly burned a brilliant scarlet by the reflected white heat of the sun against the ice, and reported having reached Camp I without difficulty. A good route had been found through the icefall, several routes in fact, and the passage, although tedious and hot, was not difficult. We celebrated their accomplishment with a special brew of ice-cold Jell-O, which revived Molenaar, who had been confined to bed with fever and weakness.

During the afternoon each man was given the special high-altitude clothing he would need, and each sorted and re-sorted such personal items as books, mittens, "snorkels" (a type of breathing tube made from the upper 6 inches of a woolen stocking and worn over nose and mouth), and bright and fanciful caps. From here on we would be limited to 40 pounds of clothing and gear per man, and cutting down came hard to some. George Bell, our ace photographer, objected, "How about this three-foot telephoto lens for my Leica? Does it have to be included in my weight allowance with my other cameras and their film?" Schoening and I, with movie cameras and tripods, were sympathetic, and finally cameras were allowed in excess, as was film.

Over tea, which dragged on into dinner, we discussed plans. We had reached Base Camp despite frustrations, worries, and delays, within a day of schedule, losing only a small amount of food and equipment. The theft of Streather's brand-new boots was a serious problem, and we would also have trouble in finding mountain footwear for the

Hunzas to replace those boots which had been stolen. Apart from these minor worries we were in good shape, well and strong and ready to go.

Tony's report on the treasury was not exactly reassuring. After paying off the porters he was able to muster four annas, approximately eight cents, and this only after each individual had given up all his own funds to the expedition treasury. This sorry financial position seemed unimportant among the splendid peaks which surrounded us, and with our own mountain squarely above us. I knew we would have mail runners to pay, however, to say nothing of the wages for the forty-five men who would return from Skardu on August 10 to carry home our equipment. I put the worry away until tomorrow, and we talked over plans.

There are three main ridges on the southern wall of K2: the Southwest, a steep, short rock ridge which plunges directly from the summit to 20,000-foot Savoia Pass; the 5-mile-long Northeast Ridge, a fearsome knife-edge of ice with fantastic towers and cornices, which runs from the summit pyramid down to Skyang Kangri; and the Southern Ridge—Abruzzi Ridge—which is a cluster of rock ribs in the steep southern face rather than a discrete and separate ridge. Bates and I saw no good reason to doubt that the Southern Ridge was our best choice. Our inspection of the Northeast and Southwest Ridges in 1938 had convinced us that they were not practical routes to the summit, nor did

95

we fancy the avalanche-swept precipices between these tremendous ridges. Wiessner's party in 1939 had also chosen the Southern Ridge after inspecting the others.

Nor was it difficult to decide upon campsites, for there is not much choice on K2. Camp I would be near the foot of Abruzzi Ridge, far enough out on the glacier to be safe from avalanches. This would be reached by a tedious march through the crevasses of the upper Godwin-Austen Glacier. From Camp I to Camp II we would follow the route found in 1938, for Camp II was too good a site to bypass. Camp III presented a serious problem. In 1938 we had narrowly escaped injury on several occasions when rocks dislodged by climbers above had fallen through our tents, once even knocking a cup from the hand of an astonished porter in the old Camp III. This had been a poor site, cramped, exposed to wind and stonefall. This camp we must either bypass or place differently. But could another location be found on that ever-dropping slope? If not, the section from II to IV would be a long and difficult climb, perhaps too long to be done in one day. Camps IV, V, and VI could be located in their old sites. Camp VII we felt might be placed somewhat higher, though this was uncertain. Camp VIII would obviously be placed near the foot of the summit pyramid, while somewhere in the rocks less than a thousand feet from the summit we hoped to pitch Camp IX, a small bivouac tent with food for two men for three days.

Our task was to build a pyramid of food and supplies up

the mountain, with its apex resting at Camp IX. In order to accomplish this, between 1,200 and 2,000 pounds of food and equipment would have to be carried to Camp I, with smaller amounts to each of the higher camps. It was imperative to leave food and fuel and some equipment at every camp to provide a reserve at each in case we should be forced to retreat during storm.

For this task we did not have much carrying power. Thanks to the help of the Mir of Hunza, we had brought with us from Skardu ten excellent Hunza porters. We intended to keep six or eight of these with us on the mountain, feeling confident that some would choose to return home with the other porters, which proved to be the case. The six strongest remained with us to serve as mountain porters. To be sure, the word "mountain" applied to these tough, cheerful fellows was a misnomer, since only one of them had ever been on a glaciated mountain before. They were strong, however, courageous, energetic, and willing. With the training we had given them on the march in we hoped that they would develop into capable climbers. These men would help us to carry loads at least as high as Camp II, and possibly to Camp III. Above this the terrain would be too difficult, the campsites too cramped, and supplies too limited to take them higher.

Base Camp was a busy place. Upon our arrival it seemed the wildest, most desolate, most remote spot in the world. Within a few hours it became home, and when we came down to it from weeks above, it seemed a luxurious resort. Our tents were pitched on a thin moraine, only a few inches of small rocks covering the snow, with tall, white ice cliffs on either side. The heat of the sun, when the sun did shine, beating upon the glacier, melted the ice beneath its stony cover very rapidly, whereas the tents protected the ice beneath them. As a result we found our tents "rising" above the glacier at the rate of some 6 inches per day. Each week they had to be removed to another site, or else a ladder would have been necessary to reach them.

Reorganization of our supplies was not complicated. All of the "soft" rations, such as cereal, sugar, rice, and fruits, had been carefully packaged in Exeter, and one day's supply for two men packed in plastic bags. To these bags there now remained to be added only tinned goods, and the other "hard" articles. This packing required time and some ingenuity, and even so we were later to find some bags that had an excess of one item or lacked another. Our work was cheered by the discovery of photographs, notes, clippings from magazines, pin-up girls, and other items from home, inserted by our packing assistants and our families. Our afternoon was not untouched by nostalgia.

The following days were filled with activity. Large amounts of food and supplies were gradually carried up to Camp I, sometimes in the burning heat of the sun, which turned the glacier into a white-hot furnace, but often in a cold blowing mist of snow and wind which chilled us to the

TO THE FOOT OF ABRUZZI RIDGE

bone. On the hot days we found ourselves plowing through slushy snow, falling into hidden lakes and rivers. On cold days we walked firmly on the crust and often wore crampons.

After returning from the daily pack trip, there were many chores about camp to be done. Molenaar professed to have had experience as a barber, which his sample demonstration did nothing to confirm. There was little choice, however, and most of us preferred to have our hair cut by a "hack" than not to be clipped at all. Bathing was a slipshod affair because we did not think we could spare fuel to heat water, and the only other available water was that which flowed in the glacial stream at a temperature a tenth of a degree above freezing. We went off on several short exploring trips across the glacier or around the corner toward Savoia Pass, but we did not climb any of the lesser peaks around Base Camp because we felt that acclimatization would proceed satisfactorily during the packing period without other climbs. In retrospect I think that this was something of a mistake, and I now believe that on a subsequent trip a period of a week or ten days might be allotted to climb smaller summits from Base Camp, thereby increasing the thoroughness of acclimatization.

Our evenings "at home" were spent in writing letters, making tape recordings, and sorting food and supplies for Base Camp. Ata was now determined that he would remain at Base Camp while we were on the mountain. Since we had become more and more fond of him, we were loath to send him packing homeward. As he pointed out, it was obvious that he could be of considerable help to us in Base Camp, and his cheerful support and energy would be invaluable. There was the complication of finding supplies for him, however, since we had brought no great surplus for ourselves. Bates, in charge of the commissary, was somewhat dubious, but finally conceded that there would be plenty for Ata if we were all careful. The die was almost cast; it appeared that he would remain.

Wild life at Base Camp was scarce, but curiously enough a half-drowned squirrel, or at least a member of the squirrel family, came floating down the brook one afternoon. He was rescued by the Hunzas, restored to life with a little food, and after playing around camp for several days set off jauntily down the glacier. What this poor animal was doing at 16,500 feet where no natural food could possibly be expected is still a mystery. There were many birds about camp, mostly of the chough family.

Here and there among the rocks on the mountain itself, and less frequently in a tiny patch of sandy soil on the glacier, we saw small primula of the most gorgeous colors. A few spiders and flies were apparent on the hottest days, but in general there was very little animal or plant life in this remote and barren land. We saw no trace of the "Abominable Snowman," that half-mythical ape or man alleged to live only above the snowline in the Himalayas. Tracks were not seen, nor did we hear any noises, smell any odors, or see any shapes which might have contributed to the notoriety of our expedition.

So the days passed. The initial lassitude, shortness of breath, and slight headaches which most of us had experienced upon arrival at Base Camp disappeared within a few days and we felt stronger and more eager every day. The Hunzas, too, were gaining more confidence in glacier travel as well as in the curious white-skinned sahibs whom they followed. The weather seemed to smile upon us; the mountain appeared to welcome us. How little we knew of what lay ahead!

6. The attack is launched

CHARLES S. HOUSTON

6. The attack is launched

All the peaks about us were glittering in the cold, clear dawn on June 26 as I broke the skim of ice on the little brook before the cook tent and started breakfast. This was to be the great day when our attack would begin.

Bates and I were to move up to Camp I, from there to examine the route to Camp II, while the others carried supplies to I. Once we had found the route to II, another pair would move to that camp while the rest packed up supplies. And so we would creep up the steep slopes: reconnoitering, establishing camps, packing supplies, and reconnoitering still higher. In about five weeks we hoped to have ten or twelve days of food at a camp around 26,000 feet, from which to push a party of two within striking distance of the summit. All lay ahead of us on this shining day: all the work, the excitement, the joy—and the heartbreak.

There were many last-minute details to attend to, and not until after ten did we set out, Bates and I carrying extra-heavy packs. Tony and Bob Craig and all the Hunzas were to have a rest day in camp.

The first part of our march lay along the edge of an enormous fan of avalanche debris deposited by the spring snowfalls. This was slushy by the time we crossed, so that we sank to our knees or blundered into lakes and rivers hidden beneath the snow. The upper icefall was hard work in the hot sun and Bob and I, tailed out behind the others, regretted the added books, the extra socks, the little specialties we had tucked into our packs. We reached Camp I—still only a cache—by midafternoon and sent the others back to Base while we pitched the tents and settled down.

With sunset the cold fell upon us like a blanket, and a bitter wind blew up the valley. At six I put on my warmest clothing and set out a few hundred yards to the lip of the icefall, where I could have direct line of sight with Base Camp to try out the radio. Tony Streather's cheerful voice came in on the stroke of six-thirty, and I was much relieved to have such excellent contact. I rejoined Bates, walking gingerly across the crevassed glacier, and we settled down in our tents.

The next morning was beautifully clear. We hurried through breakfast, examined our prospective route through field glasses, and fumbled through the maze of cracks and séracs (ice towers or pinnacles) to the "shore." Then we started up Abruzzi Ridge. For the first two hours we climbed steep scree (loose stone) and snow slopes, crossing a few little ribs, exclaiming "I remember this chimney" or "Do you see that cairn? I'm sure we must be on the old route." We could see the snow slope below Camp II tantalizingly above us, but we could not seem to find the route to it. Over and over again we hopefully worked up a ridge or gully, only to come to an impassable section and retreat.

By noon we had to confess that we were lost. Climbing over increasingly loose and exposed rock, we simply could not find the old route. Far below we could see the rest of the party crawling up to Camp I under huge packs, and we returned desperately to our search. Another few hours found us hopelessly entangled with a precipitous gendarme (a rock pinnacle) and, at last, rather than retrace our steps, we admitted defeat and started directly down a gully to the glacier below, a route that had nothing save directness to commend it. About five we straggled into camp, freshly burned by the hot sun beating on the rocks, footsore, weary, and most embarrassed.

"How did you experts make out?" greeted us as we arrived.

Bob and I exchanged glances, each waiting for the other.

"Well, we couldn't seem to hit on the 1938 route. We worked across a couple of gullies and over two main ridges, but then we couldn't find a way over or up the big ridge that you can see leading up to Camp II," I said. "On this side the slabs are pretty easy, but the whole damn thing over-hangs on the other side. I don't know how we got over it before."

"I think we were too high," said Bates. "I think we ought to cross that gully low down and go up the scree slope all the way. Remember that long, miserable slope?"

"No," I argued, "the big gendarme on that overhanging ridge must be crossed high. The lower part is worse than the upper. We have to get onto the Camp II ridge higher up. We were much too low." The others laughed at us, and we retired in some confusion.

Next morning George Bell, Bob Craig, and I set out to tackle the upper route, while Schoening, Gilkey, and Bob Bates took the lower; Streather and Molenaar went down to Base Camp to bring up a last relay of loads. About eleven someone called, "Look, isn't that a rope?"

"Yes, and here's an old piton and another cairn. This must be the old route for sure."

We crossed a gully, puzzled over some intricate towers, toiled up a loose, steep slope to a chimney, which I certainly recognized, and finally there was Camp II before us. Our shouts reached the second rope far below and they started back to Camp, Bates first doing a spectacular lead through a keyhole in a ridge which was little thicker than his body.

We found lots of surprises here: several dozen tins of jam

and pemmican scarcely rusted in the thin air, some gas containers, stoves, and best of all, a Logan tent carefully wrapped and sheltered beneath a tarpaulin. We couldn't resist pitching the tent, which to our surprise was in good condition despite its fourteen years of exposure, and we turned back to Camp I happy in the realization that Camp II could thus be said to be "established." We joined the others on the descent and spent some time in fixing ropes over some of the more airy passages, especially across the smooth, worn slabs in the gullies, and reached camp after four, tired and more than ready for the thick brew of Jell-O which had become our standard "afternoon tea."

The early evening was broken by the shouts of the Hunzas, who had been sleeping massed together like sheep in one of the large tents, and suddenly rushed out into the darkness calling, "Sahib, come quickly; you must get up. The glacier is cracking. Camp will fall into a crevasse." The groans and creaks of the ever-moving ice had scared them badly and it took some persuasion to get them back to bed.

The wind howled in a crescendo toward morning and snow beat upon us; yet we managed to pack loads and start out, hoping at least to get more supplies part way. Though the visibility was poor, we worked our way up to the tent platform built in 1909 by the Duke of Abruzzi, where the 1939 party had established their Camp I. Huddled in the lee of those rocks, we decided to leave our loads there. Returned to camp, we passed a happy afternoon in bed, reading and

109

writing letters, while the wind—there was little snow in the scudding mist—played about us.

June 30 found all of us, Hunzas and sahibs together, packing 40-pound loads to Camp II, a round trip which took us nearly eight hours. Ata made the trip for the first time and was tremendously enthusiastic. "Charlie," he said as we reached the snow hollow, "Charlie—I'm going to spend the night here."

"No," I said, for, having an inkling of his plan, I had purposely not brought any sleeping bags on this trip. "What would you sleep in?"

"In the Logan tent with a stove and my down jacket I'll be fine," was his reply. But I would have none of this, and the others equally disliked the thought of leaving him there alone, so down we all went.

We were a bit strained that night, probably having forced the altitude too fast. Only two weeks previously we had left Urdukas, now 6,000 feet below. I was distressed by the length of the pack to II, and felt that we could not manage so long a day regularly. We discussed moving Camp I up to the old Abruzzi site, using that as our jumping-off place, but decided instead to try a few more days on our present plan. From the Hunza tent came groans and pleas for medicine. Headaches, backaches, nausea, and generally low spirits indicated that they, too, were feeling despondent. A joint council of war and generous doses of aspirin for all hands put us all in a better humor for early bed.

Now Bob Craig and Art Gilkey would take over the lead, and we all packed up to Camp II, leaving them to enjoy the luxury of the large Logan tent the next night. July 2 was especially clear and hot, and the packers from I continued to build up supplies at Camp II. That evening the radio brought gleeful word from Craig: "We found Camp III all right, and it's not too far. We plan to make two trips tomorrow."

"Did you get fixed rope placed?" I asked.

"Well, you don't need too much," replied Craig. "We put in some, and we'll do the rest tomorrow. Most of the climbing is pretty easy, and you can get away without fixing many rope handrails. Art and I were thinking just now that we might even *move* up to III tomorrow." We all thought nothing of this idea, and Bates and I wondered aloud if they really had found Camp III, a doubt which was strengthened the next day when they reported having made the round trip, with loads, in three hours, and in the afternoon having gone back to lay out and attach the rope handrail on the lower part.

We were now enjoying a real stretch of good weather, similar to the corresponding period in 1938 during which we had first reconnoitered the Abruzzi Ridge. Rest days must wait upon the storms which we were sure would come. On the third of July Bell and I left soon after sunup for the glacier below Sella Pass for a detailed telescopic examination of the summit cone. George had brought along the enormous telephoto lens for his Leica, at least five times as large

111

and five times as heavy as the camera itself. Laden with this monstrosity, movie cameras, and film, we wound our way through snow-choked crevasses to the foot of Sella Pass, staying well away from Broad Peak's ice cliffs, which avalanched regularly. The chill wind hurried us along to a point about a thousand feet above and 2 miles beyond Camp I, where we sat down to inspect the mountain.

K2 is an incredibly striking sight from this point. The Abruzzi Ridge seems vertical, a tangle of small ridgelets, black gendarmes, and glistening ice slopes. Fresh avalanche tracks could be seen high up, but we were glad to see that few of these reached the base of the steep ice slopes. Through the glasses we could see House's Chimney and could trace our route to Camps V and VI, only to lose it in the forbidding cliffs which form a roughly triangular rock face at the top of the climbing ridge. This grim section, its apex reaching above 25,000 feet, is called the Black Pyramid and contains some 2,000 feet of the steepest and most tricky climbing on the mountain. We filmed for half an hour, and then saw the tiny dots of the packing party working up the slopes toward Camp II. For another hour we lingered, bitterly cold, hoping to photograph a good fall of ice and snow from Broad Peak. But nothing fell, and we finally hurried down to camp to prepare vast amounts of milkshake for the hot and thirsty packers.

Craig and Gilkey were somewhat chastened that evening. They had discovered what we had expected all along: that

their previous "Camp III" was in reality only halfway to
the real site, and that distant camp had taken a great deal
more hard work to reach. However, they had taken two loads
all the way, and one pair of loads was halfway; fixed ropes
had been placed over the most trying sections below, and
the climbers were sure the route would go. We decided to
move two more men up to Camp II, and on July 4, which was
still bright and sunny, Bell and Molenaar were established
there while the rest of us carried up loads and returned to I.
Our celebration of the Fourth was mild: a nip from our
precious Scotch in which we graciously allowed the Brit-
isher, Streather, to participate. But the day was really made
noteworthy by Ata's announcement from Base Camp that
mail had arrived, our second in two weeks. Two Hunzas went
down to get this next day, and brought Ata back with them.

Now came our first supply problems. In planning an expedition such as this where weight is all-important, where
ounces as well as pennies have to be counted carefully, quantities are measured closely. Only a moderate surplus is allowed. In all our supplies we had a reserve of perhaps 25
per cent for unexpected bad luck, a slender margin. During
the next two weeks, gas became our main worry. With Ata
and the Hunzas steadily cooking at Base Camp (which we
had not anticipated in our plans) while the rest of us
worked slowly up the route, would our 40 gallons of gasoline be sufficient? Like the Sherpas, the Hunzas are a prod-
igal lot. Their happy philosophy is: "If there is food, eat

it all; tomorrow something will turn up." In their estima-
tion gas was intended to be burned, and for hour after hour
their stoves roared. It was time, past time, to stop this. We
set up strict gas rationing, but continued to worry.

Meanwhile the packing was going splendidly. All of us
felt stronger each day, and the nasty scree slopes between
I and II seemed easier every day. We made better time,
halted less often, felt better when we returned to I. Still the
splendid weather held; not even a cloud lay over the summit.
The sunsets, though lacking the flaming reds and luminous
greens so often seen in Alaska, were superb. We felt the
great freedom of expedition life. The party was working
together smoothly and well.

On the sixth we all assembled at Camp II—four of the
six Hunzas in the 1939 Logan tent, the others paired off in
mountain tents. Khareel, who was too old, and Ghulam,
who had passed a large intestinal worm, had been sent to
Base Camp, where Ata looked after them and chafed with
impatience to join us. We were still teasing Craig and Gilkey
about their "Camp III," but in the meantime loads were
accumulating at the real Camp III, the route was safe and
well established, and excitement was mounting.

All of us carried packs to Camp III the next day, en-
countering one of the serious problems of K2—rockfall.
So steep is the route, and so directly upward does it lie,
that rocks accidentally knocked off by the first climbers fall
upon those below. Since many thousand feet of climbing lie

over loose and rotten rock, it is almost impossible to avoid this hazard. We had faced it in 1938 unhappily, and had realized the danger. Now we planned to move closely together, never allowing a second party to straggle more than a short space below the first, taking advantage of all the natural shelter afforded by cliffs and buttresses.

About noon we reached a large outcrop of rock below and to the right of the old Camp III.

"Charlie," said Bob, "this may be the answer to our problem. Couldn't we somehow dig in our tents beneath this overhang, and avoid the exposed campsite we used in 1938?" This was a good suggestion, because the old Camp III had been placed on the open slope, directly in the line of rockfall from above. Several times in 1938 stones knocked off by climbers had whizzed through camp, tearing tents. We had finally taken down the tents each day and covered them with stones for protection, and I had expected that we might have to skip Camp III entirely, moving from II to IV in one long day. But Bob's site looked pretty small.

"Maybe," I agreed, "but we have a lot of construction to do to put two tents here." The eye of faith prevailed. Hidayat led the others in a furious burst of construction. From all over the slope big slabs and small were tossed to the masons in the gully. The job seemed hopeless for several hours, but we all worked with vigor, and by late afternoon a solid revetment nearly 10 feet high had been built up the gully to end in a platform about 5 feet wide and possibly

115

8 feet long. Above this rose a slight overhang, which would keep off rocks falling from above; below the long steep slope dropped clear to the glacier below.

Meanwhile a second crew was hacking away at ice and imbedded rock on a little outcrop, and bursts of profanity were punctuated by cheers as stubborn stones were broken away. A good platform was finally built there, more exposed, for on each side the rocks fell away steeply, but at least both tents were safe from stonefall from above.

This tiny camp was spectacular. We looked directly across at Broad Peak—still well above us—and down 5,000 feet and perhaps 5 miles away to the gracefully curving moraine where Base Camp lay hidden. Masherbrum dominated the eastern view, just as Skyang Kangri filled the western side. Hundreds of lesser peaks, unnamed, unmapped, unknown, lay before us. I have always been fascinated by the wasteland that lies to the southwest. There the peaks bear very little snow and few glaciers, but stand in stark black and red and yellow aridity, 5,000 square miles of unknown country where little rain or snow falls, vegetation is almost unknown, and no people live. At dawn tiny wisps of cloud floated over these dry valleys, and their deep, shadowed scars accentuated the peaks above. Always my favorite was Masherbrum, its distinctive triangle usually wearing a snow plume.

The shadows were longer and the cold more bitter as we hurried down to Camp II, well pleased with our day's work.

After supper, which each tent pair cooked themselves, we drew lots and thus selected Bell, Bates, Molenaar, and me to move up to III the next day. Over the radio Ata asked if he might come up with another load of mail to Camp I, and Gilkey and Craig planned to go down from II to meet him. All went smoothly. As usual, those to be residents at the higher camp found their packs much heavier and larger than expected (the sleeping bags were very hard to compress!), and it was a relief to settle down that night in the two tents pitched on the cramped platform at III. The day was cold with a very high overcast, and gray clouds were thickening in the east. Masherbrum was covered. The radio warned "storm." But July 9 was still good, though cloudy again. Bates was feeling poorly because of an abscessed tooth which had bothered him increasingly for ten days. We forced him to stay in camp, full of codeine, while Bell, Molenaar, and I eagerly started for Camp IV. Schoening and Streather were to make a late start from Camp II, reaching the foot of the open slope not earlier than noon, by which time we hoped to be out of the zone where we would kick stones down upon them. From twelve to two the slope would be theirs, and only after that would we start down. In this way we hoped to reduce rockfall danger to a minimum.

Above Camp III there are two short, steep snow slopes, up which we slowly kicked a staircase, fixing rope handrails freely. We found two caches of pitons and lots of old

117

and rotten fixed rope left by the 1939 party. We moved slowly, feeling the altitude. Soon we were among the steep, broken rock which Bates and I recalled so bitterly from 1938. Molenaar, feeling strong and eager, led off to the left and soon had us spread-eagled over a most disagreeable rock face, clutching small holds and cursing "Molenaar's Madness," as the pitch was obviously christened. Once back on the ridge we worked on up to the front of a big gendarme, a rock tower known to the 1938 party as "Petzoldt's Overhang." Having spent many hours chilled to the bone on a narrow ledge while belaying others up this pitch, I remembered it well from 1938. I pointed out the flake, the ledge, and the overhang up which the route lay—a bit of gamesmanship made unnecessary by the obvious old fixed ropes. George Bell led up this section neatly, but it took time and hard work, and we were glad to rest above it before climbing some disagreeable down-sloping slabs to Camp IV.

There another surprise awaited us. The wreckage of the 1939 camp was all about us—tents reduced to shreds, several large Thermos flasks, fifteen or twenty tins of jam, pemmican, powdered eggs, and a large tin of Ovaltine half used but still in perfect condition after fourteen years. Two stoves, several cooking pots, some gasoline, and three good sleeping bags were also there. Though the sleeping bags were frozen and filled with ice, we were able to dry them out and would bless them several weeks later.

7. Storm warning

CHARLES S. HOUSTON

7. Storm warning

Camp IV lies directly beneath a great vertical cliff of fer-ruginous limestone from 150 to 400 feet high. This seems to be a great dike or intrusion, standing sheer and steep across the climbing ridge like an enormous wall without a gate. In 1938 we considered it the key to the whole climb, and spent some time in trying to pass around the lower end—an impossibility. Bill House, supported by Bob Bates, finally worked out a spectacular route up a narrow vertical crack, doing about 150 feet of very difficult climbing. House's Chimney was made practicable by many pitons driven into the rock crack, and by hundreds of feet of fixed rope. Once above this obstacle we had felt in 1938 that the hardest single stretch of climbing was done, but while above it we had always worried about getting down safely. To descend that chimney in a storm might well be impossible.

I remembered this chimney with awe, and had wondered about it for many months. During the past ten days I had been mulling over different schemes which would put me in position to try this lead myself without being too obviously unfair to my companions. Now the time had come and I hesitatingly turned to George and Dee, both more competent climbers than I. "Would you fellows mind too much if I tried to lead this?" I tried to make it sound off-hand, but they must have sensed the eagerness behind the words, for they both agreed readily.

With considerable misgiving I led off, first up the steep snow to a little rock island, and then across an icy traverse to the base of the chimney. For the first 30 feet I worked on the face, clutching at tiny holds, and trying not to appear too clumsy to the experts below. More by luck and will power than by good technique, I reached the deep cleft, where I huffed and puffed, all the while pretending to get out pitons, adjust the rope, or blow my nose. The upper section was strenuous, though not too difficult. With considerable exhilaration I reached the top finally, and shouted to the others, "Come on up; I've got you belayed like a house." Remnants of the 1938 and 1939 ropes were here in the chimney, both too rotten to use, but both frozen too tightly in the ice to be removed.

This accomplishment meant a great deal to me, for I had secretly feared that House's Chimney would be beyond my ability. I felt that somehow I had crossed the line, that having done this I could do anything above. It was one of the great days for me.

From the top of the chimney one has about 300 feet of disagreeable snow and rock slope to Camp V, disagreeable because it is steep, exposed, and very slippery. At Camp V we found nothing but trash and platforms for three tents. By now the ominous clouds were dark gray and we hurried down to Camp III, delaying only to fix ropes in the chimney and on Petzoldt's gendarme. At III I found Streather established in my tent, for Craig, having brought up more loads with all the Hunzas, had then escorted Bates down to II, leaving Tony in his place.

Bob's tooth was bothering him enough so that he was ready for its extraction, but the dental forceps were in the medical stores at Base Camp, and I was at Camp III. After some conversation on the radio, it was arranged that Craig would go down to I, taking with him Hidayat, who was having trouble with bladder stones, a common ailment in this country, there to meet Ata coming up with the forceps, novocain, and a few odds and ends from Base. With another Hunza, Craig would then come back to II while I came down from III to perform the operation. The day had been a full one for all of us, and after making these plans we crawled into our warm sleeping bags with great satisfaction.

A sense of urgency began to penetrate our thoughts. Up to this point the climbing had been relatively easy, the weather mostly fair, and the altitude barely noticeable. The next few weeks would bring success or failure to our efforts, and each day would become important. We must waste no time. Our supplies, painfully carried up so high, must be used to the greatest advantage. Plans for each day were carefully weighed. We were entering our crucial period— those few weeks toward which a year of hope and work had been aimed. How long would the fair weather last? Would our good health and our acclimatization continue? Our talks, our thoughts, our diaries, and our letters home became more serious.

The weather was still fairly good on July 10. Bell, Molenaar, and Streather started early to carry supplies to IV, while I waited in camp for the packing group from II, who could reach me only after the upper party had left the slope of loose rocks above. It was a pleasant, slack morning. I fussed about camp, drying all the sleepers as best I could, counting our food bags, figuring plans, and often just sitting, wrapped in the immensity of my surroundings.

My reveries were interrupted by the arrival of the party from II, who urged me to hurry down before the truce was over and stones began again to be knocked down from above. Leaving Tony Streather in my tent, Gilkey and I climbed down, reaching Camp II just as Bob Craig came up from I with dental forceps and mail. After a leisurely

124

tea, I assembled my equipment for the first dental extraction of my career, somewhat embarrassed by Mohammed Ali, who, despite his lack of any training, was reputed to be a very proficient tooth puller in his village. He was said to be so good that natives came from long distances to consult him. As I boiled up the forceps and prepared my syringe of novocain, his attitude all too plainly was, "What's all this fuss about? Why not let me take care of this simple business while you get on with the main job?" Clearly my prestige was at stake. With Bates seated on a comfortable rock, his head pillowed in Craig's lap, I injected novocain, carefully seized the offending tooth, and to my intense relief and surprise, with one great pull obtained the tooth intact. The Hunzas were astounded, and from that time on I had considerable stature with all. Bates felt immediately better, and after a few days of Aureomycin was quite restored to his usual happy and energetic self.

In the meantime, Bell, Schoening, and Molenaar were carrying loads to Camp IV, now almost completely stocked. Ata had returned to Base with the unhappy Hidayat. The six o'clock "news" from Ata brought the report of Beria's arrest by Malenkov, but it also brought warnings of storm, which meant much more to us in our present situation. The clouds really burst upon us that evening, and heavy snow fell all through the night. Bates and I, enjoying the unaccustomed luxury of individual tents, found the snow piling in about our heads through our tent door openings, and breakfast next morning was disorganized and unpleasant. The storm, though not severe, continued all day. We lay contentedly in our tents, reading, writing letters and diaries, and enjoying the first rest in over two weeks. The Hunzas, too, seemed quite happy, piled on top of each other in the crowded Logan. Radio contact that evening reported that all was well at Camp III, although the wind was more disagreeable in that exposed site.

This was our first real storm. The Karakoram Range lies beyond reach of the monsoon, which so limits the climbing season on Everest. But as on all mountains, occasional storms occur here all through the summer, and the higher we climbed, the worse these storms would be. A week of storm above Camp VI or VII might put us in real danger. Trapped in our small tents by fierce winds, or unable to move up or down because of the danger of avalanches of fresh snow, we would consume our precious supplies, exhaust our strength. Herein lies the real difference between climbing in the Himalayas and climbing in the Alps. "Rush tactics" are too risky to use on great mountains. One must painfully build up supplies, stocking each camp, ready to live through days of immobilization during these great storms. To climb in storm above 23,000 feet is to court disaster. Frostbite is swift and insidious in the thin air at great altitude. Cold and exhaustion bring accidents. Judgment fails and disaster follows. The mild storms of late

126

July made each of us more acutely aware of weather and its influence on our destiny.

Although nearly a foot of snow had fallen and the weather was still cold and windy, we set off on July 12 to make a final pack to Camp III, waiting until Bell and Molenaar, who were moving up to IV, should have climbed above the danger zone of rockfall. It was a nasty trip. The new snow made each foothold and handhold a problem and cut our speed in half. We floundered in some places, and felt precarious in others. The rock ridges and towers on this part of the climb protected us from avalanche danger, but small waterfalls of powdery snow fell over us, filling our footsteps, hiding the rock handholds. Gilkey and I were glad to settle down at III while the others hurried back to II before the cannonade, signaling the descent of Schoening and Streather from IV, should begin.

We parted from the Hunzas with honest regret. They had long since become a real part of the team, and their climbing had improved each day, until they now seemed thoroughly reliable. Their early cockiness, bred of ignorance, had been succeeded by overcautiousness, which in turn was being replaced by the confidence which comes of knowing the problems and your own ability to solve them. After their initial demoralization at Camp I (and what mountain porters have not gone through this?), they had performed splendidly. We discussed the possibility of taking them

127

higher, but discarded the idea for several reasons. First was the character of the Abruzzi Ridge. Such campsites as had been found in 1938 and 1939 were cramped and scarcely gave room for even three or four tents. We saw little prospect of lodging more than six or eight men in any camp, nor was there much chance of finding better sites. Secondly, so continuously steep was the route that stones knocked out by climbers above raked the entire route below. Parties had to climb very close together, or take shelter while the higher party was working. To have more than six or eight men on the mountain at one time, we believed, would expose the whole party to considerable risk. Nor had we equipped our porters with food or clothing for the higher altitudes, and we did not have sufficient gas, stoves, tents, or food to give to them and still maintain the reserve necessary for a safe retreat for the larger party. Most important of all, we knew that they had much to learn, and might well become liabilities on the harder rock work above when altitude had dulled their reactions. Considering all things, we thought it wiser to send them down to Base Camp with Ata and to carry the packs ourselves. We parted sadly, after exchanging many embraces and prayers. Before they disappeared below the large buttress at Camp III, we heard a last cheer: *"America zindabad; Pakistan zindabad!"*

The next day, another gray, cold one, found us all moving loads up to IV, while Bates and Craig escorted the Hunzas down from II to I, where Ata met them and returned to Base. George Bell and Dee Molenaar carried loads up House's Chimney, and worked on the platforms at V. It was a depressing day despite our accomplishments. The weather had not cleared completely after the storm as we had expected, and more storm was obviously coming. We were close to our planned timetable, but the continued wind and cold was wearing on us all. The sense of urgency quickened.

About midnight great gusts of wind awakened us. Snow hissed upon the tents and sifted in the ventilators. Tony Streather and I discussed the storm sleepily and then dozed off; nothing could be done. Sometime later I dreamed vividly that I was being frozen between two blocks of ice, compressed harder and harder as the blocks froze together. I awoke in a panic, tried to sit up, felt a firm cold wall against my nose. It took a few seconds to collect my senses, to realize that snow had drifted in between the tent roof and the mountain wall, pressing down and out, flattening the roof over our heads. With great effort I wriggled toward the center of the tent (I was on the inner or mountain side), arousing Tony. The wind beat great blows against the fabric; the tent ridge sagged dangerously.

"The poles will break if much more snow piles on the roof," said Tony in a matter-of-fact voice. I disagreed. "The cloth will tear first, or else we'll be crowded off the outer edge. We've got to shovel."

"In this wind? There isn't room to stand outside, and besides, it's pitch-dark. Let's wait until morning," said

Tony. But in another half hour we had to decide: shovel or be buried. We drew straws; I lost, and wriggled out of my warm sleeping bag, feeling very sorry for myself as I tugged on stiff, cold boots, parka, and mittens. We slept now in most of our clothes. Muttering and complaining, I opened the tent zipper and faced a wall of snow which I finally cleared away. This gave me a few square inches to stand on while I shoveled and pushed and cursed. Fumbling my way in the howling blackness, I took half an hour of the hardest work to shovel off the accumulated snow, tighten guy ropes, and clear the tent. By then I was wet with sweat and melted snow, thoroughly out of sorts, and glad to crawl into the tent. I did not lose the opportunity of brushing a little fresh snow in Tony's face to emphasize what a hard time I had had. (Once before I had been caught in a half-buried tent, in the high camp on Nanda Devi in 1936. But there the shoveling was easy, for there was space to walk around outside the tent.) Bed was most welcome as I crawled in, and I enjoyed it the more when Tony took his turn at shoveling around dawn. The second tent, exposed on the ridge, had no such trouble, for the wind, although worse there, kept the snow blown clear. Over the radio Camp II reported heavy snow, and Ata chimed in with news of at least 6 inches of snow clear down at Base Camp. Bell and Molenaar had no radio at Camp IV, but I was confident that their location would be safe.

All through the day and night of July 14 the snow blew

about us, and Tony and I took turns shoveling out our narrow tent every three or four hours. We read, we slept. Dinners had become real occasions, because our appetites were still good (they were to fail higher up) and considerable ingenuity was usually exercised by the cook. Sometimes he added Triscuits to the boiled meat bars, or fried raisins to the chicken. Sometimes we had oyster stew (minus oysters) by mixing Klim, butter, salt, and tuna fish—a delicious concoction adapted from the "Klim Skardu" of 1938. Bates and I had noticed recently that our companions, heartily sick of our everlasting reminiscences, were now again showing interest in these memories, particularly when they involved some of the epicurean dishes then conceived.

The second night of storm was less severe, but July 15 was clearly another rest day. More than 20 inches of snow was measured at Camp II. Once again we dozed and read, talked lazily, nibbled on hoarded raisins, nuts, or chocolate, and shoveled every four hours. Our schedule was further delayed, and we worried again about our prospects for the summit. That night saw an end to our troubles, for the wind dropped and the stars appeared. We all slept well, hoping that finally the scudding clouds of the last ten days would be gone. But no hot sun greeted us in the morning; instead we found more overcast and a chilling wind. We were determined to waste no more time if possible, and so we made up heavy loads and began the laborious struggle through deep snow to Camp IV. Tony and I felt the chill immediately, and did not move as rapidly as those ahead. By the time we reached Petzoldt's Overhang, we were thoroughly chilled. There we decided to leave our packs, and hurried down to Camp III. Schoening and Gilkey, made of sterner stuff, pushed through to Camp IV, where they joined Bell and Molenaar, whom they found snugly established and none the worse for the storm. No snow had accumulated on that exposed slope across which the wind swept furiously.

Below us Bates and Craig were trying to pack loads from II to III. All morning they struggled through waist-deep snow in the gully above Camp II. By noon both were thoroughly chilled and wet, and wisely they returned to camp. The six o'clock radio contact brought us the startling report of a real "air raid" at Camp II. Craig had left his air mattress on the rocks to dry, while he packed up to Camp III. When he and Bates returned, they found the mattress deflated—with seven jagged puncture wounds. At a loss to explain the damage, they finally realized that the angry chough which was screeching around the rocks had dive-bombed the mattress, thinking it a tasty morsel. These birds are quite large, with a wingspread of 3 to 4 feet, look something like ravens, and often fly as high as 25,000 feet. They have voracious appetites and are incorrigible scavengers about camp, but this was the first time we had heard of them eating rubber. Craig, with a few choice words, hoped that the bird had the bellyache; the mattress, though repeatedly patched, was never again the same.

On the seventeenth our long awaited good weather seemed to have arrived, and we all worked furiously in the bright, calm daylight. Those at Camp IV moved loads up House's Chimney, using an ingenious device made in Seattle by Schoening. An A-frame of tubular aluminum, about 6 feet high, was firmly anchored atop the buttress. Through a pulley at its apex a long doubled rope was led to a second pulley anchored on the small rock island in the snow slope below the foot of the chimney. Loads were tied to one of the ropes and hoisted to the top. This was hard work, and time-consuming. But it was nowhere near so hard as carrying loads up the narrow chimney. This work continued next day while loads were relayed up from III by the rest of the party. On the nineteenth, the gray, cold weather returned. Our spirits sank. We managed to establish the whole party at Camp IV, with most of the supplies for the higher camps already up at V. Tony Streather, George Bell, and Bob Bates and Pete Schoening climbed House's Chimney once again and moved up to V late that afternoon in the hope that all of us working together could finish lifting the six or seven hundred pounds up the chimney the next day. This we did despite intermittent snow, cold, and wind.

Ata reported that night that mail runners had arrived two days late, having been unable to find Base Camp in the storm, and asked if we wanted to send out letters. Each of us wrote a brief note which I read over the radio to Ata, who copied it down, adding an explanatory paragraph of his own. What a sense of isolation this little episode gave us all! It would be two weeks or longer before these messages reached a post office, and another week before our friends received them. By then our destiny would have been resolved, our success or failure would be history. For one of us this would be the last message home. "Camp V, by radio to Base Camp, July 19." The letters comforted us and warmed us, but we felt the more removed from civilization.

We were a week behind schedule by now, but the supply train was well enough laid and we had enough food with us and in the camps below to be reasonably safe—unless the storm should continue several weeks more. However, the constancy of bad weather, the continual wind and cold and blowing clouds had a depressing effect upon us. Gone were most of the jokes; the banter had become more serious. We were more determined now than ever, but the picnic was over; the true struggle had begun. Gas rationing had been profitable and gas was now in long supply, but a new shortage had developed: matches. As the altitude had increased, we had had more and more trouble lighting our excellent little Army stoves, sometimes using ten or twenty matches for one lighting. From home we had brought what seemed to be an enormous supply, recalling the shortage of 1938. Having a surplus, however, during the march in, we had generously given many away here and there to the natives, for whom matches are a great luxury in place of their customary flint and steel. No one had paid much attention as the match supplies dwindled, but now a hasty count showed only four or five hundred left to last us for at least two more weeks on the mountain. For many nights I dreamed of matches and we used many tricks to save them —like lighting a candle in a tin can from which to relight the stoves when they sputtered and blew out—as they often did. But matches were to remain a worry for the next ten days.

8. Steep rock and steep ice

CHARLES S. HOUSTON

8. Steep rock and steep ice

High cirrus clouds again hid the sun on July 21, but we all packed loads to Camp VI, the route having been scouted the day before by Bates and Schoening. Above Camp V lie first several hundred feet of steep, loose rock, then an upward traverse across a gully choked with loose snow. Here several ropes of two elected different routes, some high, some low, and soon each pair was vainly extolling the merits of his choice above that of the others. Each party, though, had trouble getting onto looser and looser rock plastered with new snow, and steeper and more difficult pitches. It was a great relief to get onto the ridge itself and to see Camp VI above. Here, at about 23,500 feet, we noticed the altitude more. Only a few hundred feet of loose scree lay below

139

Camp VI, but this steep slope seemed endless as we puffed up to the old platforms first built in 1938, and used again in 1939.

Bates and Schoening had prepared us for the moving sight that confronted us there. On two small platforms nestled under a big overhang lay the wreckage of the last camp which the heroic Sherpas had used when they tried vainly to rescue Dudley Wolfe, sick and alone at Camp VII. Two tents had been torn to shreds. A stove, gasoline, and sleeping bags, rolled and ready to be strapped to the carrying frames, lay nearby. A small bundle of tea wrapped in a handkerchief lay inside an empty stove box beneath the snow. As we dug through the wreckage, we tried to imagine that day, July 28, 1939, when Pasang Kikuli and Tsering had climbed from Base Camp to Camp VI, an incredible climb of 6,800 feet in one day, to join Phinsoo and Kitar, who had come up from Camp IV in the attempt to rescue Wolfe. On the thirty-first, Kikuli, Kitar, and Phinsoo went up to Wolfe again, leaving Tsering at VI. There he had waited for them alone for two days before returning to Base Camp. The others were never seen again. Whether they fell trying to bring Wolfe down or whether they were lost while going to him nobody knows. Whatever their fate, the history of climbing has no braver story, no more generous chapter than theirs. Their sleeping bags, and the pathetic bundle of tea, were sad reminders of their courage.

But we had our own work to do. After rummaging through

the wreckage, we left our loads and returned to Camp V early in the afternoon. Then Streather and Gilkey started down to Camp II, where they planned to meet Ata coming from Camp I with Korean boots for all of us, mail, and more fixed ropes. I went down with them as far as Camp IV, where I was to spend the night alone before helping to hoist a few more loads up the chimney in the morning. It had been a long, hard day and I slept well despite the rising wind. After the loads had been hoisted up Schoening's aerial tramway next morning, I joined the others at V, belayed up the chimney by Bell, but the wind was too high to work more that day. Down below, Gilkey and Streather were climbing up from II, having exchanged news with Ata. We worried about them as the storm grew worse, hoping that they would spend the night at Camp III. Bell and I went down to the top of House's Chimney to look for them during the afternoon, and again about sunset, when we saw them through the driving snow. Obviously they were far too cold and tired to join us in the storm, but they managed to collect enough energy to climb to the bottom of the tramway and tie on a small packet which we hoisted. It was precious mail, which brightened the evening for us.

All through the next two days and nights the storm howled. Tony and Art had a radio at Camp IV, and we were able to keep good contact with them and with Ata, who had by now returned to Base. But there was nothing else to do save lie in bed, reading, dozing, and talking lazily. I couldn't help re-

141

calling Tilman's wry remark on Everest: "The chief danger faced by the mountaineer at great altitudes is bedsores." As the hours passed, we thought of the future. We had no worries about getting down, even if it were necessary to climb through the storm. But the weather was steadily deteriorating. Each week seemed worse than that before. We could have no hope for the summit if this should continue. Yet we were determined to press on. Bates and I recalled this same week in 1938, when the party was making its highest climb in hot, fair weather.

Dawn on July 25 was unforgettably beautiful. Tags and tatters of clouds shredded by the high wind lay scattered in the valleys below. Infinite myriads of tiny ice crystals sparkled in the air about us. The sky was deepest blue. Across the valley below us range after range of unknown peaks faded to the horizon. The rising sun colored all. But it was cold, terribly cold. Slowly we dug out our supplies, made up our packs, and set out for Camp VI. The wind numbed toes and noses, and within an hour we had all had enough, dumped our loads, and hurried back to camp, where we found Gilkey and Streather, who had moved up from IV. Next day it was still cold, but the wind had fallen, and the others moved Bell, Craig, and me to Camp VI to examine briefly the route ahead.

Directly above us was a steep tower, which we climbed on the right, the hard way, for we later found an easier route to the left. Above this, we followed a narrow, upward sloping shelf, and by some gymnastics gained the ridge again. For a while we could work a way up this tiny ridge, forced sometimes off to one side and sometimes off to another. Once we came to a short, slightly overhanging buttress, which was climbed by a spectacular wriggle up and over a granite needle some 10 feet high. Gradually the ridge emerged into the relentless steepness of the Black Pyramid. The rock was solid, steep, polished by icefalls through ages past. The holds were small for hands and feet, and often choked with ice. Bell, who was leading here, was in his element. He spoke very little, moved with deceptive slowness, but never seemed at a loss for the way. Sometimes Craig or I took over the lead to relieve George of the labor of kicking steps in some short, snow-choked gully. Despite the threatening sky, the ceaseless wind, the cold, it was climbing at its best. Seldom easy, seldom obvious, the way required skill and care and engrossed all our attention. The day wore on. It was too cold to stop to eat. Indeed for hours on end there was no place to stop save on narrow footholds where handholds were uncertain. We found no ledge on which to sit for nearly a thousand feet.

Finally, tired, cold, but excited, we reached the upper end of the Black Pyramid, where the slope eases a bit. Snow piles in here and some ice freezes on the slabs, making treacherous footing. Up a narrow gully below a huge boulder we crept, one at a time, carefully belaying each other. This took more time, and by then I was almost too cold to move.

143

Urging the others to climb on only far enough to find a possible site for Camp VII (we had seen nothing even remotely possible so far), I unroped and tried vainly to warm my frozen body on a cramped ledge beside the boulder. For what seemed an eternity Bell and Craig climbed on, clear to the beginning of the green ice slope which we had crossed in 1938. I shivered, not too hard, for my ledge was narrow. Only a few feet beyond, a great precipice fell away to the ice slopes which slid 7,000 feet to the glacier below. Suddenly I heard through the wind roar a warning shout, then another. Small rocks whizzed past, then a huge one. I could see nothing as I clung to my shelter. The cannonade stopped but I dared not stick my head out. When Bell and Craig finally returned, both looked shaken. "I had a little spill," was George's laconic answer to my anxious question. "Little spill my eye," said Craig. "George stepped on a big rock the size of a barrel; it turned under his foot. That's when I shouted to warn you. Then down he went, sliding on his face. I saw him claw at the ice slope with his ax and finally he stopped—a beautiful self-arrest. And a good thing too, for I was in no place to stop a fall."

"Pretty slippery spot," was George's only comment as I roped in and we started down.

The return to camp seemed endless to me, and I was happy to collapse in my sleeping bag under the tender nursing care of the others, who had moved up from V. Bates took charge of my hands and feet and I was filled with hot drinks, but it was more than an hour before I became warm.

The wind made climbing next to impossible on the twenty-eighth, and again we idled in our tents. The afternoon was made memorable by a great conference in Craig's tent, where six of us piled in together until the walls bulged like an over-stuffed pillow. Discussion of the next move led to reminiscence of things past, and soon Tony got off on tales of the frontier. For several hours he regaled us with accounts of intrigue and adventure, with near escapes and capture during the war years, and the hectic summer and fall of 1947 when India and Pakistan were divided. It was an exciting afternoon, for Streather has seen much and is a born raconteur. At supper time we regretfully crawled back, each to his own tent, in a real gale. The radio message from Ata that night brought word of the signing of the Korean armistice, but also warnings of more storm to come. Fortunately the warnings did not completely materialize, but high cirrus clouds next morning showed that the storm was still not spent, although the wind had dropped, and we carried 35-pound loads up to the cache near the tentative site for Camp VII in dubious weather. The added new snow made climbing difficulties even worse, and we all felt the cold bitterly.

At last on the thirtieth of July the sun shone hot and warm, and the sky was cloudless. The long awaited spell of good weather had arrived. With high hopes we made up heavy

145

loads. Art Gilkey and Pete Schoening were to move up to VII, and we carried enough food and supplies to insure their safety there. With the large party and heavier packs, we made slow progress, each rope delayed by the belaying of the party above. As the hours passed, the sunlight grew fainter, high clouds came in again to hide the sun, and the wind rose. In the middle of the afternoon, cold and tired, we reached the ice slope where Camp VII should be placed. Vainly we searched for some spot where the "eye of faith" might see a tent platform. In this sloping waste of rock and ice we found nothing. A few small stones were there, but not enough to build up a wall, and nowhere could we find snow deep enough to carve out a ledge. It was far too late in the day to try to cross the ice slope to find shelter in the broken séracs on the far side, where we had camped in 1938. All were tired and cold. We were reluctant to retreat with Schoening and Gilkey to Camp VI. As we sat dejectedly on the rocks, Craig chopped idly at the slope. His ice ax broke through; he had hit upon a shallow cave roofed with ice. In a few moments all of us had hacked into the slope and soon a sort of platform was built. It was not the most inviting spot, measuring at most 6 by 4 feet, and floored unevenly with chips of ice. Worst of all, it lay at the foot of a steepening ice slope, which disappeared in the clouds above. New snow on that slope might mean avalanches unless the wind blew it clear. But, considering everything, it seemed reasonably safe to leave Pete and Art here for that night; indeed we

146

had no other choice if we were to proceed higher with the climb. Unhappily, we left them to pitch their tent, and hurried down to Camp VI, where we were much relieved to hear over the evening radio that they were settled in reasonably comfortable style.

By now we had all become reconciled to wind and cloud, although we hoped against hope for the few clear days we needed. I think that by now we had all decided that we must climb in doubtful weather if we were to have any chance of getting higher. To remain in camp, waiting for the long anticipated spell of clear weather which we had every reason to expect at this season of the year, would exhaust our supplies and spell defeat. The seventeen days of food and fuel which we had carried up to Camp VI would, I felt, be sufficient to allow us to push ahead, trying to get in position for our final climb when—and if—the weather cleared.

The thirty-first was definitely not a climbing day, at least not a day on which to tackle the Black Pyramid. Schoening and Gilkey, facing the dangers of a second day at Camp VII, rightly chose to search for a better site. As we lay snugly in our tent, they reported over the radio every two hours. First they managed to cut steps across the ice traverse to the séracs among which the 1938 and 1939 parties had camped. They found the whole area greatly changed and after an hour of search found no adequate campsite. Returning to the tiny tent which we called Camp VII, they next carved steps directly upward until they reached the snow where they could

147

kick a stairway. Up this slope they labored for several hours through the clouds, emerging at last on a flat area on the very edge of the great precipice which falls toward the east and Base Camp. From this campsite they radioed the cheerful news: Camp VIII was found. It would be a long and difficult climb from VI, almost 2,000 feet, but there was no choice. Back to their narrow ledge they went, stopping only to fix ropes over the steepest ice. Theirs was a magnificent accomplishment, carried out under hard conditions, and it made possible all the events, both good and bad, which followed.

9. The highest men in the world

CHARLES S. HOUSTON

9. The highest men in the world

August 1—Swiss day. We saw the sun again, through racing clouds which said, "Go on, the storm is over. The sky will soon be blue, the sun warm." Leaving Bates and Streather to follow next day, the rest of us broke camp, taking all save two tents and a little food and fuel with us. We started up the long, hard climb to Camp VIII. Schoening and Gilkey were busily packing food from VII to VIII as we struggled up the last stretch of the Black Pyramid, moving very slowly with our packs, for even 35 pounds weighs heavily at that altitude. Five hours later we reached Camp VII. As we passed the now empty ice ledge, we met Schoening and Gilkey returning through the clouds at VIII to guide us up. We strapped crampons on our clumsy Korean boots, added

151

more supplies to our packs, and climbed on up the huge steps carved in the ice by our pioneers. It was a nasty stretch, pure green ice as smooth as a skating rink, with only scattered stones here and there. We were all frankly relieved to reach the snow, where our footing was secure although more difficult.

I thought that day would never end. I was counting steps, my hope being to climb ten steps before stopping, but I found that I had to stop more and more often. Finally, in the deep snow, I unroped and set my own pace, for the men above seemed tireless. Often the clouds hid them from me, but I had their tracks, knee or thigh deep, to follow. About six o'clock, close to exhaustion, I reached Camp VIII, where a tiny tent in this white wilderness would be our home. The rest were equally tired, but we all managed to pitch two more tents, blow up our air mattresses, cook supper, and crawl into bed. It is surprising even now to recall how quickly we recovered. Morale was magnificent. We were within striking distance of the goal. The summit might still be ours.

We spent a sleepless night with the wind beating about us, but next morning the sun shone hot and full and we dragged out our snow-caked sleeping bags and our wet clothes to dry. Gilkey and Schoening felt miserable. They had shared one of the "impermeable" nylon tents, a fabric which does not "breathe." Both men blamed this semi-suffocation for their illness. Both had severe headaches and felt nauseated.

Schoening saw double. Neither was able to do much for an hour or two.

Over the radio I made plans with Bates and Streather at Camp VI to meet them at Camp VII around noon. After enjoying the unaccustomed sunlight for an hour or two, we hurried down to the empty ledge at VII to bring back what few loads of food remained there. The wind and clouds were so bad again that we felt certain that our friends would have turned back. We packed up loads and started upward. Through the storm Craig heard a shout. We listened. Sure enough, a hail from far down the pyramid. They were still coming, but far, far below. We held a hurried conference. Without tents it was too cold for us to await them there. Late as they were, it seemed almost impossible that they could reach Camp VIII that day, and neither they nor we had a tent in which to sleep at VII. They must be sent back to Camp VI. Altogether we shouted again and again, "Go back, go back." The wind mocked us. Finally we started to climb again to VIII, certain that our message must have been received.

But some little voice within reminded me of the strong determination of these two men. From the Camp at VII I gathered up the pile of willow wands, 3-foot wooden dowels painted black at one end. Passing these out to the others in the party, we planted one dowel every 50 feet up the slope as we climbed. This would guide the others if they should

153

come through the snow which had already completely buried our morning track, and would soon hide the tracks we were then making. We arrived at Camp VIII late in the afternoon, thoroughly cold and exhausted. It was growing dark. "They will never come now," said Pete. As he spoke there came a weary shout. It was our friends, exhausted, triumphant, cold, and hungry.

"Yes, we heard your shouts," said Streather. "But we thought you meant *we* are going back." "So we kept on," added Bob. "Thank God for your willow wands. We had no idea where your camp was and couldn't see a thing. Your tracks were completely gone above the ice steps."

While Pete and Art pitched a tent for them, George and I hastily boiled up a pot of tea, only to spill the whole pot as we poured. Our tent floor was flooded, our sleeping bags soaked, but who cared? The party was all together, all well. We had the men, we had the food, we had the will, but would we get the weather? It was a happy evening with high excitement which kept us talking until late.

The night was long and our sleep broken. Battering gusts of wind flapped the fabric of the tent against our heads with malicious force. Snow sifted through tiny holes in the tent and through the ventilators, covering us with powder. Crowded as we were with boots and clothing, food bags, stoves, and pots, there was little room to turn or stretch. Sleep was fitful and broken. The wind screamed about us; snow hissed on the tent walls.

Day broke a sickly gray. No sun penetrated the dense white mist of cloud and tortured snow. Only our watches advanced the hours. Snow piled in drifts about the tents until a sudden change in the wind swept them clear and piled new drifts elsewhere. We were disinherited from the earth, our only horizon the tents. Once or twice during the day a man would move from one tent to another, chat for a while, and then stumble off. But no one could live long in that white hell of wind and driven snow; fine sharp ice crystals penetrated our lungs, smothered and choked us. Only by cupping heavy gloves about his mouth could a man draw a breath. Though it was not terribly cold, perhaps 0°F., the chill of the tearing wind was bitter and we were cold even in all our clothing. There was nothing to do save lie in our sleeping bags, where fortunately we were warm, and wait—and hope —and wait.

Our one contact with the world, the world of people and things (not the world of tents and snow and wind), was the radio. Every morning at seven and every evening at six I took the wonderful little Raytheon walkie-talkie out of my sleeping bag, where I usually kept it to warm the batteries. Anxiously I would wait for the stroke of six.

"Hello, Base Camp. Hello, Base Camp. This is Camp VIII. Can you hear me? Over." And a cheerful voice would answer, "Hello, Charlie, I hear you very well. Give me your news, please. Over."

"Well, Ata, the storm keeps on up here. There is nothing

155

to see, and we can't get out. But we are fighting-fit and ready to go. What is your news? Over."

"Here too we have storm, Charlie. Even at Base a foot of snow fell today. None of the peaks can be seen. The wind is terrific. Over."

"Ata, tell me the weather forecast." And Ata would answer sadly, "Charlie, tonight Radio Pakistan said, 'At 24,000 feet the weather will be cloudy with heavy snowfall. Winds will be westerly, blowing 40 to 45 knots, occasionally gusting to hurricane velocity.' I'm sorry, Charlie, but if the forecast is right, you will have more storm tomorrow." I could feel the sorrow and the anxiety in his voice. I knew how he longed to help us, how powerless this energetic and determined man must feel. But his presence at Base Camp, his voice on the radio, gave us new strength.

As we lay in our tents, or visited each other through these stormy days, our thoughts were always on the summit. Endlessly we discussed plans. Over and over again we made out careful lists of the supplies we would carry to Camp IX, supplies for two men for three days. Three days that might give us victory. But three *good* days they must be! Three clear, calm days. On the first day the whole party would move two men to a camp as high as possible on the summit cone, somewhere in the black towers to the east of the ice, perhaps above 27,000 feet. On the second day these two would make their bid for the summit, returning that night to Camp VIII. On that same day a second team would move

BASE CAMP

up to Camp IX to help the first party down if successful, to replace them and make a second try on the third day if they had failed.

"Three days—just three clear days," we said.

August third and fourth were like the first and second. Wind and driven snow. Mist and cloud. Tents flapping against our heads and shoulders. For an hour once or twice in those days we saw a sickly sun, were able to crawl out and stretch our legs in the deep drifts.

Despite the continuing storm, our spirits were so high, our confidence so strong, that we selected the summit teams on August 3. I had anticipated that various factors would eliminate three or four men from a possible summit try, but here were eight climbers, all apparently fit and eager to go higher. The philosophy of our expedition had avoided one-man decisions, and I was reluctant to choose by myself the men who might have the great chance for the crowning effort. We took a secret ballot, therefore, selecting our two best men by vote of all. Each of us thought carefully and long, and when I crawled back from the other tents through the blizzard, I was prouder than ever before of my party. When the ballots were counted, Bell and Craig were to be the first team, Gilkey and Schoening the second. But I asked Ata not to tell their names to the porters when I radioed him that night, for one of our cherished hopes was to preserve the anonymity of the summit pair—if they succeeded. We hoped to report, "Two men reached the top"—no more, no less. We felt that this would doubly underline the team nature of our enterprise. It would emphasize as strongly as we could the interdependence of the climbing party. But this was not to be.

The lulls were rare and brief. During the fourth night the wind gained new force. George Bell and I watched the nylon walls of our tent stretch and pull. Runs appeared in the fabric. We knew that the cloth could not last long.

I wondered aloud, "George, shall we get out of our tents now and make a dash for another?"

"I think we'll last till daylight," was his calm answer. "It will be tough to get into boots and move our gear in the dark."

"Even if we could survive the wind," was my mental note.

So we slept fitfully, and every time I looked up the runs were wider and longer. With dawn came a little lull, then terrific gusts. Our tent was going, and George and I rushed into boots and parkas, and blundered out into the storm as the tent went down, its poles snapped and the fabric torn. Each pulled his sleeping bag from the wreckage and crawled into another tent. A second trip for food was all we could manage in the wind and cold. Streather and Bates pretended to be glad to have me crowd into their tent, a French model with lining which made it very cramped even for two. George piled in on Dee Molenaar and Bob Craig. The storm reached its peak. The day wore on.

Can such an ordeal be remotely conceived as "pleasure"

159

or "sport"? Are we masochists to "enjoy" such a battering, such cold, such wind, lack of food, lack of sleep, lack of water? Emphatically not. Our stay at Camp VIII, ten days of hardship and anxiety, was terribly hard. It brought each of us down to fundamentals. The deepest springs of character were tapped for our survival. The lack of oxygen at great altitudes may dull the mind and weaken the body, but there is an inner strength of spirit, a bigger power which emerges undiminished, even magnified, to bring a man through such an experience. We faced nature's wildest forces with our pitifully feeble tents and clothing as our only weapons, plus our inner determination. Perhaps it is this conquest, conquest of one's self through survival of such an ordeal, that brings a man back to frontiers again and again. It may be a storm at sea, the arctic cold, or the desert heat. It may be a frontier of the spirit or of the mind. By testing himself beyond endurance man learns to know himself. He endures and grows. Each generation passes the limits defined by its elders; the passage of the oceans, the reaching of the poles, flight, the four-minute mile, the theory of relativity, atomic fission. In a small way the conquest of a great peak is such a frontier.

But we did not think much about *why* we had come. Our whole energies were focused on survival, though we still planned to go higher. Not one of us but wished the job were done; not one of us but longed for Base Camp and for home. Apathy grows strong on high peaks, the body becomes feeble,

160

the force to advance declines. Simple jobs—writing a diary, taking photographs, cleaning the cooking pots—loom as major undertakings. It seems too hard, too tiring to do anything but lie still and rest, and yet someone managed to go out for more food bags, and at the same time to supply the other tents. Someone tightened the guy ropes on all tents. When we could melt snow, someone had strength to clean and fill the pots, and someone else took tea to those in the other tents. Bob Bates read aloud to us for hours. Dee Molenaar painted. We all wrote diaries; my own was now over 200 pages long. Weakened, hungry, thirsty though we were, I was able to say truthfully to Ata over the radio on August 6, "We're fine; morale is excellent. George and Tony have slightly frosted toes, and we're all thirsty, but things look pretty good."

Ata's reply, "Radio Pakistan forecasts more wind and snow," was hard.

The sixth of August was an anniversary for me, for on that day in 1934 three of us had made the first ascent of Mount Foraker in Alaska, returning late in the night through a storm much like the present, but at an altitude little more than half our present height. Surely this date must bring good luck. But when we awoke the wind was as bad as ever, and I spent the day writing in my diary a long account of our sensations, our hopes, and our fears.

During the afternoon for the first time we discussed retreat. George Bell had two frostbitten toes which had grown worse even in his sleeping bag, and Bob Craig had ominous spots on his heels. Dee was feeling poorly. Schoening, Streather, and Gilkey seemed to be the strongest, but all of us were weaker than we had been a few days before. We could not sleep much in the noise and pounding which the wind gave; we had little to drink and only cold food to eat. Retreat seemed wise, but perhaps we could recoup at Camp VI and return when the weather cleared for a final summit try.

Was this an irrational hope at this point? Was our judgment so warped by altitude that we really believed that we could go higher? Ata says no. He says, and I am inclined to agree, that we seemed in full possession of our faculties, and that our radio discussions and decisions were sound. We now believe that we were still strong enough to make the attempt, that had the weather cleared on August 7 we could have gone much higher.

We were not to be so tested. On August 7 came the cruelest blow. The day began brighter, the clouds were higher, the wind blew less. We crawled from our tents and stumbled around camp like castaways first reaching shore. As Art Gilkey crawled out to join us, he collapsed unconscious in the snow. We rushed to him and he smiled feebly. "I'm all right, fellows; it's just my leg, that's all."

We half carried him to his tent, pulled off his clothes. As soon as I examined him, I knew with a sinking heart that real trouble had hit us.

162

"I've had this Charley horse for a couple of days now," said Art anxiously. "I thought it would be gone by now. It's sure to clear up in another day—isn't it?" The last was added in a voice that carried no assurance. The diagnosis was all too clear. Art had developed thrombophlebitis. Blood clots had formed in the veins of his left calf, cutting off the circulation and jeopardizing his leg. Already the ankle was swollen and an angry red. Reassuring him as best I could, I wrapped both legs snugly in Ace bandages and rejoined Bates and Streather in our tent. One look at my face sobered them as I explained the situation. "What's more," I concluded, "sometimes bits of clot break off and are carried to the lungs. At sea level this embolism is often fatal, and up here—" I shrugged, not having the heart to finish.

"Whatever caused this?" asked Tony. "I never heard of such a thing. Art didn't have any sickness or injury, did he?"

"I can't tell you what caused it. It's a disease which usually hits older people, or surgical patients," I explained. "I have never heard of it in healthy young mountaineers."

Then Bob asked the question we were all thinking, "How soon will he get better, Charlie? What are his chances?"

This was hard to answer. Under ideal circumstances the condition often clears in ten days to three weeks, though it may last longer. Under our conditions of dehydration, cold, and anxiety, it seemed unlikely he would improve. I didn't have the heart to add the latter, but optimistically I predicted ten days, and I explained to them the possibility of a

163

pulmonary embolism. Bob went out to tell the other men. I sat for a few minutes, then crawled to Art's tent. I did the best I could to explain his condition, leaving out the complications, taking as optimistic a note as I could, trying to hide my awful certainty that he would never reach Base Camp alive.

By this catastrophe our whole fortunes had been changed. Before, we had been clinging to our camp, hoping for the clear weather which might bring success. Now we could only hope for weather good enough to try to lower Art down the mountain. I talked with Schoening and Craig, both of whom had done a great deal of mountain rescue work. Both said we could somehow manage to get Art down, but their statements lacked conviction. I did not believe them. I knew, we all knew, that no one could be carried, lowered, or dragged down the Black Pyramid, over the dreadful loose rock to Camp V, down House's Chimney. My mind's eye flew over the whole route. There was no hope, absolutely none. Art was crippled. He would not recover enough to walk down. We could not carry him down.

But we could try, and we must. The day seemed settled, though cloudy and cold. We packed quickly, taking sleepers, camera, food, and only one tent because Camp VI was adequately stocked. Art Gilkey, in his sleeping bag, was wrapped in the wrecked tent, and a climbing rope secured about him. In the sickly sun we took some pictures of the party. The Third American Karakoram Expedition at its highest point! About ten o'clock, with a last look around, we started off.

Just then we came close to an action which would have been fatal. I have what amounts to an obsession about leaving tidy campsites, and I hated to leave, even here, such a messy camp. So I began to throw over the cliff all of the surplus food and to pull down the tents. Someone stopped me. "Come on," he said. "The snow and wind will take care of all this mess." We started down. At first it took all our strength to pull Art through the powdery snow, waist deep. Soon, as the slope grew steeper, we had to hold back, and hold back hard. Within a few hundred yards, what we should have anticipated became obvious: the whole slope of fresh snow was ready to avalanche. New snow had piled in even deeper on the ice, snow so cold that no consolidation could occur. As we cut down this slope, jarring it, the whole mass, tons upon tons of powder snow, would have plunged down the cliff. We had watched hundreds of these powder-snow avalanches from below. Now we were too close to one. Thanks to Pete Schoening and George Bell, we saw the danger in time and started back.

Our return to camp was terribly difficult. We could neither carry nor drag Art; instead we hauled on the ropes and on his arms as he gave great leaps with his good leg. It must have been harder for him than for us, and we were

165

close to exhaustion when we reached our tents, those tents and that food which I had come so close to casting over the cliff.

Our position, bad enough before this discovery, was now desperate. There seemed to be no real hope that Art would recover enough to climb down or even to help us lower him. We could not ourselves survive much longer under these conditions at this altitude. Already we had lived longer than any other climbers at such a high camp, and the privation and strain had taken its toll. But our escape route was cut off. It would take many days—if no new snow fell—for the slope to consolidate. I could see no hope, no way out of our position.

"Charlie, Pete and I think we can find a route down the rock ridge to the east of the ice slope. You know, on the left as you look up from Camp VII. Remember that rock ridge?" Bob Craig broke in upon my thoughts, trying to sound hopeful. "We want to have a look at it."

"Yes, I remember the ridge," I answered. "It's terribly steep; it's plastered with new snow; but it certainly will be safe from avalanches. It will be easier to lower Art down that than to drag him through the snow, and safer. Go ahead if you feel like it today."

Despite the wind and clouds, now returned in almost full force, Schoening and Craig set out. Some two hours later, while the rest of us settled in our tents, their weary shouts reported success and they straggled back to camp. Despite the wind, they had gone down the rock rim for 400 feet, and through the blown snow and driven mist had looked down and across to the ledge at Camp VII. Their route, though difficult and dangerous, was safe from avalanches. They were convinced that the unknown section between them and Camp VII could be done. At any rate, it was a way down, and it was free from avalanches.

I slept that night the sleep of utter exhaustion. Mind and body were beaten and numb. As I lay in the hazy half-light between sleep and wakening next morning, I was conscious that the wind had slackened. "This may be our chance to get Art down," I thought again and again in the dull repetition of fatigue. For an hour I lay thinking; then the stirring beside me showed that Bates and Streather too were awake, and we started breakfast.

So simple a phrase does not do justice to the complex operation involved. I lay in a narrow hole between Bob and Tony, who had the outside berths. We had changed places each day, for the two men on the outside got colder and wetter, while the middle man slept poorly on the crack between the two air mattresses and was pommeled by his neighbors on two sides instead of one. As middle man it was now my job to make tea. I twisted and crawled and wriggled, dragged a dirty pot from beneath someone's boots, filled it with snow drifted into the tent. Balancing the stove on a pot lid between my two inert companions, I was able to light it after only six matches. The *dekshi* of snow was carefully placed on top after I had wiped dry the bottom of the pot, for drips of excess snow would put out the stove. For nearly an hour I balanced the stove and dekshi till tea was made, protecting it from the flapping tent, which blew out the tiny flame several times. Finally the water boiled. Some water went to another pot for cereal, but most was for tea. Prospects of food aroused my stuporous neighbors, and in a very complex series of maneuvers they sat up and we ate. We had had so little to drink the preceding week that this meal tasted delicious and raised our spirits.

"This looks to be a good day—maybe the beginning of the good weather," said Tony.

"If it is, then we've got to decide what to do," Bob answered. "Start down with Art or wait another day or two. Do you think his leg will be well enough for him to climb down soon, Charlie?"

Sadly I destroyed this optimistic thought: "I don't think there's a chance of his climbing today or for the next week or so. We must choose between carrying him down in this dubious weather today or waiting until tomorrow in hopes it will be better."

We talked this over among ourselves for a while; then I crawled to the other tents. In each I found cheerful faces.

"Charlie," said Bob Craig, "what about a dash for the summit from here? We could do it easily."

"Or maybe we could move two men up to IX today,"

1. More than 125 miles had to be covered to reach Base Camp. The rope bridges of Baltistan are a terror. Made of twisted willow shoots, they are reputed "never repaired until broken."

2. Back row: Dee Molenaar, the late Art Gilkey, Charlie Houston, Bob Craig, Bob Bates, Tony Streather. Front row: George Bell, Colonel Ata-Ullah, Pete Schoening.

4. Native porters on the snout of the Baltoro. Above the loose moraines of the glacier rise astounding pinnacles. The constantly moving ice mass produces arduous walking and climbing conditions.

3. Hot spring near Askole. Just below Askole, the last village on the long, hard route to K2, the expedition relaxed for hours in natural hot sulfur pools.

5. K2 from Base Camp. For two months this was home to the expedition. From this camp, Colonel Ata-Ullah kept in daily radio communication with the climbing party.

6. Heavy loads being packed between Base Camp and Camp I on Godwin-Austen Glacier. The big build-up of supplies for the long climb has begun.

7. Pete Schoening on pinnacle between Camps II and III. Danger of rockfall from above was always present.

8. Capt. Tony Streather clearing tent at Camp III after a storm. A short, severe storm threatened to shove the tent clear off the mountain.

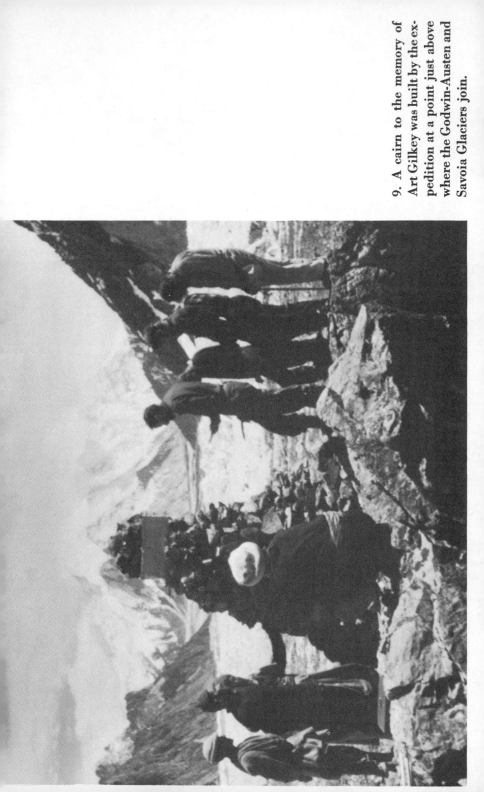

9. A cairn to the memory of Art Gilkey was built by the expedition at a point just above where the Godwin-Austen and Savoia Glaciers join.

chimed in Pete. "I'm game. We might as well do something while we wait for Art's leg to get better."

I looked at them closely to be sure they were in earnest. Here was no foolish, blind bravado, no desperate "summit or die" attitude. Nor was there any idea of retreat without our friend. Their courage was tremendous, their morale superb.

"It seems to me we can do one of three things," I said seriously. "We can sit tight today, hoping tomorrow will be better. Carrying Art will be bad enough, and we shouldn't try it except in reasonably good weather. Or we can start for VII now, even in the clouds, because tomorrow may be bad again. The forecast just now said clouds and wind. Or, and I think this is the best idea, all of you fellows can hurry down to VI today, leaving me to take care of Art. The supplies up here will last the two of us for at least ten days, and you can all come up to help us down, well rested, when the weather is really settled.

The others were reluctant to split the party at this point, and after some discussion we decided to wait another day. Then we would either all go down or, if necessary, Streather, Art, and I would remain at VIII while the others descended.

Art felt and looked better, and his leg hurt less. "I'll be climbing again tomorrow," he said. It was heart-rending to see his courage, to know that his hope could not possibly come true. But I did hope a better day would come for the

177

terrible work ahead of us, a day when we could see, a day without storm.

Meantime the wind decreased somewhat and the sun's heat could almost be felt through the dense cloud which enveloped us like cotton. We staggered around camp in the deep drifts, locating supplies, repitching tents. I made my daily medical rounds, looking at George's toes, which were by now badly frosted, and at Bob Craig's red and painful heels. For a long time I talked with Art, rebandaging his legs. He did seem better, but now the right leg was slightly tender, too. It was clear that he would not climb.

For several days we had talked about moving *up*. We did not want to retreat with bowed heads, beaten, discouraged. We would go down with colors flying. One last puny gesture of defiance must be made. Schoening and Craig were our fittest climbers now. They put on their warmest clothing, tied on their climbing rope, and set out—upward. For an hour they climbed through the steep new snow, over hummocks and across wide cracks. They could see nothing in the dense clouds but they were going *up*. After two hours they returned, having climbed perhaps 400 feet. They were still far from the summit cone. But their gesture underlined our spirit. We were not beaten.

At six o'clock I called Ata. "Hello, Base Camp, Hello, Base Camp. This is Camp VIII. How do you hear me?"

Cheerful as always, Ata replied, "I hear you very well,

Charlie. How is Art? How are you all standing up in this storm?"

"We are very good, Ata," I tried to sound sure. "Art seems a little better today, but I don't see any prospect of his being able to climb for a long time." I went on, "What have you to suggest for therapy, Ata?"

"Charlie, that isn't my field," said Ata, an eye specialist. "I can't suggest anything to do for him but what you're already doing. But I do strongly urge that I come up to help you. After all, you have two or three frostbite cases besides Art, and I can share your burden. Over."

My eyes watered at this new sign of this wonderful man's affection for us, his determination to share our ordeal. "Ata," I replied, "you can't possibly get up here in this weather."

"I could try," he broke in.

"And furthermore," I went on, "there isn't anything you can do. We must handle this from here."

I talked over our plans with him and he agreed with our decision: if the next day were not good enough to carry Art down, the others would proceed to VI, leaving me with Art and Tony, who insisted on staying with us.

"Pray for good weather, Ata," I concluded.

"You are fighting now for all your lives," said Ata. "We here in Base Camp have been praying for you for many days."

August 9 was grim and cold. The storm returned in all its fury. Snow screamed against the tent; wind beat upon us in renewed viciousness. Nothing could be done. We could not leave the tents and live.

This was our lowest time. For the first time I thought we might all perish here in this pitiless storm. We would never leave Art; none of us had even thought of it. But we could not move him in storm; indeed, we could not move ourselves in the storm of that day.

Art had begun to cough during the night, a dry, hacking cough. My fears were confirmed as I listened to his chest. At least two clots had been carried to his lungs, for I could hear two congested areas. He looked dreadful; his pulse was pounding at 140 per minute. But his courage never faltered. He had no pain—he said—but he admitted that the cough was a nuisance. I moved in with him that morning and Schoening took my place. Through the stormy afternoon we talked briefly or read. There was little to say. We knew the odds against us, but we had made our plans. Art said nothing of himself. He had never talked about his death, though he was too wise not to see its imminence. He apologized for being a burden upon us. He encouraged us, spoke of another summit attempt—after we got him down.

The embolism to his lungs made retreat even more imperative. He could not live long up here. He would probably not live through the descent, but we must give him all the chance we could. We must do it soon. That evening I called

Base Camp. "Ata, Art has had a pulmonary embolism. His condition is poor. We *must* get him off the mountain. We are going to start down tomorrow unless the weather is impossible. All of us are weaker, but morale is very high. I will call you tomorrow morning at seven. If possible we'll start soon afterward."

On that note we slept.

10. The accident

ROBERT H. BATES

10. The accident

We all knew now that some of us might never get down the mountain alive. Each had long recognized the near impossibility of evacuating an injured man from the upper ledges of K2. We had told one another that "if somebody broke a leg, you never could get him down the mountain," but now that we were faced with Gilkey's helplessness, we realized that we *had* to get him down. We didn't know how, but we knew that we had to do it.

Schoening in particular, and also Bob Craig and Dee Molenaar, had done a lot of mountain rescue work, and the rest of us placed great confidence in their faith that somehow we could get our casualty to Base Camp. Gilkey's high morale and his confidence in us was a great boost to our

185

spirits and we faced the job ahead with strong determination. When on the morning of August 10 Charlie Houston thrust his shoulders through the tunnel entrance of the tent where Schoening, Streather, and I, shoulder rubbing shoulder, had tossed during the long night hours, we spoke almost in unison: "How is he?"

"We've got to take him down," said the doctor. "His other leg has a clot now and he can't last long *here*."

The wind was hammering the tent fabric so hard that we had to yell at one another. Drifts of fine powder snow were sifting in through a strained seam in the tent vestibule, though we had done our best to keep the shelter airtight, and we could feel the whole tent vibrate as gusts stretched the fabric to the utmost.

"What? Move in this storm?" said someone.

"We've got to," said Houston. "He'll soon be dead if we don't get him down."

Nothing needed saying after that, for we knew what this decision meant. All of us had fought mountain storms before, but we had never seen anything like the duration and violence of this furious wind and snow that was still battering us. We all knew the story of the storm on Nanga Parbat in 1934, when nine members of a German expedition had died of exhaustion while battling the wind and snow. Willy Merkl, Uli Wieland, and Willi Welzenbach had been famous mountaineers, but a storm had exhausted them and killed them one by one. Here on K2 we had not only the storm to

186

fight but the steepest part of the mountain, and we were trying to bring down these precipitous slopes a crippled companion as well!

We all realized that our adventure had now become grim, for the odds against getting Art down were obvious, and our own position was getting more critical all the time. While Houston and Schoening were easing Art out of his tent into the storm, the rest of us began packing light loads to take down. We would need one tent in case of emergency, and we took the Gerry tent, our lightest one. We also might need a stove and pot, and some meat bars, chocolate, or quick-energy food that needed no cooking. Often the effects of altitude so weaken one's determination that doing nothing becomes a positive pleasure, but this was no time for lethargy, and as we moved purposefully out of the tents into the stinging blasts of snow, we knew that we had to move fast, while fingers and toes still had feeling. Little was spoken. Each of us realized that he was beginning the most dangerous day's work of his lifetime.

Gilkey seemed in no pain as we wrapped him in the smashed tent, put his feet in a rucksack, and tied nylon ropes to him in such a way that they cradled him. Four ropes, tied to this cradle, could be held by one man ahead, one man behind, and one on either side. We had already put on all our warm clothing—sweaters, wool jackets, down jackets, and nylon parkas—and stripped our packs to the minimum. As we worked, the disabled man watched the preparations silently. He was an experienced mountaineer and realized what all of us were up against. But he knew also that we would never leave him, and that we would bring him down safely if it were humanly possible. Art's cap was pulled down over his face, which looked drawn and bluish-gray, but he gave a wan smile whenever someone asked, "How is it going?"

"Just fine," he would say. "Just fine." And his mouth would smile. He never showed a moment's fear or the slightest lack of confidence, but he realized of course that he had been stricken by something that was likely to be fatal, that his condition was getting worse, and that he was 9,000 feet above Base Camp in a terrible monsoon storm. The nearest tent, at Camp VI, was 2,000 feet below. He knew that we could not carry him down the tricky route we had come up, and that we must go only where we could lower him. Even in perfect weather with all men in top physical condition, the task might prove impossible—yet Art Gilkey could smile, and his smile gave us strength.

While we were adjusting the tow ropes, Schoening and Molenaar strapped on their crampons and disappeared into the storm. They were to find the best route past the dangerous avalanche slope that had blocked us a few days before, and to go over to the Camp VII cache to get a climbing rope that was strung on the ice slope just above. It would be useful in the descent. After their departure Houston called Base Camp on the walkie-talkie and told Ata-Ullah our plans. "It's pretty desperate, Ata," he said grimly, "but we can't wait. We're starting down now. We'll call you at three o'clock."

Each man took his place on a rope tied to Gilkey and for a couple of hundred yards we lunged hard at the tow ropes to pull Art through the knee-deep drifts of powder snow; then gravity took over and we had to hold back just as strongly to keep our helpless 185-pound load from plunging into the abyss. The steep slope we were on disappeared below us into nothingness. Was there a cliff there, a jumping-off place? We strained our eyes peering into the storm, but we could not wait for clearing weather. Instead we had to depend on Schoening and Molenaar, who had gone ahead to scout out the way. As we descended, Craig and Bell pulled the front ropes, one on each side, and Houston directed operations from a point immediately behind Gilkey, while Streather and I anchored the rope higher up. Gradually we worked our way to a rock ridge, climbed down alongside it, and then began to lower Gilkey down a steep snow slope leading to a snow chute and an ice gully below. This route was not the one we would have taken had Gilkey been able to walk, but now we had no choice: we could go only where we could lower our companion, and we had faith that the two men ahead would find a route down. Once we were well started, return to Camp VIII would be impossible for any of us.

The wind and cold seeped insidiously through our layers of warm clothing so that by the end of the third hour none of us had feeling in his toes any longer, and grotesque icicles hung from our eyebrows, beards, and mustaches. Goggles froze over and we continually raised them on our foreheads in order to see how to handle the rope. Moving the sick man was frightfully slow. We had to belay one another as well as Gilkey, and our numb fingers would not move quickly. Somehow, when we got to the steepest pitch, however, someone managed to tie two 120-foot nylon ropes together and we started to lower Gilkey down, down in the only direction the slope would permit. Houston and I, braced on the storm-swept ridge, backs to the wind, could feel the terrible gusts trying to hurl us off the rocks. We could not see where we were lowering Art, but we could hear faint shouts from Schoening and Molenaar, who were out of sight below. As we slowly payed out the coils of rope, thankful that they were of nylon and would not freeze in kinks, Bob Craig unroped from us and climbed down alongside the injured man to direct the descent. Soon he was completely obscured, too, but Streather climbed down to where he could see Craig's arm signals, yet still see us, and so we belayers had communication with Craig and Gilkey and knew whether to lower or to hold the rope. Alternately we anchored and payed out line until we were nearly frozen, and our arms were strained when Tony Streather, whom we could barely see, turned and shouted, "Hold tight! They're being carried down in an avalanche!"

We held. Our anchorage was good and the rope stretched

taut. For a moment snow flurries blotted out everything, and then we could hear a muffled shout from Streather. "They're still there!" The rope had broken loose a wind-slab avalanche of powder snow that had roared down over both men, blotting them from sight. Craig clung to the rope to Gilkey, and held on to it for his life. The pull of the hissing particles must have been terrible, but the avalanche was of unconsolidated snow. The falling powder slithered out of sight and down off the side of the mountain, where it must have kept falling long after we could hear it. When it was gone, Craig still clung to the rope, gray and very chilled. Both men were safe. The grim descent continued.

Schoening and Molenaar, who were not far from Camp VII, soon were able to reach Gilkey, but it seemed like hours to the four of us on the icy rocks of the wind-swept ridge before they shouted up that they had him strongly belayed "on the edge of a cliff," and we could climb down. Stiffly we shifted from our frozen positions, and climbed clumsily down the steep, crumbly rocks to the snow chute above the ice gully. Houston and I were on one rope, Bell and Streather on the other. All were so cold, so near exhaustion, that moving down over dangerous, snow-covered ice stretched us to the limit. Through the murk of blowing snow we saw Schoening standing in front of a large, rounded rock that had become frozen onto a narrow ledge. His ice ax was thrust deep into the snow above the rock, and the rope with which he held Art Gilkey was looped tightly around the shaft of

191

the ax. The sick man was at the edge of a 20-foot cliff, beneath which we could glimpse the ice gully dropping off steeply into the storm toward the Godwin-Austen Glacier nearly 2 miles below.

Schoening looked like a man from another world. So much frost had formed on our beards that faces were unrecognizable, and we knew that we were fast reaching the breaking point. We could not continue much longer without shelter from the driving storm and food to renew our energy. Some 150 yards below us to the east was the tiny shelf, nicked into the ice slope, where Schoening and Gilkey had spent the night of July 30 during their reconnaissance above Camp VI. We had called it Camp VII, or Camp VII cache. None of us had expected anyone to spend another night there, but Bob Craig, whose struggle against the avalanche had so completely exhausted him temporarily that he could hardly tie a crampon strap, had been belayed over to this site to rest and clear some of the avalanche snow that had seeped under his parka. We yelled to him to try to enlarge the ledge. Meanwhile, with Schoening anchoring the rope, we lowered Gilkey slowly over the short rock cliff until he was resting against the 45-degree ice slope. Streather, who was roped to Bell, climbed down to Gilkey. Schoening held Gilkey's rope firmly while Houston belayed me across a delicate pitch of steep, hard ice, and then Houston climbed down to a point opposite the man suspended against the slope. The problem now was not to get Gilkey down, but to swing him across

192

the steep ice slope to the ice shelf at Camp VII. Our plan was to get a firm anchorage and then pendulum him across, but unfortunately the ice near him was too hard for axes to be driven in and the slope was relentlessly steep.

Even during the best weather conditions the maneuver would have been dangerous, and our position at that moment I shall never forget. Schoening was belaying Gilkey, who hung 60 feet below him, suspended against the sharply angled ice. On the same level as Gilkey, and 40 feet across from him, five of us, facing into the stinging, drifting snow, were searching for a place where we could stand and anchor the rope to Gilkey as we pulled him across the ice in the direction of Craig on the ice shelf. With our spiked crampons biting the hard ice, Streather, Houston, Molenaar, and I stood close together. Bell and Streather were roped together, Houston and I were on a rope together—and Molenaar had just "tied in" to a loose rope to Gilkey. He had done this when Craig had unroped and gone over to the ice shelf to rest, and it was Molenaar's precaution that saved us all. For George Bell, who was some 60 feet above us, began to descend a delicate stretch of hard ice in order to help with Gilkey's ropes. At that moment, what we had all been dreading occurred. Something threw Bell off balance and he fell.

I never saw Bell fall, but to my horror I saw Streather being dragged off the slope and making desperate efforts to jam the pick of his ax into the ice and stop. Streather had been standing above the rope from Houston to me. In al-

most the same instant I saw Houston swept off, and though
I turned and lunged at the hard ice with the point of my ax,
a terrible jerk ripped me from my hold and threw me backward headfirst down the slope. *This is it!* I thought as I
landed heavily on my pack. There was nothing I could do
now. We had done our best, but our best wasn't good enough.
This was the end. Since nobody was on the rope with Houston
and me, there was no one else to hold us, and I knew that
nothing could stop us now. On the slope below, no rock
jutted on which the rope between us could catch. Only thousands of feet of empty space separated us from the glacier
below. It was like falling off a slanting Empire State Build-
ing six times as high as the real one.

Thrown violently backward, with the hood of my down
jacket jammed over my eyes, I had a feeling of unreality,
of detachment. The future was beyond my control. All I
knew was that I landed on my pack with great force, bounc-
ing faster and faster, bumping over rocks in great thumps.
The next bound I expected to take me over a cliff in a terrible drop that would finish it all, when, by a miracle, I
stopped sliding.

I was on my back with my hood over my eyes and my head
a yard below my feet. My arms, stretched over my head,
were so completely tangled with the taut rope that I could
not loosen them. I was helpless, and when I tried to move, I
realized that I was balanced on the crest of some rocks and
that a change of position might throw me off the edge. The

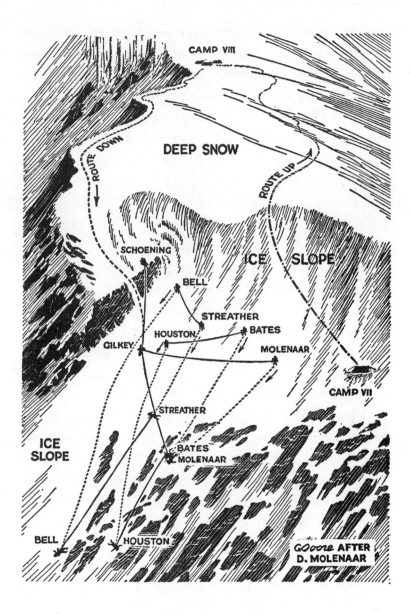

CAMP VIII

ROUTE DOWN

DEEP SNOW

ROUTE UP

SCHOENING

ICE SLOPE

BELL

STREATHER

HOUSTON

BATES

GILKEY

MOLENAAR

CAMP VII

STREATHER

BATES
MOLENAAR

ICE
SLOPE

BELL

HOUSTON

Goore AFTER
D. MOLENAAR

rope had apparently snagged on a projection—though how and where I couldn't imagine—but it might not be securely caught. Whether it was firmly held, whether anyone else was alive, I did not know, but I didn't need to wait. Almost immediately I heard a groan coming from nearly on top of me. "Get me loose," I called, and immediately I felt the pressure of a leg braced against my shoulder and the rope was pulled off my arms.

Grabbing a rock, I swung my head around. Dee Molenaar and I were clinging to a rocky outcrop at the side of a steep ice slope, studded with rocks, about 150 to 200 feet below the place where we had been working on the ropes to Gilkey. Blood from Dee's nose trickled across his mustache and beard, and he looked badly shaken. My rope was tight to someone or something above, and I heard a distant yell, "Get your weight off the rope!" Fifty feet higher, through a mist of blowing snow, I could see Tony Streather staggering to his feet, a tangle of ropes still tight about his waist. Below me I heard a cry, "My hands are freezing!" and, looking down, to my amazement I saw George Bell, who seconds before had been 60 feet above me. Now about 60 feet *below*, he was climbing up over the edge of nothingness. He wore neither pack nor glasses and was staggering up over the steep rocks, obviously dazed, with his hands held out grotesquely in front of him. His mittens had been ripped off in the fall, and already the color of his hands had turned an ugly fish-belly white. If his hands were badly frozen, of

196

course, we might never be able to get him down off the mountain.

Turning to Molenaar, I thrust my pack into his arms. Most of the lashing had ripped loose and the walkie-talkie radio, which had been on top, was gone; my sleeping bag was half off, held by a single twist of line. Without sleeping bags we were unlikely to survive the night, no matter how we tried! Since Molenaar wore no pack, I imagined that his sleeping bag also had been torn off in the fall. Whether or not the tent someone had been carrying had survived the fall, I didn't know. "For God's sake, hold this," I yelled above the wind, placing my load in Molenaar's arms. (For all I knew, mine was the only sleeping bag to survive the fall, and we must not lose it now.) The loose pack was awkward to hold securely while we were standing on such steep rock, but Molenaar grasped it and I unroped and started to climb shakily down to meet Bell. As I climbed down, I wondered about the ropes that had saved us. They were snagged to something up above, but the driving snow kept us from seeing what was holding them. Luckily I had a spare pair of dry, loosely woven Indian mitts in the pouch pocket of my parka, and when I reached Bell, whose face was gray and haggard, I helped him to put them on. Already his fingers were so stiff with cold that he couldn't move them, but balancing on projections of rock on the steep slope, we struggled to save his hands and finally forced the big white mittens past his stiff thumbs and down over his wrists.

Bell's fall had ended with him suspended over the edge of a ledge, below which the slope dropped away precipitously for thousands of feet. The weight of his pack pulled him head down, and he had lost it while trying to get right side up and back over the ledge. While Bell crouched down, working desperately to warm his hands under his parka, I left him, for Molenaar and I had seen a crumpled figure lying below a 30-foot cliff on a narrow shelf that seemed projecting over utter blankness below. It was Houston. Somehow a rope to him was snagged high above us, too. Climbing unsteadily but cautiously, for I was not roped and felt shaken by the fall, I worked my way down the steep rocks and across to the ledge. Houston was unconscious, but his eyes opened as I touched his shoulder. When he staggered to his feet, I felt relief it is impossible to describe.

"Where are we?" he asked. "What are we doing here?"

He was obviously hurt. His eyes did not focus and he appeared to be suffering from a concussion. Again and again I tried to persuade him to climb up the cliff, while Molenaar anchored the rope still attached to him from above. He didn't understand. "Where are we?" he kept saying, for my replies did not convey any meaning to him in his confused state.

The wind and blowing snow were searing our faces. We were all near exhaustion and in danger of crippling frostbite. If we were to survive, we had to get shelter at once, or we would be so numbed by exposure that we could not protect ourselves. What had happened in that Nanga Parbat storm which had taken so many men was a grim reminder. All of us working together did not now have strength enough to pull or carry Houston up the steep rock and snow to the ice ledge, 150 feet above, which we had called Camp VII.

"Charlie," I said with the greatest intensity, looking directly into his eyes, "if you ever want to see Dorcas and Penny again [his wife and daughter], climb up there *right now!*"

Somehow this demand penetrated to his brain, for, with a frightened look and without a word, he turned and, belayed by Molenaar, fairly swarmed up the snowy rocks of the cliff. Instinct and years of climbing helped him now in his confused condition, for he climbed brilliantly up to Molenaar. I followed more slowly because, being fully conscious, I had great respect for this steep rock wall, and with great care I pulled myself up over the snow-covered slabs. When I reached Molenaar, he was looking puzzled and very unhappy as he tried to answer Houston's repeated question, "What are we doing here?"

11. The bivouac

ROBERT H. BATES

11. The bivouac

When I reached Molenaar, I still did not know what had caused the near disaster or how all five of us who fell had been saved. Up above, through the murk of blinding snow, I caught glimpses of Art Gilkey, anchored where he had been before the fall, but now Bob Craig was near him. Tony Streather, in a direct line above me, seemed to be untangling himself from a confused snarl of nylon climbing ropes, one of which led down to me.

Much later I learned the sequence of events that had put us in this position and marveled even more at our escape. When Bell fell, he pulled off Streather, who was hurled into the rope between Houston and me and became tangled with it. We were in turn knocked off by the impact, and all three

203

of us—Streather, Houston, and I—began tumbling in a blind, uncontrolled whirl toward the glacier far below. Nothing we could do could stop us now. But our time had not come. For Molenaar was standing below us on the slope, farther away from the sick man, and he had just tied one of the loose ropes from Art Gilkey about his waist. That circumstance saved us, for our wild fall sent us all into and across the rope from Gilkey to Molenaar, and somehow Streather fouled onto this rope too. But our impact had thrown Molenaar headfirst down the slope, and we all bounded on unchecked until stopped by the tightening of the rope from Gilkey to Molenaar—a rope in which Streather was now completely tangled. Gilkey was not pulled loose, for he was anchored by Schoening, who stood on a rock ledge 60 feet above him, and the whole strain of the five falling men, plus Gilkey, was transmitted to Schoening, the youngest member of the party. Fortunately for us all, Schoening is an expert belayer, and his skill and quick thinking saved our lives. Later he told us how he did it.

By the time I returned to Molenaar and Houston, it was clear that through some miracle every climber was still able to move under his own power, but our exposure to the wind-driven snow was chilling us dangerously; we had to move fast to take shelter before we became too numb to set up a tent or became so crippled by frostbite that we would never be able to continue the descent. Since Molenaar's leg hurt and he didn't feel like moving much, I took Charlie Houston's rope and began climbing slowly up toward the ice ledge at Camp VII. I couldn't hurry, to save my life. Houston was obviously confused, but by instinct he climbed well and did what was asked. I hadn't climbed far when Tony Streather threw me a rope-end, and then Bob Craig returned from anchoring Art Gilkey and he and Streather took over the task of escorting Houston to the ledge. Craig had not seen the fall, but had looked up suddenly and been horrified to see the slope bare except for Schoening and Gilkey and a solitary ice ax with its pick end jabbed into the ice. At that moment a cloud of snow had blown across the ice, blotting out everything. When it cleared, Schoening, whose tight grip on the rope was freezing his hands, called to Craig to help him to anchor Gilkey. The sick man had not fallen, and he lay suspended against the ice as he had been at the time of the accident. He was probably the warmest of us all, but we could not continue to move him until the injured were cared for and we had more manpower to help get him across the slope.

When Craig reached him, Art handed over his ice ax, which he had retained for use in the descent. To make a secure anchorage was not easy, and Craig, still exhausted from his struggle against the avalanche, was not secured by anyone while he did it, but he skillfully found firm snow and drove in Art's ice ax right up to the head. He told the sick man that we would return for him as soon as we had a tent up. Gilkey understood. Not until then, when Craig had an ice ax firmly embedded, could Pete Schoening release his grip—which had held six men!—and begin to warm his freezing hands. Craig had not been involved in the accident, but all the rest of us owed our lives to Schoening's skill, courage, and technique.

Fortunately the tent had not been in one of the lost packs, but as I started to unroll it, the wind threatened to sweep it off the mountain. Craig and I were trying to wrestle the corners of the tent into position when Streather, who had now anchored Gilkey with a second ice ax, joined us to help pin the flapping edges under loose rocks till we could get anchorage for the guy ropes. The slope was so steep that the outer third of the tent was off the ledge and overhanging, so that it was impossible to keep the wind from sucking under the tent and trying to tear it away.

We were fortunate that this was our smallest two-man tent, for it held the ledge better than a wider one. Actually, in Exeter before the expedition, we had thought it too small for two men and had almost failed to bring it. Pitching the tent was frustrating, for each time we would secure one corner, another corner would shudder loose. Finally we tied the front guy rope to a rock piton and lashed the inside corners as well as we could to projecting rocks. When Bob Craig later pounded in a Bernays ice piton, we felt somewhat safer, though the nylon shroud line attached to it didn't look too strong and the outer section of the tent bulged out over the slope. If someone inside forgot how precariously the tent was poised and leaned against the outer wall, we knew that the fabric would probably tear or the whole tent pull loose from the little ledge, and with everyone in it roll down the mountain into space.

The moment the tent was up, we moved Bell and Houston inside, where they would be under shelter and their weight would be useful in anchoring the tent. Molenaar at this point joined them to help take care of Houston, for Dee by now had lashed my loose pack together and carried it to the ledge. His left thigh hurt and he had a cracked rib.

While these men were trying to warm themselves in the tent, the rest of us began to hack out another platform in the ice for Schoening's bivouac tent, which had previously been cached on the ledge as a safeguard for Streather and me on the day when we climbed from Camp VI to Camp VIII. This tent was meant for one person or in an emergency two, but if we could get it up, we meant to use it for three men to huddle inside.

At this moment Peter Schoening climbed down to us and declared laconically, "My hands are freezing." He too crawled into the tent to try to save his hands. All of us were still too busy to find out how Schoening had held us, for it seemed as if we would never get a platform flat enough or wide enough to pitch the bivouac tent. All our strength and energy went into chipping out an ice platform, for we had to get shelter from the bitter blast for everyone; but when we did get an uneven floor carved out, the wind

207

whipped the fabric violently. It was like working in the slip-stream behind an airplane as it taxied across the snow, spraying stinging particles behind. Finally Pete crawled out to help us insert the poles and we fastened the tent insecurely to rocks and pitons near the shelf of ice. It too overhung in an alarming manner.

The moment the bivouac tent was up, three of us prepared to go back for Art Gilkey. He was only 150 feet away, but a low rib of rock hid from sight the ice gully where we had left him suspended from the two widely separated ice axes, each firmly thrust into the snow. Gilkey had called to us a couple of times while we were desperately hacking at the slope to make a platform for the bivouac tents, but the severity of the storm and the position of the gully made it impossible to distinguish words. Gilkey sounded as if he were shouting encouragement, but the wind blurred his words, as it must have muffled our answering shouts to him. He knew that we were making a shelter and would come for him as soon as we could.

About ten minutes after Gilkey's last shout, Streather, Craig, and I roped up and began to cross the slope to reach the injured man and move him somehow to the ice ledge where we now had two small tents. We knew that moving him even this short distance would take every bit of strength we had left, and we roped together carefully and braced ourselves for the effort.

Schoening would have come with us, but as he emerged

from the tent, he began a fit of coughing so long and painful that it doubled him up and made us urge him to crawl back into the tent. Pete had gulped in deep draughts of frigid air while climbing up to collect the fixed rope above Camp VII earlier in the day, and apparently the cold had somehow temporarily affected his lungs. He coughed until he seemed exhausted. At the moment we were particularly dismayed by Schoening's near collapse, because he had always been strong and we were counting heavily on him to help in moving Gilkey and in getting the party down the mountain. We didn't know at the moment what his trouble was or how serious it might be, and in great distress we started out into the wind to traverse the slope to Art Gilkey. Streather and I had had our snow glasses off most of the day, because snow had frozen over the lenses, turning them almost to blinders. Apparently we had developed a touch of snow blindness, because we now seemed to be seeing everything through a very light mist. This mist was hard to distinguish from blowing snow, and we seemed to be moving in a dream. Fortunately, the wind had dropped as we reached the rock rib and looked into the gully where Art had been left suspended. What we saw there I shall never forget. The whole slope was bare of life. Art Gilkey was gone!

Our sick comrade, who had called to us a few minutes before, had disappeared. Even the two ice axes used to anchor him safely had been torn loose. The white, windswept ice against which he had been resting showed no sign that anyone had ever been there. It was as if the hand of God had swept him away.

The shock stunned us. Blowing snow stung our faces as we silently stared and stared, but the slope remained empty. Something about it had changed, however, for there seemed to be a groove on the lower part of the slope that had not been there before. A snow or ice avalanche must have swept the sick man away scant minutes before we came to get him. As Craig and I belayed Streather out onto the center of the gully, he looked down past his cramponed feet to where the slope disappeared into the storm below. We called and shouted, but all of us knew that there would be no answer. Nobody could slide off that slope out of sight and remain alive. Dazed and incredulous, we turned and plodded back to the tents.

Gilkey's death, though anticipated for other reasons, was a violent shock. He had been very close to us, and we could not forget his many kindnesses to each of us in the past weeks. We had admired him and loved him. But too many immediate problems faced us to permit brooding over our loss now. Several men were injured. Whether they were in condition to climb down the mountain without help, we didn't know; nor did we know whether we could get them down if they could not walk. We would never leave anybody, but our struggle to lower Art Gilkey had shown us that to get a helpless man down the upper slopes of K2 under storm conditions required more strength and manpower than we now had. The route down from Camp VII to Camp VI would be longer and infinitely more difficult for rescue work than anything we had yet descended.

At Schoening's request, I moved into the Gerry tent along-side Houston. Four of us were now crowded into this little shelter with our backs to the ice slope and our feet resting lightly on the one-third of the tent which bellied out and overhung the slope. Luckily we had an air mattress, and once this was inflated and worked under the men inside, it gave some insulation from the cold. I opened my sleeping bag and placed the outer bag under our feet on the droopy side of the tent, while the inner half I wrapped around Houston, who was in a state of shock.

By this time the sky was darkening, but to our great relief the wind had dropped. We wore all our clothes and though they were damp we were not too cold, yet the night was a ghastly experience. George Bell, his hands and feet frozen, had jammed his great bulk into one end of the little Gerry tent. He cannot see well without glasses, and the pair he was wearing and the spare pair in his pack had disappeared in the fall. That night he must have realized the effort that would be required of him next day, for the steepest part of the route lay immediately below our ledge, and it would be impossible for us to carry him if he could not climb down. At the opposite end of the tent lay Dee Molenaar, a deep cut stiffening his left thigh and a bruised or cracked rib making his breathing painful. What he was thinking during the long hours of darkness I don't know, but he insisted on covering up Houston in his down jacket, even though he himself was lying exposed just inside the doorway of the tent.

Between Molenaar and Bell were Houston and I. Charlie Houston usually is bursting with energy, and if he had had his normal strength that night he would have been far too powerful for us. At first he was in a state of shock, but he soon stopped shivering and began to ask question after question, "Where are we?" "Where is Pete?" "How is Art?" Some things he seemed to understand, but he would ask the same questions again and again. A dozen times at least during the night he would ask, "How's Pete?" I would say, "He's all right," but Charlie wouldn't believe me. Then I would call across to the tiny bivouac tent, which was swelled to bursting by the three men inside, "Hey, Pete, tell Charlie you're all right."

Pete Schoening would call out, "I'm fine, Charlie. Don't worry about me."

"Oh, that's fine; that's fine," Charlie would say, and for a moment he would be quiet. Then again he would say solicitously, "How's Tony?" and the rigmarole would begin all over again. We were touched by his anxiety about us but we were more concerned about him.

During the fall Houston had evidently struck his forehead against a rock, causing a concussion and a hemorrhage which blurred the vision in his right eye. Another blow had given him a painful chest injury, which so affected his breathing that any deep breath was painful. In his confused state he thought that the pain in his chest when he breathed was caused by lack of oxygen in the tent, and so he tried to remedy the situation by clawing a hole in the fabric. Then, to keep from breathing deeply, he would take short breaths, faster and faster, until he would slump over unconscious and breathe normally until he became conscious again. When he became unconscious, we would shift position and try to get more comfortable, for the moment he was conscious he would become active again and we would have to restrain him.

Somehow—I still don't know how—the three men crammed into the bivouac tent, which was just as precariously pitched, were able to make tea and pass it in to us occasionally. There wasn't a great deal, but those swallows of tea were a godsend. They helped us to keep awake. Molenaar even opened the tent door to humor Charlie, but he still wanted to cut a hole in the tent. "I know about these things," he would say. "I have studied them. We'll all be dead in three minutes if you won't let me cut a hole in the tent." And again his breathing would speed up tremendously and he would collapse.

The night seemed unbearably long, but at least we could converse with those in the other tent and the tea cheered us. During the long darkness we asked each man about his injuries and each man told a compressed story of what had happened to him in the fall. Schoening wasn't saying much, but we kept calling over to him, "How did you do it, Pete?"

"What kind of a belay did you have?"

"If you can stop five men at 25,000 feet, how many could you stop at 15,000?"

Pete's story was brief. "Well, I was lucky," he said. "My ice ax was driven into the snow and braced against the upper side of that big boulder frozen in the ice. The rope passed around the ax to where I stood in front of the boulder, and went around my body, so that the force was widely distributed. Of course I was belaying Art anyway, and when I saw George slip and then Tony and the others pulled off, I swung weight onto the head of the ax and held on as the rope slid a bit. The force must have come in a series of shocks. The strain on me was not too great, but at the ice ax that seven-sixteenth-inch nylon rope stretched until it looked like a quarter-inch line, and I was scared stiff the boulder would be pulled loose. If that happened, the ax, which was braced against it, would go, too, and we would be lost. For minutes, it seemed, the rope was taut as a bowstring. Snow squalls blotted out everything below, and I couldn't tell what was happening. My hands were freezing, but of course I could not let go. Then the air cleared a bit and I yelled to Bob Craig, who was over at Camp VII, to come and anchor Art. By the time he reached him, most of the weight was off the rope, and from below I could hear someone calling, 'Charlie's hurt.' Once Art was secured, I came down to thaw out."

This simple story failed to stress the remarkable fact that

one man had held five men who slid 150 to 300 feet down a 45-degree slope and that he had done it at nearly 25,000 feet, where the mere job of survival absorbs most of the strength of a man. Such magnificent belay work has rarely been recorded in mountaineering anywhere. Nor have I read of any other climbing miracle when three separate ropes fouled together to save the lives of five men. Bad luck had forced us to move in storm and had placed us where the fall had swept us off, but good luck, the resilience of nylon rope, and a remarkable tangle had saved our lives.

When the long hours finally wore away and the first rays of daylight came, a dour gray sky showed that more storm was coming fast. Silent, haggard, exhausted, we waited until Bob Craig had first made some tea and then cooked a little cereal. We had only one pot. During the night someone had placed the other pot outside the door of the crowded tent and it had immediately slid off the mountain. At the first light Houston crawled to the door and thrust out his shoulders. He seemed astonished that he didn't find more oxygen or easier breathing outside the tent. The morning air was raw and we were sore and weary. Everyone's eyes looked dead. But there was no question about the next move. We had to go down.

12. From camp VII to camp II

12. From camp VII to camp II

During the long hours of darkness we had had much to think about, and in the morning we soberly assessed our situation. Art Gilkey, who had camped here so cheerfully a few days before, was gone. Houston seemed physically able to climb but he was weak and still out of his head, had a chest injury, and couldn't reason. Whether he had internal injuries we didn't know. George Bell was an almost greater worry. His hands were covered with frostbite blisters and his feet were blotched with deeper frostbite. He wasn't sure that he could get his swollen feet into his boots again. In addition he could not see well without his glasses. Whether he and Houston could climb down, we didn't know, but we realized that we didn't have the manpower to carry them if they couldn't.

Schoening's chest seemed better during the night, but it was still a potential cause for worry. Fortunately, his hands, which he had nipped when he held the fall, had not suffered damage and did not give him trouble. Molenaar had a cracked rib and a cut on his thigh which would slow him down, but his morale was good and he was anxious to get started. Craig, too, looked exhausted, but the early morning light showed him to be obviously in better shape than he had been the evening before. Tony Streather, who with Craig and Schoening had been brewing tea for us all during the night, looked more himself than anyone did.

Craig and Streather teamed up again to cook breakfast, and though we somehow didn't feel hungry, we drank the tea, forced down the thick cereal, and made Houston eat some. There would be many problems before we reached Base Camp again, but from now on it wouldn't do to look too far ahead. The essential thing was for us to get down out of avalanche danger to Camp VI. Once there, the most treacherous climbing would be behind us, we would be close to the food cache at Camp V, and even short periods of good weather would permit the descent to lower camps.

The wind was already rising when we finished breakfast and it took an effort of will to crawl out into the raw morning, stiff and sore, and begin to pull our packs together for the descent. Houston's crampons were hard to strap on, because there was no flat place for anyone to stand or for him to put his foot. And yet they must be strapped on tightly. George Bell was having similar problems. His neck was so stiff from his cramped position in the tent that he could not straighten his head, and for dreadful minutes it seemed that he could not force his swollen and frostbitten feet into his vapor-barrier rubber boots. Fortunately most rubber will stretch, and after much pulling and straining both boots went on.

Schoening and Craig wanted to take Houston down, for he was still suffering from the concussion, and we were all very worried about how he would climb. If he stopped climbing, if he decided to act independently or if he slipped, he might bring disaster to the teammates whom he would have risked anything to save. We knew that this day's descent was the most dangerous we faced. If we could get the whole party down to Camp VI, there was a good chance that we would all get safely off the mountain. Accordingly, when everyone's crampons were on, Houston was tied carefully into the middle of Craig's and Schoening's rope and they started to climb carefully down over the snow-covered slabs. Schoening, whose ability at belaying had been established for all time, went last and anchored the rope. Those of us who were to follow on the second rope watched breathlessly as the three started down. We knew how close to exhaustion everyone was, and we worried over whether Houston would be able to climb. As we watched, he started off all right, but

221

after going 20 feet he sat down in the middle of a steep snow patch, put his chin in his hand, and looked around as if to say, "What are we doing here?" Schoening looked perplexed. After a few moments he shook the rope and called down, "Come on, Charlie. Let's go!" And Charlie, still looking bewildered, got up and continued to climb down.

Perhaps this was a good time to have no inhibitions, for we were faced with a problem similar to climbing down a wind-swept, steeply slanted house roof, 1,700 feet long, with snow and ice covering many of the slates. The exposure was so severe that any slip would be hard to check and might pull the whole rope of men down off the mountain. We knew that we were physically exhausted and climbing under conditions that would have been extremely dangerous even when we were at our strongest. Each one of us had to climb with all the strength and skill he possessed. No one could slip.

The first rope had descended 100 yards and all were making good progress when the rest of us turned our backs on Camp VII and started to descend the relentlessly steep slopes. The storm clouds had risen a little, but the wind was sweeping great plumes of snow whirling across the rock slabs. Footing was dreadfully uncertain, and since Streather seemed strong, we had him go first. Next went Bell, whose uncertain steps because of his missing glasses and his frostbitten hands and feet were alarming, and finally came Molenaar and I. Molenaar's leg was bothering him but he kept as sound a belay as he could on Bell, and obviously did everything he could to secure me when I moved down behind him. We had moved down only a couple of rope lengths when we saw 100 feet to our right an ice ax sticking into a snow slope at a crazy angle. Molenaar made a careful traverse across the snow to reach it. It was Houston's ax, which had disappeared in the fall, and we quickly handed it over to Bell, whose ax had also vanished in his headlong plunge down the slope. This chance find helped Bell tremendously, for now with the ax he could probe places where he could not see clearly; but to watch George lean out over the slope and tap around with the tip of the ax was anything but reassuring to the other three men on the rope who, standing on slabs covered with powder snow, were trying to safeguard the party. Under these conditions Bell's poise and steady climbing, despite his handicaps, were magnificent. He knew that his own life and ours were at stake, for we were all so near exhaustion that a slip could easily drag all four of us thousands of feet in a fall. And if Bell reached the point where he could not walk, we might be too weak to get him down.

In the back of our minds was the terrible lesson of the fatal storm on Nanga Parbat. We had more food on K2 than the Germans had had, but that wouldn't help if we couldn't reach it. Our feet and hands were numb as we cleared away the snow to find handholds and footholds. In some places the savage wind even helped us, for it had so firmed the snow that we could kick steps down it, but as a rule the powdery coating over the slabs did not adhere well, and climbing on

223

this uncertain surface with such exposure below strained the firmest nerves. The accident of the day before and our miraculous rescue appeared to have developed in most of us a fatalistic attitude about our dangerous position. We had the feeling that matters were beyond our control. We seemed to be puppets pulled by a string, as if things were fated to happen in a certain way, do what we would, and nothing in the world could change them. Under the circumstances this fatalism, caused no doubt by the series of accidents of the past few days, was almost comforting, for we did not lose strength through nervous worry. We were doing our best. If that wasn't good enough, there was nothing else we could do to change things. What would be would be.

I have never had this fatalistic feeling before, but I certainly had it as we moved out onto the exposed col (pass) at the top of the steepest slope. Here, in an utter maelstrom of wind and whirling snow, we had to take off our crampons to climb down the smooth, steeply angled rock. We were already cold and as we eyed the slabs, which were here too steep for snow to cling, we faced a wind that was eddying furiously up the mountain directly at us. I have seldom been so cold.

With numb fingers we got George Bell's crampons off, pulled off our own, and then Streather climbed over the edge and disappeared. Thank God our fixed ropes there were clear of snow! But despite their help, this steep section of the descent seemed to take hours, and my feet had lost all sensation before the third man on the rope, Molenaar, reached a good belay point and called to me to start down from the col. Like the others, I could not move fast, but the blessed handlines helped, and putting my faith in the pitons that supported them, I stiffly lowered myself off that storm-swept col and onto the steep face. I still had confidence that we would get down that cliff, and on down to Camp VI. I wasn't going to worry, but I was terribly anxious to get all of us under shelter so we could start work to save our feet.

One at a time we moved down across the steep slabs, along the ridge and down another fixed rope on the other side. Here, on loose rocks precariously poised, we had a brief respite from the wind. Our strength was ebbing fast, and Molenaar, who had belayed so well above, was now climbing entirely on reserve strength and hardly able to take care of himself. At 200 feet from camp, Streather, the strongest man on our rope, climbed 20 feet down the wrong place and had to climb back. Reascending cost him frightful effort! Ahead was one more slippery traverse, but no one slipped, and after descending a shallow gully we stepped down almost onto the tents of Camp VI.

The others were already there when we arrived. They had found both tents full of snow, one of them right up to the top, for a couple of small rocks had fallen and made slits in one, and faulty closure of a zipper had provided a tiny opening in the other. Through these small entrances the driving monsoon winds had forced powder snow until the tents were drifted full.

Fortunately for us on the second rope, the others had just finished clearing out the powder snow when we arrived, and they had started a stove. As we climbed into these tents, the most blessed sense of relief came over us. We had come down safely. We had passed the worst part of the route. Here were shelter and food. No matter how exhausted we were now, we had faith that we could get down.

Uncomfortable though we were, the next hours in camp seemed by contrast to be almost luxury. Charlie Houston seemed far more himself. Schoening and Craig reported that he had climbed extraordinarily well for a man in his condition, only occasionally sitting down in the most unexpected places and looking around as if to wonder what he was doing there. All of us looked years older than when we had been here before, but there was a confidence in our voices that had not been there that morning. Nobody made optimistic statements, but morale had improved.

While snow was melting for tea, we blew up the air mattresses which had not been abandoned above, arranged some 1939 sleeping bags we had found there, and took off our boots to work on our feet. My toes had no sensation, but neither did anybody else's, and I was glad to remember that my feet had not hindered my climbing down. Since the tent Houston and I were sharing stood in the lee of the other, and our tent had no holes that let in the wind, we called to

George Bell to trade places with Bob Craig and move into the warmer tent. Bell's feet were a great worry to us now, for they were in the most dangerous condition of all. George shouted, "Okay," and started to crawl across the space between the tents. As he did so, he saw a little bag about 15 inches long and 8 inches high in the passage between the tents.

"Where did that come from?" he called, and without waiting for an answer he picked it up and pushed it into our tent ahead of him.

"Why, Tony found it about 1,000 feet below Camp VII," I said. "He thinks it's something of Art's. I haven't looked at it yet, but I'm going to take it to his family."

"It isn't Art's," said George huskily. "It's mine. It was in my pack when I lost it in the fall."

Eagerly he pulled at the zipper, drew it open, and began to fumble frantically inside. And now, to our utter amazement, George let out a gasp of joy and pulled forth his spare pair of eyeglasses—unbroken!

What the discovery did for Bell's morale we couldn't tell, but his delight did us all a lot of good. Also in the bag were the expedition accounts, for George was the field treasurer, but at that time we had no interest in such matters. The rest of his pack, however, with camera, exposed film, and diary, like Charlie Houston's, had completely disappeared, and we never saw it again.

All the way down, of course, we had been looking for Art

Gilkey's body, but we never found it. We did see, however, a
tangle of ropes and a broken ice ax about 1,000 feet below
the ice gully where we had last seen him. The wooden shaft
of the ax, broken in its fall down the mountain, had jammed
between two rocks. Our friend must have had an instant and
merciful death, the swift death that is the best kind, before
his body was swallowed forever beneath the snows of the
Karakoram.

That evening at six o'clock Charlie Houston was so far
recovered that he could use the spare walkie-talkie, which
was at Camp VI, to call Colonel Ata-Ullah at Base Camp. The
emotion and relief in that good man's voice when he learned
that we were alive was tremendous. "Thank God," he said,
and for a moment or two he said little more. He had listened
constantly since we had failed to keep our schedule with
him at three o'clock the day before, and by now had practically given us up for dead. Next day he was planning to
search the glaciers for us, and then, when weather permitted,
climb as high as he could to look for us before accepting the
fact that we were lost. He had told his fears to the Hunzas,
and together they had had a mournful time.

That night at Camp VI we had a magnificent dinner of
tomato soup, canned ham, rice, and cups and cups of tea,
but darkness overtook us before the cups were cleaned and
the sleeping bags arranged. Pushing aside the stove and
dishes, Houston and I fell asleep almost before we could
pull ourselves into the two parts of my sleeping bag, for

Houston's bag, of course, had disappeared in the fall. Drugged as I was by exhaustion, my sleep was fitful, however, for Houston was out of his head again and all night long he kept getting out of the inner half of the sleeping bag, which he was using, and crawling about the tent. He was most anxious not to waken me and kept steadily apologizing for the trouble he was causing. "If I can just get out of this warehouse," he would say, "everything will be all right." Then, as best I could in the darkness, I would find the opening to his sleeping bag and try to get him inside. The next thing I knew, I would be awakened again by Houston crawling around the foot of my sleeping bag. "I'm terribly sorry to bother you," he would say. "If I can only get out of this warehouse. . . ."

Next morning the storm had increased in violence and we were apprehensive about starting down to Camp V for fear that George Bell would extend the damage already done to his feet. We were deeply worried about his condition. We feared that he might reach the point where he could not walk, and we hated to think what would happen then, for in our exhausted state and with a storm raging we could not carry anybody, let alone our biggest man, down along the ridges below. Since food and gasoline were short at Camp VI we were anxious to move some men down, and Schoening and Streather took advantage of a lull in the storm to push their way down to the next camp, but the lull ended and the rest of us stayed behind. Supplies of fuel were low and that night

229

we went to bed with a cold supper and the realization that we had to start down again next day. Bell was now the main problem, for Houston was gaining strength and clarity of thought with remarkable rapidity.

August 13 was cold and windy with light snow falling, much like the day we had moved down to Camp VI. Craig and Molenaar had had a cold night in the torn tent, and after cold meat bars for breakfast, they pulled on their packs and started down. Putting George Bell in the torn tent for shelter, Houston and I began trying to free the bottom of the tent we were in from ice, for it was necessary for us to carry down one tent, and the other one was ripped. Our tent had become iced-in during previous use, and our hands became frightfully cold as we hacked at the ice and pulled at the knots. Meanwhile the wind was getting at the tent Craig and Molenaar had emptied, so that by the time we had freed the tent that was to go down, the wind had torn the other one from end to end with Bell in it, and the whole fabric began to shred apart as we huddled in it to try to bring back sensation to our nipped fingers. Then, swinging on heavy packs, we started down to Camp V.

To our delight, Bell climbed steadily and safely. The route from VI to V was normally not particularly difficult, but with fresh snow on the rocks some of the route was dangerously coated with loose snow, especially in one gully. Here Houston did a fine job of anchoring the rope as I went ahead. He seemed almost his old self as we moved down onto a tiny scree slope and around a corner into Camp V. Craig and Molenaar were already there, and they made way for us to move in where Schoening and Streather pumped the stove to a red-hot roar and poured cup after cup of orange juice—flavored tea down our still dehydrated throats. They had battled the storm the day before and had been glad to reach camp safely.

Our descent was going well now and the storm had let up a bit, but there was no indication that another frightful blow wasn't on the way. "If we can only get below House's Chimney," someone said, "it will take mighty bad weather to hold us back after that." We were still going on reserve energy and it was now about two-thirty in the afternoon, but the thought of putting the last major barrier behind us spurred us on. Normally we could climb from Camp V to the top of House's Chimney in five minutes, and from there look down on the tents of Camp IV almost directly beneath.

Now it took over an hour of the hardest work to get to the top of the chimney. Craig and Molenaar, who went ahead, shouted up to watch out for the ice, for everything was glazed over and there was great danger of a slip's pulling a whole rope of men off the mountain. We had heavier loads now, Houston especially, and we concentrated grimly on crossing this dangerously exposed section safely. Even so, Houston and I had a number of unpleasant moments and cut many steps before we climbed to the base of the A-frame and looked down the fixed rope Craig and Molenaar had set

231

up in House's Chimney. And 150 feet below us we could see them working on the tents at Camp IV.

The hour was late enough so that not a moment could be wasted if we were to make the descent before dark. Houston insisted on belaying each man down in turn, and then we began to lower the packs to Schoening, who had climbed up the snow slope across from the foot of the chimney and made himself a platform there. These operations took time, for each pack had to be well secured, and it was almost dark when I climbed down the chimney and, guided by Schoening, crossed the ice steps to the rock outcrop from which we had hoisted loads three weeks earlier. Houston had been first man up the chimney and he wanted to be the last man down it, but it was nearly pitch-black by the time he left the tiny platform where he had been crouching so long and backed off the plunging cliff into space. Such a tangle of old and new ropes hung in the chimney that in the blackness the terrible thought swept over him that he was hanging on the wrong rope! Swinging out over this sheer cliff with the awesome gulf below is an impressive experience at any time, but it was doubly so to Houston, as with numb hands he launched himself out over the blackness, hoping that the rope was the right one and that it would reach the line of steps cut in the snow at the bottom.

The rope held, and Schoening was soon helping to guide Houston across the slope. A few minutes later we were all at the tent platforms of Camp IV, too tired to do more than

1. Telephoto of K2 from across the glacier. This photograph was taken by Bell and Houston from a cirque below Sella Pass.

2. The expedition en route to Camp II. About 1,500 pounds of supplies were packed to Camp II, which served as a sort of advance base camp.

3. Bell on the ice above Camp II. Fixed ropes were extremely helpful between Camps II and III.

4. Bell, Bates, and Molenaar, carrying loads from Camp II to Camp III.

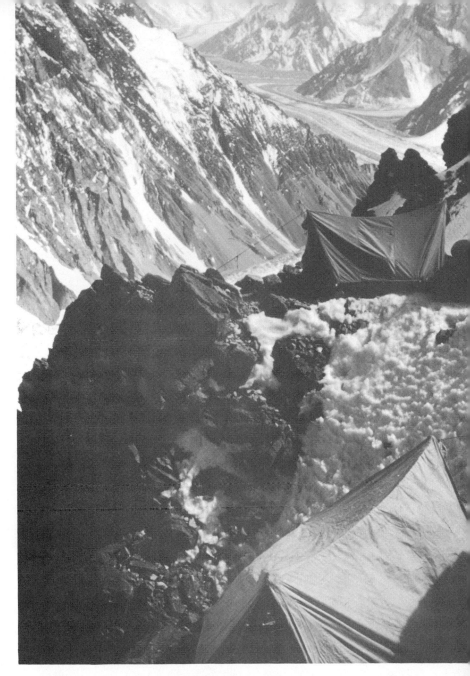

5. These two tents were on platforms that overhung a 3,000-foot snow slope. They were, however, protected from rockfall, which had endangered the 1938 expedition.

6. Climbing overhang below Camp IV. A short but severe pitch here required careful climbing, while loose stones threatened the men belaying below.

7. Broad Peak at sunset. Giant avalanches were constantly falling off 26,400-foot Broad Peak.

8. Hauling load up House's Chimney by pulley. This gash in an 80-degree cliff well over 100 feet high is the only route found over the reddish buttress which blocks the Abruzzi Ridge.

11. Avalanche off flank of Broad Peak. Giant avalanches in the Karakoram sometimes sweep completely across the Godwin-Austen Glacier.

9. One of these tents at Camp VI was eventually shredded by the force of the monsoon winds.

10. The climbing was continuously difficult between Camps VI and VII. Here Concordia can be seen over a spur of Broad Peak.

12. Camp VIII, looking down. The continual pounding of the monsoon smashed the tent in the foreground. Bride Peak in the distance, 25,110 feet high, is now below the horizon.

13. George Bell rides back in style. Tent poles lashed to a folding cot produce a makeshift stretcher. It took ten Balti porters to carry it over cliffs and glaciers.

14. Molenaar gets a ride across a glacial stream on the back of a Balti porter. The porters crossed these icy streams barefoot, again and again showing an amazing physical toughness.

swallow some tea, eat a cold meat bar for energy, and climb into our sleeping bags. Having House's Chimney behind us was a boost to our determination to get the whole party down safely. That night Molenaar, Houston, and I shared one tent, and I remember rubbing and rubbing to try to get feeling back into my toes. They didn't hurt and they weren't swollen, but try as I would, I couldn't bring back any sensation to some of my toes. Still, the chimney, which had been long in our thoughts, was now behind us and we lay down scarcely conscious of the dampness of the half sleeping bag each of us was using.

When another gray dawn broke on August 14, gaunt, hollow-eyed men began to stumble out onto the slippery scree to collect pieces of ice to melt. Craig's feet were very painful but George Bell was an even greater worry, for he was obviously now going on nerve alone. This morning his feet were so swollen that he couldn't get his boots on no matter how hard he struggled, and at last he was forced to slit the boots with a knife in order to pull them on. These openings wouldn't increase his protection against further cold damage, but at least they would permit him to climb down with something on his feet.

This time Streather and I started down ahead to find and improve the route if possible. We found powder snow masking loose rocks and making part of our upward route unusable. Worse still, most of our fixed ropes were completely buried and we had to hack and hack to cut steps in smooth ice

241

that covered slopes we had descended with ease before. Cutting steps straight down is arduous work, and both Streather and I were feeling the strain of the past few days. A couple of hundred yards above Camp III, we checked a slip before it got started, and then Schoening took over the lead to give us a rest and began cutting the last of the steps needed to get to camp.

How rich the air seemed! We had descended the equivalent of five Eiffel Towers, or ten Washington Monuments, below Camp VIII, and that part of the mountain already seemed impossibly remote. New York and home by contrast now seemed almost around the corner. But we were not down by any means. Storm clouds shrouded the slopes above us, and we knew that if the ice we had met just above Camp III plastered the route to Camp II, the next part of the descent would be especially dangerous, for the continuous strain was having its effect on all of us.

Camp III was well stocked with food, and since the wind had dropped, we made a solid lunch there. Like starving men, we gulped down date bars with almonds in them, chunks of Gruyère cheese, dried apricots, biscuits, and chocolate. We mixed a can of concentrated orange juice with snow, beat the icy mixture with a spoon until it grew mushy, and then took turns gulping great spoonfuls. Our bodies sorely needed replenishing with hot food and sleep, but Camp II was calling to us, for we knew that our faithful Hunzas would be there. Also, it was imperative that Bell waste no time in getting as low as possible, for we realized that before long, no matter how much nerve he had, he would be unable to walk on his frozen feet.

Ice over the rocks would make the route below Camp III very dangerous, and while we were pondering whether to descend or wait until the next day, Schoening moved down to the traverse across the first gully and found not ice but firm snow. We were much impressed, for we had expected more of the ice we had found just above. Morale soared. We even added to our packs a few items that had been left in duffel bags at Camp III, and then continued the descent.

This time Houston, Bell, and Schoening went first on one rope; Streather and I followed; and Craig and Molenaar brought up the rear. More than ever we were determined not to slip, and despite the need for one delicate maneuver after another, no one fell. Luckily the ice was not so bad as we had feared, and we gained confidence as we climbed down. The mountain took one parting shot at us, however, for just before Schoening, Bell, and Houston turned off the main slope into the shelter of a safe gully, a rock plummeting with great speed and noise from high on the mountain whizzed within a few feet of their heads.

Streather had the walkie-talkie, and exactly at six o'clock he tried to call Ata-Ullah. There was no flat place near us. Actually at exactly six I was standing on one foot traversing a steep rock wall, and didn't dare to move for fear of dislodging Streather, who was in an only slightly more secure

243

position with one hand on the walkie-talkie. We hoped to tell Ata-Ullah to send porters next day to the glacier near Camp I to help Bell down, but Ata couldn't hear us and Streather finally folded in the radio aerial and went on.

As we started down the last couloir (gully) toward Camp II, we could hear the Hunzas shouting, and as we stepped onto the last snow slope, Ghulam, Vilyati, and Hidayat, roped together with what looked like string, swarmed out onto the steep slope and embraced us with tears rolling down their cheeks. It was an overwhelming welcome and almost too much for us in more ways than one, for we were clinging to small holds and standing at the top of a steep couloir which fell away 1,500 feet to the glacier below. Such a position is not suited to an uninhibited heart-to-heart embrace!

Our packs were taken from us and these hardy frontiersmen, with tears streaking their cheeks, handed us down from rock to rock as if afraid that at the last moment we would collapse. As each one of us reached Camp II, where sleeping bags had been laid out on the rocks for us to sit on, each Hunza in turn with great emotion embraced each one of us. The storm had ebbed away, the wind had dropped, and the first stars we had seen for weeks were glittering in the night sky as Craig and Molenaar climbed down the last rock pitch above camp.

Our feeling of relief and luxury at that moment is too great to describe. The ship had been saved; the lost, found. Every man who had started down from the dreadful bivouac at Camp VII had reached the safety of Camp II and the protection of our Hunzas. That evening was one of the sweetest any of us will ever spend, for a sense of supreme peacefulness enveloped us. Yet we were sad, too. We talked about Art Gilkey, and the Hunzas cried and prayed in unison for him. They wanted to know what had happened and how we had forced our way down through the storm.

And slowly as we lay there on sleeping bags with our boots off in the warm, rich air, with a stove roaring cheerily *in the open* at our feet, we began to return to life. First the Hunzas fed us rice cooked in milk; then, with three stoves burning, we started on tea. Fuel and fire were plentiful here, and we made the most of it. Stacks of the flat pancakes called *chupattis* were cooked and pot after pot of tea and milk was brought over to us as we lay talking, relaxing, rubbing our feet, too emotionally stirred to go to bed. And all this while, kindly Hunza hands were kneading our tired muscles as only Asiatics can, bringing us back to life. At that heartwarming moment differences of race and language meant nothing. We and the Hunzas by the light of a flickering flare shared a great emotional experience as we talked and talked. Those who also have faced hardship and danger can appreciate our emotions and the bond between us all as we lay there. Then, after hours of delicious rest, we hoisted ourselves to our feet, staggered to our tents, and crawled gratefully into our sleeping bags. We had done it.

13. Base camp again

13. Base camp again

When I woke from a sound sleep the next morning in a dry, whole sleeping bag, I heard a movement outside the tent door, and a minute or two later a Hunza handed in a cup of sweet tea. This simple act was a convincing demonstration that we were no longer fighting for our lives but were back on the fringes of civilization. And further proof was to come, for next a large batch of mail was thrust into the tent. The contrast was almost too much for us as we lay drinking tea, eating hot *pirattas* and reading letters, often many weeks old, full of love and well-wishes from our friends and families.

A hot *sun*, the first in weeks, was beating down, and its rays gradually drove us from the tents to sit in the warm,

windless sunlight, mail in hand and the giants of the Karakoram, buried in new snow, looking down on us. Our cups
literally and figuratively were very full. Except for the dull
ache of Art Gilkey's loss, we felt at peace with the world.
Our defeat did not rankle. We felt as if we had suffered
and passed a very special test, an ordeal—why we did not
know—but we had done our best and had survived.

While we sat on warm rocks, barehanded—even barefoot—reading mail and soaking in the sunlight, we realized
that we were not quite down yet and we were still alarmed
about the condition of George's frostbitten feet. Accordingly, after an appetizing breakfast in which the Hunzas
joined, Streather and I were elected to go on ahead to Base
Camp and send men up to the icefall with a stretcher to
carry Bell back to camp. His feet looked frightful now,
blistered and mottled in all shades of red and black. But
George Bell is a stoic, and though he looked pale and on the
verge of collapse, we knew that his iron will would keep
him from complaining and drive him on down the mountain.

Streather and I found vast changes in the route as we
worked our way down to the Godwin-Austen Glacier. In
some places we found ice and were forced to chip out steps
as we descended. Instead of going to Camp I, we tried a
route the Hunzas had been using and headed down a long,
steep scree slope to the edge of the glacier, then wound
through a mass of séracs and crevasses until we came out

on the relatively smooth ice of the center of the icefall. Here we were on our old route from Base Camp to Camp I and we made good time. Our toes felt strangely numb, however, and we walked stiffly.

We were trying to go fast, but neither of us could step out in a real stride, and rotten ice and uncertain stones made us put our feet down tenderly and a bit uncertainly. Not until we had skirted the snow fields below two hanging glaciers on the south face were we convinced that no traces of the fall from Camp VII would be found. And now our eyes turned toward the junction of the Godwin-Austen and Savoia Glaciers, for we could make out the tents of Base Camp a half mile ahead.

We could see figures about the tents, and soon some of the men came out to greet us. Our meeting was another heartwarming experience, for the simple coolies, whom we had joked with and encouraged on the march in to Base Camp, now threw their arms around us and with tears in their eyes told us how happy they were to see us return. One old rascal who had been with Shipton in the Sarpo Lago area during the Shaksgam Expedition was especially demonstrative and offered each of us a ride on his back. With this escort to accompany us, we walked on down the glacier, meeting Haji, the kindly leader of the porters, and other small groups of Baltis who had come up. Near camp, Colonel Ata-Ullah came out to welcome us. We shook hands and embraced with a feeling of the closest fellowship, for

251

here embodied was the voice we had heard so many times in our desperate position while snowbound on the mountain ledges high above. Here was our companion who had been at the other end of the walkie-talkie—in another world— sending us hope and encouragement and news, and providing a precious link with civilization and life itself.

Ata-Ullah had done some fine exploratory work while we had been gone and we viewed each other warmly and with increased respect. The camp itself illustrated Ata's efficient management, and in no time Streather and I were drinking tea, eating cheese and crackers, and telling of our experiences. "Thank God," Ata kept saying. "Thank God."

While we were talking, a stretcher party was organizing to go to the aid of our companions. George Bell we knew would need help, and there might be others. The colonel, of course, was going to lead this group, and fifteen minutes after our arrival the whole "rescue party" was clambering across the rock-strewn ice of the Godwin-Austen at top speed.

Their action was the signal for Streather and me to relax gratefully, and to look over more stacks of mail which had recently come in. Beria, labor disturbances in France—all seemed incredibly far away, interests of another world, and for the moment at least news that would normally strike our attention held no fascination. It was as if we had to learn our old set of values all over again.

Relaxing at Base Camp gave surprising pleasure to both

of us, and although we made a few preparations for the arrival of the others, the release of pressure was so over-powering that we did little but drink tea, read mail, and let the Satpura men knead our leg muscles. At that moment we craved no delicacies, no entertainment, no luxuries. We felt like swimmers from a capsized boat who had just completed the long swim to shore. Merely being there was un-speakable luxury.

Late in the afternoon the others began to arrive. Schoening was in the best shape of any, but he looked gaunt and haggard. Molenaar was limping and Houston's face showed the strain. Bob Craig was helped in by a Satpura man on one side and a Hunza on the other, while George Bell was borne in on a folding cot borrowed in June from Colonel Young in Rawalpindi for just such an emergency.

That night over pot after pot of tea we told and retold the events we had been too tired to discuss before. We were beginning to replace some of the liquid we had lost and all of us—Houston especially—had an almost unquenchable thirst. We were hungry, too, for though we had lost 10 to 20 pounds apiece, we had gained the greatest appetite of our lives. George Bell, who looked especially gaunt and ema-ciated, was particularly hungry, and though three of his toes were black, his good humor never failed. Like the rest of us, he appreciated the thoughtfulness of various Satpura porters, who kept bringing us such things as a few withered apples and a handful of dried apricots, carried all the way from Skardu. That they were deeply sympathetic was obvious.

The following morning we worked lethargically at packing our gear for the return trip. Nearly a third of the porters would be needed to carry George Bell, and we could not overload the others. Charlie Houston, who had blurred vision in his right eye from the blow on the head he had received on the mountain, worked hard on official mail despite his injuries. But the first letter he wrote was the most important. It was to Art Gilkey's father and mother in Ames, Iowa.

Art was very much in our thoughts as we boxed his personal belongings to send home, and about noon we gathered to pay him our respects for the last time. Under Colonel Ata-Ullah's direction the Hunza men had built a splendid cairn on a prominent point of rock at the juncture of the Savoia and Godwin-Austen Glaciers. It is a distinctive location, conspicuous to anyone approaching K2 from the south. From the cairn one can look down the Godwin-Austen to the vast ice amphitheater of Concordia and far beyond to the peaks of Ladakh. Less distant, the beautifully fluted snow slopes of Bride Peak rise gracefully, while across the valley gigantic Broad Peak towers. Past either side of the rock platform on which the cairn stands, the great glaciers coming down from the edge of China flow majestically. Beyond these icy highways to Savoia Pass and Windy Gap, the world of snow and rock seems endless, but most striking of all, behind the cairn, K2, awe-inspiring and immense, thrusts up toward the sky in a sweep of tremendous exaltation. It is well named the "mountaineer's mountain."

On wooden, tender feet we limped to the base of this 10-foot cairn and placed on it the aluminum box that had held Art Gilkey's personal effects. In it we reverently laid mountain flowers, a statement about our dear companion, the flags we had hoped to take to the summit, and a favorite poem. On top we placed his ice ax. Sadly, with bowed heads and heavy hearts, we read a passage from the Bible, said a prayer for our friend, and then with spirits somehow lifted, stumbled back toward camp. We stopped at the first tent to look around at the cairn, long to keep lonely vigil on the rock platform, and we realized again the uncertainty of all human endeavor and the relative permanence of the mountain giant on which the cairn stands.

14. Out from the mountain

14. Out from the mountain

On August 17 we began our trek away from the mountain. The clouds hung low over Base Camp as we prepared to leave at dawn, and we had no final view of K2. No doubt far above the Godwin-Austen Glacier and Base Camp, and above the lower camps of the Abruzzi Ridge, the savage, relentless winds still swept the heights of K2, derisively flapping the shreds of our tents. But far below these icy ledges, we on the glacier, the wreckage of an expedition, began the long trip home.

The eagerness and excitement with which we had approached Base Camp were gone. Bundled up in a sleeping bag, I was carried on a litter by relays of the strongest Satpuras. Houston trudged down the glacier in a set and

259

trancelike manner, for the injury to his chest made normal movements of his arms and shoulders painful. Craig stumbled and tripped as he forced his tender feet to carry him along. Even Molenaar and Bates carefully favored their sore feet, while Streather and Schoening had no longer the brisk, free-swinging stride which is usually the mountaineer's joy.

On the mountain we had grown accustomed to looking forward to the trip out as something easy and rapid, and now as we left Base Camp, our motto was "Urdukas today." We all longed to see there the green grass and scrubby bushes of the last oasis. On our march in, the bandobast had taken three full days from Urdukas to Base Camp, but of course that had been uphill with 150 heterogeneous, unenthusiastic porters dragging their feet. Houston and Bates had told us how in 1938 the Base Camp cook, the well-beloved Ahdoo, had walked to Urdukas for wood and returned with his burden all in the same day. This feat suggested that with our band of stalwart Satpuras, we should easily reach Urdukas in a day. But the first evening found very tired sahibs and their porters less than half the distance to Urdukas. Indeed, during all the homeward march we made about the same distance per day as on the way in.

Of course, carrying me on the litter was extremely arduous for the Satpuras. Less than twenty of them were strong enough to be useful bearers, and even they could make only slow progress over the loose rocks and slippery glacial ice.

260

But the walking wounded did not want to travel much faster than the litter bearers.

Each day between eight and twelve Satpuras would be chosen by their sirdar, Haji, or by some common consent to act as "dandy wallahs," for to them my litter was called a *dandy*. The number chosen depended on how hard they thought the day's travel would be. On the glacier, Hunzas, particularly Vilyati, Hidayat, and Ghulam were usually at hand to chop steps and help the dandy wallahs in difficult spots. Ordinarily four men would carry the dandy for about fifteen minutes before being relieved by a second team.

My dandy was a lightweight canvas and steel cot, with each side reinforced by heavy bamboo poles, which had been brought for a large tent which the Hunzas used. The poles were lashed to the sides of the cot with Balti goat-hair ropes, and extended far enough past each end of the cot so that four men could carry the dandy on their shoulders. I lay on the litter either in or on a sleeping bag, and was tied on with a few turns of goat-hair rope. The steel framework of the cot was flexible and gave the dandy an easy-riding, knee-action quality.

The Baltoro Glacier and Braldu Valley, however, were not laid out with an eye to comfortable travel. The glacier above Urdukas offered comparatively good going and only in a few places did the dandy wallahs have great difficulties. But from Urdukas on, the track became frequently too narrow, steep, or tortuous for four men or virtually any num-

261

ber to maneuver the litter. In these situations, the courage
and strength of a small group of Satpuras proved my salva-
tion. Indeed, from Urdukas on I spent about one-third of the
time being carried piggyback by one stout Satpura or another.

The need first arose shortly beyond Urdukas, where the
track entered a V-shaped trench between the moraine and
a rock wall. The trench did not give the dandy wallahs room
to maneuver, and soon a few obstructing boulders brought
progress to a complete halt. At this point the biggest and
strongest of the Satpuras took off his shoes, knelt down beside the litter, and with a gentle smile invited me to climb
aboard. His name was Mohammed Hussein, but we did not
know this for a while and called him John Ridd, after the
strong-man hero of *Lorna Doone*. When I had secured a
good hold on his broad shoulders, John rose to his feet without visible effort and began with wonderful balance to
traverse the tortuous route. Sprawled on his back with my
arms draped over his shoulders and clasped across his
chest, I could peer over his shoulder and see exactly what
went on. John for his part seldom used his hands for balance and usually held my knees with a firm grip. And so
in this position he strode from boulder to boulder, balanced
across narrow, muddy ledges or, wonder enough for me,
walked unflinchingly across a stretch of sharp stones. Each
time he carried me, John would remove his shoes so as to
obtain better purchase on the often minute and insecure

footholds, and in time I came to feel almost as secure on his strong back as I had on my own two feet during the march in.

Big John was a young and gentle strong man. Each time he put me down after a hard carry, he would turn around with a sympathetic boyish grin and inquire, *"Tik, sahib?"* (Everything okay, sahib?) It was impossible not to say yes. For all his strength, John liked nothing better than to sing in a high falsetto voice and go through a bit of a dance for his comrades.

Zafar Ali was perhaps not the second strongest Satpura, but he wouldn't admit this for all the world. He spoke a great deal and acted out each sentence with his fine mobile features and expressive gestures. He was an enthusiastic man and zealously took on his role as second strongest sahib carrier. Certainly Zafar Ali was the most comfortable-riding Satpura, for in his pride he held me high up on his shoulders so that I barely needed to hold on. Zafar Ali had something of the Arabian Nights about him, something like Shah Khan, the Hunza leader we had met in Skardu. These were glamorous men. My estimate of them was colored by imagination, but it was easy to visualize them leading a band of trusted followers over the edge of the world.

The other Satpuras were less certain of their abilities and undertook to carry my shrunken frame, now about 170 pounds, with less assurance. Smallest, most cheerful and courageous of the select band was Taki, whom we christened

Smiley. For some reason, Smiley was clothed more or less in city-made rags, while most of the Satpuras wore home-spun. Perhaps he had traveled more to acquire his Bohemian air. The two other strongest carriers came into their own only after Big John, Zafar Ali, and Smiley had carried me on several successive days and proved that the labor could be borne.

My own feelings about being carried by litter and piggy-back were mingled. Most pronounced was resignation: this was, after all, the only way to get out of the mountains. But I counted the days, eleven in all. My arms would go to sleep clutched over the shoulders of the carrier, his back and shoulders would grow weary and sore, but each ten-minute carry, which was about what Big John did in his prime, or each two- or three-minute stretch, which was about par for the others, brought us that much closer to the goatskin raft, the zahk which would float us down the Shigar River to Skardu.

I always had the feeling that except for temporarily use-less feet, I was essentially a healthy man. True, my fingers were lacking skin and swollen, but they were improving every day. I was also weak, but I had a good appetite, which has often seemed to me a good criterion of health. My feet did not hurt enough to bother me so long as anything interest-ing was happening, but at night Bob Craig and I often would be kept awake by our feet.

Each morning Houston would hold sick call. He could

do little for himself, but he would always wash my toes in soap and hot water, rebandage them, and give me a shot of penicillin. A couple of times really sick people showed up to destroy any illusion of real physical misfortune that I might have. The second day out of Base Camp, one of the most cheerful of the Satpuras approached Charlie with a wry turn to his accustomed grin, complaining of headache and cough. He was given an aspirin or something similar. By the time we reached Urdukas the next day, however, he was very much worse, racked by a deep cough, and barely conscious of his surroundings. Charlie diagnosed pneumonia, shot him full of penicillin, and probably saved his life. Two days later, to our utter amazement, the near casualty wore his cheerful grin again and insisted on carrying a full load.

The attitudes of our porters toward Charlie's needle were strong and varied. One old reprobate with an infected gum was greatly disappointed when he recovered and could no longer be stuck with the potent needle. But later a younger Satpura with an infected finger fled in terror when Charlie approached with the needle, and no amount of persuasion could induce him to submit to treatment.

Most of the patients at sick call had vague complaints and were apparently looking for free pills. Others from villages we passed through came with little hope. For instance, once a father appeared before Charlie carrying his lovely young daughter of about thirteen in his arms. Some weeks before she had been playing in a high tree, had fallen, and since then had been unable to walk or move her legs at all.

On the route from Urdukas to Askole, we had much difficult travel. At first the chaotic, boulder-strewn glacier at times must have caused my carriers to wonder what they had done to be cursed even in this life with such burdens. Perhaps this is not orthodox Moslem reasoning, but I should think the sentiment inevitable. When we had escaped from the barren chaos which men call the Baltoro Glacier, the dandy wallahs and I grinned at each other with mutual pleasure.

Beyond the glacier our way lay close beside the raging Braldu River. Often we saw no suggestion of a trail; but only a precarious system of ledges, which even an unladen man might eye with misgivings. Here Mohammed Hussein was invaluable and I often wondered what would happen to me without him. In time, when Mohammed was sick for a few days, I learned that other Satpuras, inferior in strength perhaps but not in courage, would carry me on.

The first rope bridge posed an interesting problem. Needless to say, no one was particularly eager to carry me across, nor was I particularly eager to be carried across. The Satpuras crossed the bridge to eat a meal on the other side, perhaps thinking that if the problem was ignored for a bit it would vanish. Mohammed Hussein was frankly terrified by rope bridges. Zafar Ali had waved good-by to

OUT FROM THE MOUNTAIN

me with a wry smile and copious gestures to the effect, "Just wait a little while, sahib, and I will be back to carry you over with no trouble at all." But before he returned, Houston and Craig came over with a pair of thick felt overshoes which belonged to Ata and I tried to cross the bridge on my own. The struggle turned out to be much easier than we had expected. The side ropes or railings were low, so that I could sit on the center strands and still hold on to the side ropes firmly. I then progressed by placing my weight on my arms and heels in front and shifting forward to sit a little farther along on the bridge. Bob Craig went ahead to spread the side ropes appropriately, and in this manner I crossed the first rope bridge without even breaking my blisters.

The two subsequent bridges below Askole were not so easy because their side ropes were higher and could not be reached while sitting down. Hence a certain amount of more or less upright walking was necessary, and the rushing torrent beneath proved a more than adequate stimulus. Truthfully, I cannot think back on the crossing of the rope bridges as entirely unpleasant. After all, in these places I was able to do something for myself above and beyond merely emulating a sack of potatoes.

Beyond the last rope bridge, two extremely grueling days were needed to traverse the rock walls of the desolate Braldu Valley. At times the trail lay along banks of crumbling rubble close beside the foaming water; then it would climb a disintegrating wall of glacial debris to circumvent a precipice. The first day was backbreaking labor, and the dandy wallahs swore they could do no more. Accordingly, for the last day we enlisted the help of six strong men from a nearby village, who together with Zafar Ali, Taki, Rustum, Hassan, and Mohammed Hussein succeeded in hauling me over a last fearful section to Niyil, close to the goatskin zahk.

We had all been sure that the trip out would be much faster and easier than the journey in. Some of us had even toyed with the idea of making interesting side trips, such as a short detour to look at a ridge on the fabled Mustagh Tower, a ridge which the eye of faith might construe to be a possible route. Craig wanted to spend some days in Hunza getting better acquainted with that friendly land, its people, and its Hunza *pani*—literally Hunza "water," but actually wine. Art Gilkey and I had planned to relax on a houseboat in the Vale of Kashmir.

The reality was, of course, a far cry from these dreams, but we had certain compensations. The terrible days of storm, struggle, and death high on K2 had welded us together with a bond which was hard at the time to appreciate. There had been other pressing preoccupations then, and it was only when we had escaped the inhuman world of the wind and heights that we could appreciate in some leisure the depths of common experience and understanding which were ours. When men climb on a great mountain together, the rope between them is more than a mere physical aid to the ascent; it is a symbol of the spirit of the enterprise. It is a symbol of men banded together in a common effort of will and strength—not against this or that imagined foeman of the instant, but against their only true enemies: inertia, cowardice, greed, ignorance, and all weaknesses of the spirit. These things were hard to realize at the time. It was only in some tranquillity and leisure that we who together had ventured far and nearly lost all could appreciate what had happened.

Each time we got together for breakfast or dinner on the homeward trip was a memorable occasion. At first, as at Camp II and at Base Camp, merely being able to sit down and eat enough and drink enough and be together seemed heavenly. This was a stage when all we seemed to be able to do was to recount over and over again what had happened above, letting no detail escape us. And when the wholly remarkable facts had settled to the bottom and no longer needed to be retold at each gathering, there remained the warmth of comradeship. It is sad that usually such a spirit arises among men only in war. Charlie Houston put it well when he said, "We entered the mountains as strangers, but we left as brothers."

Forgotten delicacies appeared to make the meals memorable as we came to Askole and other villages. We stuffed ourselves with apricots, chickens, eggs, grapes, apples, pears, and cucumbers, for the fertile valley was yielding

269

luxuries unknown to the grim regions beyond. I can remember lunch on the day when we were supposed to reach Askole. A few days previously some of the Askole men had been sent ahead to bring back atta for the Satpuras. They brought it and also some dainties for the sahibs. The going had been hard and the dandy wallahs and I were far in the rear of the bandobast when we came upon Ghulam and Haji Beg with "lunch for the sahib." My lunch turned out to be ten hard-boiled eggs, two small chickens, and chuppatis. The dandy wallahs were perhaps a bit depressed by seeing me eat with such gusto, but that did not detract from my enjoyment of the entire meal. At Chokpyong and Niyil, the apricots were just ripe and we made hogs of ourselves. I can recall Tony reclining against a tree, helping himself for the fiftieth time to a large basket of apricots with a wistful "I shall very likely be sick tomorrow, but. . . ." And then at Yuno, just before the zahk voyage, we had a king's feast of apricot seeds, dried mulberries, cucumbers, and grapes.

At Askole, Ata, Schoening, and Bob Bates diverged from the Braldu Gorge to take a short cut over a 16,400-foot pass, the Skoro-La, and thence go directly down to Shigar. This would save them three days' travel and offer splendid views of peaks along the Braldu. Their trip was favored by perfect weather which, if it was clear back in the high peaks, was the first pleasant weather there in well over a month. Ata was impatient, as his leave was coming to an end, and he spurred his party to a rapid crossing.

Meanwhile the rest of us marched and lived for the day when we would come to the zahk (goatskin raft) which we were certain would carry us in painless splendor the remaining 50 or so miles to Skardu. We were supposed to meet the zahk at Niyil, where we had first crossed the Braldu on the way in. The river was high, however, and so we spent the better part of another day climbing up and down along the Braldu.

The Satpuras could almost see where their home village lay as we swung into the wide Shigar Valley. Their hearts were cheered, and every now and then they would break into song. Their favorite was a sort of leader and chorus ballad, where Mohammed Hussein would chant something in a high falsetto, and the others would join in on the refrain. I have no idea what these songs were about, but very likely the Satpuras recalled their women, children, homes, and fields, which they would soon see again after their long, hard journey into the great mountains.

The zahk wallahs soon appeared and ferried everyone over to Yuno on the other side of the Shigar. This crossing was no mean feat in itself, for here the river was divided into many turbulent channels, each one of which was a powerful stream. But the zahk wallahs were Yuno wallahs as well, and at home in these channels.

August 29 was the day of our great zahk ride. This particular zahk was made of about thirty goatskins and floated high and easy with its eight passengers: Houston, Streather, Molenaar, Bob Craig, and me, and the three zahk wallahs. Oldest and most experienced zahk wallah was a small, gray-haired Balti, who looked just the part of a river pilot. After a leisurely start, we soon found ourselves bobbing down to Shigar at about 10 knots. The multitudinous channels of the Shigar River sprawled over an extensive gravel plain, and the zahk wallahs skillfully poled and paddled their craft, striving to keep it where the water flowed swift but not heavy. A few times we ran some fair rapids and once we nearly grounded, but on the whole the travel was smooth. Lulled by the warm sun and easy motion, our spirits were high. Charlie spoke of 1938, and how in that year two expedition zahks had held the first Harvard-Yale zahk race on the Shigar, a race which (as I recall) Harvard was winning by several lengths until their zahk ran aground. Displaying my scientific background, I convinced Bob Craig that the cup of water which he was drinking from the Shigar River almost certainly contained atoms from the first glass of water that he had ever had in his life. And Tony told another of his great tales of life on the Northwest Frontier before partition.

Three times the zahk pulled in to shore for minor repairs, mostly the blowing up of goatskins which were becoming deflated. Below the village of Shigar, the river was confined in only one or two big channels, and here we made rapid progress. In the afternoon, the huge rock outcrops by Skardu came in sight. Soon we approached the confluence of the Shigar with the great Indus River. Their waters met in conflict and turmoil, but our old river pilot and crew treated the place with caution and safely brought the zahk to the far side of the Indus, whence Skardu was only about a mile away. Two farmers were enlisted to carry me to Skardu. Since darkness was coming on, Houston and Molenaar hurried ahead to get a regular litter and bearers from the hospital, but my two carriers proved so strong that I reached the hospital before the litter bearers were organized, and indeed quite a while before Bob Craig could hobble in.

Thus, after long travail, we were returned to the world of men. The new, young, and energetic political agent gave us a delicious curry, and soon I was comfortably ensconced in a bed of the civil and military hospital.

The next day we said good-by to the Hunzas, who had stood by us so faithfully during the entire course of the expedition. "Perhaps we shall come again," we said.

"Or I shall go to America," answered Hidayat with his most infectious smile.

On August 31 we boarded an Orient Airways DC-3 and flew to Rawalpindi, where Charlie's wife, Dorcas, had traveled halfway round the world to meet him. The Indus Canyon was as spectacular as before. When the pilot took the DC-3 up to 20,000 feet we could see close by such

273

mighty summits as Rakaposhi, Haramosh, and the high and deadly Nanga Parbat, which had finally been climbed only two months before by a German-Austrian party.

Far, far in the distance there stretched out jagged range upon range of storybook mountains, and above all the others the symmetrical, ice-encrusted, and wind-swept summit pyramid of K2.

Appendixes

1. Chronology

JULY (cont'd)

to Camp III; others move to Camp II

6–7 Packing to Camp III

8 Bates, Bell, Molenaar, Houston move to Camp III; others packing

9 Bell, Molenaar, Houston reconnoiter to Camp IV, climb House's Chimney to Camp V

10 Bates has tooth pulled at Camp II; others packing

11 Brief storm

12 Bell and Molenaar move to Camp IV; others packing

13 Packing from Camp III to IV and from II to III

14 Storm

15 Storm

16 Storm

17 Packing to Camp IV and up House's Chimney

18 Packing to Camp IV and up chimney

19 Bad weather; packing up House's Chimney

20 Bad weather; packing; Bates and Schoening reconnoiter to Camp VI

21 Packing to Camp VI; all move to Camp V

22 Packing Camp IV to V and V to VI

23 Bad storm

24 Bad storm

25 Very cold; packed part way to Camp VI

26 Bell, Craig, Houston move up to Camp VI; others pack from V to VI

27 Bell, Houston, Craig reconnoiter to Camp VII; others move to VI

28 Storm

29 All pack to Camp VII cache

30 Gilkey and Schoening move to Camp VII; all packing to VII

31 Gilkey and Schoening reconnoiter above Camp VII; others stormbound at Camp VI

AUGUST

1 Gilkey and Schoening move from Camp VII to VIII; Bell, Craig, Molenaar, and Houston move from VI to VIII

2 Bates and Streather move from Camp VI to VIII; others descend from VIII to VII and return with loads

3–9 Entire party stormbound at Camp VIII. On August 7 Gilkey found to be ill and attempt made to bring him down. Craig and Schoening reconnoiter new descent route

AUGUST (*cont'd*)

10 Descent begins about 9 A.M. Accident occurs at 3 P.M. Gilkey lost. Bivouac at Camp VII. Skardu porters arrive at Base
11 Descent to Camp VI
12 Stormbound at Camp VI. Craig and Molenaar descend to Camp V
13 Descent to Camp IV
14 Descent to Camp II
15 Arrival at Base Camp
16 Base Camp
17 Base to Glacier Camp

18 Glacier Camp to Urdukas
19 Urdukas to Lilipru
20 Lilipru to Paiju
21 Paiju to Biange
22 Biange to Askole
23 Ata-Ullah, Bates, Schoening climb nearly to Skoro-La; others to Chondo
24 Ata-Ullah, Bates, Schoening cross Skoro-La and down to Shigar; others to Chokpyong
25 Chokpyong to Yuno
26 Yuno to Skardu
28 Flight to Rawalpindi

Approximate elevations of camps used in 1953:

Base Camp	16,600 feet	Camp V	22,000 feet
Camp 1	17,700 feet	Camp VI	23,300 feet
Camp II	19,300 feet	Camp VII	24,500 feet
Camp III	20,700 feet	Camp VIII	25,500 feet
Camp IV	21,500 feet		

2. Equipment

As usual for an expedition of this scale, selection of equipment took considerable time and effort, aroused a good deal of discussion, and produced a variety of judgments on many items. On shoes and snorkels, goggles and gauntlets, each seasoned climber has his own cherished opinions, which are good for many long winter arguments. Accordingly I shall try here to give only the skeleton of our 1953 equipment lists with the virtues and faults more generally agreed upon (see page 293 for itemized personal equipment list).

This was largely purchased by the expedition and distributed at Base Camp. In retrospect I believe that it might have been better to allow each member to supply his own kit, following certain broad principles and assuming of course that the personnel have had considerable expedition experience. A common pool of extra clothing is essential, and certain basic items (down jackets, parkas, sleeping bags) might best be supplied by the expedition.

DOWN JACKET, made by Eddie Bauer to our design, was unanimously considered our best item of clothing. It proved very warm and tough, was made from scarlet K2 cloth for visibility.

NYLON WINDPROOF PARKA, by Cunningham, was of double-thickness nylon, tightly woven, windproof, and was excellent except for a minor problem of closure around the neck. Lightweight windproof pants were also good.

WEATHERALL JACKETS AND TROUSERS, of quilted nylon with "insulite" material in place of down, were warm and light in weight. Most men used the trousers but only few needed the jacket, except in camp.

WOOLEN UNDERWEAR, of newest Army type, was excellent.

SOCKS: Army "cushion-sole" type were favored as a lightweight sock. Heavy Army wool ski socks were standard. Raw wool Indian knit socks, provided in two sizes, color-coded so that the larger would be worn over the smaller, were excellent, even when damp. Most found these their best socks.

INSOLES: Army plastic type were the most used, with a heavier felt insole as second choice, for the latter were difficult to dry.

TROUSERS: Individual choice varied from tight-weave gabardine ski trousers to whipcord work trousers. The windproof, coverall trousers had a drawstring belt and drawstring to obtain snow seal at boot top. Pockets, slit access to inner trousers, were needed.

SHIRTS: Individual choice varied from light- to heavyweight wool, with colors from conservative gray to flaming scarlet.

SWEATERS: Individual choice from heavy Army type to multiple lightweight Shetland wool with turtle necks.

GLOVES: Unsatisfactory as always. On lower stretches we used insulated gloves, wristlets, fine wool gloves, mittens, or nothing. Several pairs of ordinary cotton work gloves would be of help on glacier stretches and on the lower rocks, where protection from cuts and scrapes is as important as protection from cold. Higher on the mountain most men liked the Indian knit raw wool mitten. The standard Army wool mitten was condemned as too cold. Heavy Air Force lined gloves were favored by one man. Army ski gauntlets with palms of nonfreezing leather were fairly good, though poorly tailored. Six- or eight-inch tape, sewed to each glove and buttoned to a large button on the parka or jacket sleeve, was used by some to prevent loss of gloves. Many extra gloves and gauntlets must be taken high on such a mountain. Very fine, light woolen gloves would help in photography, to be worn under mittens.

BOOTS are the perennial problem of high-altitude climbers, with no two men agreed. We used several types, none ideal. Probably best for high work was the Korean boot, large, heavy, and clumsy though it is. The usual sole is too flexible and has inadequate treads for the rock on K2. Cleated soles were welded to one pair, and helped a lot but were heavy and even more clumsy. To our surprise these excellent boots did not keep our feet warm at extreme altitudes (but see Appendix 4 for other causes of cold feet). One pair of Lawrie Everest boots—a light leather boot with fur insulation between layers of fine nonfreezing leather, was excellent up to 23,000 feet; above this it was too cold. Custom-made boots by Tyrol were heavy, clumsy, and cold, though well made. A lighter boot by Protiaux had too pointed a toe and was too small. We all preferred rubber cleats to straight nails or a combination nail and cleat. Felt boots were not used, for we feared they would not stand up on the sharp continuously difficult rock on K2. The ideal high-altitude boot must be light; it should be insulated along the lines of the Korean boot, and it should not freeze. A stiff, rubber-cleated sole is necessary. Easy lacing, or hooks, a pull-on strap (sadly lacking in the Korean boot), and a watertight tongue are important features. The boot should be large enough for several pairs of socks and insoles, and stiff enough to hold crampons firmly.

HEADWEAR: Individual choice ranged from colorful Peruvian bonnets to homemade woolen helmets. Good ear protection is essential. Face masks were neither taken nor missed. Several men used "snorkels," made from the upper 6 inches of a long woolen stocking, and held over mouth and nose by elastic passed around the back of the head. By breathing through this elephant-trunk appendage cold air was to a certain extent warmed before entering the lungs. Its advocates thought it essential; the skeptics were unconvinced.

GOGGLES: Army-type snow goggles, old Everest goggles, or dark glasses ground to the wearer's prescription were all adequate. All gave trouble from fogging in our worst weather. The goggle design is *not* essential, for a dark spectacle gives adequate protection against snow blindness.

PACK FRAMES: The Army molded-plywood frame was excellent, though some type of detachable sack was often needed. A tubular steel and nylon frame (Cunningham) was preferred by some because it was slightly lighter and had a rucksack which could be removed or used. Clothing was kept in multiple plastic bags of various sizes, which were excellent; the old-fashioned canvas duffel bag was widely used.

MARCH-IN CLOTHING: A wide choice was used. Protection from fearful sunburn by light, long-sleeved shirts and trousers is essential for the first few days. An extraordinary collection of felt hats, sun helmets, topis, etc., was used. Ponchos are useful even if it never rains, and they can double as tarpaulins on the mountain. Well-broken-in walking shoes or boots are essential, but even then blisters are almost unavoidable in the first week.

TENTS: Volumes could be written here. Our slender purse forced us to use a variety, including three veterans from the 1938 trip (Meade type by Burns), whose fabric stood up surprisingly well. Duplicates of the Meade made by Camp and Trail were good. One French tent, used by the Swiss on Everest, was taken, with a fine nylon liner; the tent was excellent, but the liner was poorly suspended and undesirably cut down living space. One Cunningham tent was our lightest, smallest, but had cooking vestibules which were highly thought of, as well as a well-designed liner. Condensation is significantly less, and warmth appreciably greater in a lined tent. Two large Army hexagonal tents were used on the march in and at Base Camp and Camp I; these were outstanding: easy to pitch, spacious, conveniently dimensioned, and warm. An ideal tent for K2 should fit the following specifications: floor area from 44 to 48 inches by 76 to 80 inches, with peak 44 inches high with a vestibule on either or both ends. Fabric should be light in color, permeable to moisture but tight to wind. The liner should be removable, of very light weight, not inflammable, and attached so as to provide an air space not less than 1 inch nor more than 3 inches wide on walls to peak. Floor must be of tougher, waterproof material, extending to ends of vestibules. A door

285

at each end is desirable, either of tunnel type with draw-string, or with a large, strong, full-length zipper, with gentle curve, and a 2-inch safety flap on the outside, having snaps every 4 inches to close the opening in case of zipper failure. Four-inch, tubular ventilators with wire supports and a suitable closure device are important at each end. Poles should be of strong, lightweight aluminum alloy, $\frac{3}{4}$ inch in diameter, in two sections. Tents should be of standard dimensions so that all poles—and many extra sets should be taken—are interchangeable. A light "Gothic wand" should fit midway along each side, meeting at the peak, to hold side walls from sagging in. Worthy of mention is the 7-foot-by-7 Logan tent which was left, rolled in its bag, on the rocks at Camp II by the 1939 party. Though the fabric was a bit rotten in one or two spots, we used the tent all summer. On the long climb to Camp VIII, Tony and Bob made good use of a 10-ounce bivouac sack which sheltered the two of them from the bitter wind.

SLEEPING BAGS (Swiss Foundation): Our outstanding double, down-filled bags were always warm. They weighed only 7 pounds and their only fault was bulk—it was hard to compress them into a respectable pack. The fabric was very thin, very tough nylon of the tightest possible weave. It is important to be sure that the tallest member of the party has a long enough bag—George was rather bitter about this oversight. Despite initial disagreement, we all concluded that a double bag (one inside the other) is preferable to a single bag of the same weight.

AIR MATTRESSES: The full-length Army plastic mattress was very good, light in weight, tough, easy to inflate. Half-length rubber pads of $3/4$-inch foam rubber were about as comfortable, warmer, about the same weight, and required no inflation.

KITCHEN EQUIPMENT: The Army mountain stove was light, compact, efficient, and such repairs as were needed were easily made in the field. We burned gasoline, which is relatively clean and free of fumes. Any stove becomes less efficient as the altitude increases, but failure of these stoves at 25,500 feet during the storm was due to the tremendous flapping of the tents, from which we could not manage to shield them. Aluminum dekshis, bought in Pakistan, were used as cooking pots. These are light, strong, and shallow, without a bail, but using instead a narrow lip. A "kitchen box" (containing all cooking utensils, a stove, and staples) which could be converted into a table and a sheltered spot for the stove would be a worthy addition. Army 5-gallon gas tanks were satisfactory, though two out of eight sprang leaks under rough handling. On the mountain these are too heavy, and we used instead a multitude of lightweight, 1-liter aluminum bottles. Wide-mouth, 1-quart Thermos flasks were helpful in keeping water from freezing overnight, but were not adequate to preserve heat. For eating and

287

drinking we used a 1-pint plastic cup, plus a square, plastic "deep-freeze" container. Both were light, almost indestructible, did not conduct heat and so kept food warm longer than a metal or enamel cup. One spoon per man sufficed, and plates were seldom used except for "state" occasions on march in and out. Plastic canteens were very useful and light.

CONTAINERS: Supplies were carried mostly in wooden plywood boxes (12 by 14 by 24 inches), packed and strapped in the U.S.A. and carried intact to Base; others were carried in a hinge-top aluminum box (12 by 10 by 24) with hasp for locking. These excellent boxes were made for us by the Aluminum Company of India and were most valuable. Boxes should be numbered in large letters and have keys and locks with matching numbers for easy access on the approach march. Supplies needed on the approach march should be concentrated in a few boxes so that only these need be disturbed each night. Gunny sacks and miscellaneous boxes were used less satisfactorily, as even tough tinned goods are badly battered if carried in sacks over such trails.

PORTER SUPPLIES: K2 presents few campsites with tent space for more than two or three tents, and the danger of knocking down stones is so great that only a small party can move safely on the mountain, so that a large corps of mountain porters is not very practical. Hunza porters, properly trained, will in the future provide an excellent supply of mountain porters, but I am dubious about using many men above Camp III on K2. For the above reasons we did not equip our men for high-altitude work, but provided only the following items. Except for the boots (Korean type would have been better), and the heavy woolen porter underwear (bitterly described as too itchy), the gear was good.

PORTER CLOTHING AND EQUIPMENT

Windproof parka and trousers	1 pair
Woolen sweaters (turtle-neck)	2
Woolen socks	4 pair
Woolen mittens	2 pair
Canvas gauntlets	1 pair
Boots (Army ski-mountain)	1 pair
Wool helmet	1
Woolen underwear	1 pair
Sleeping bag (Army mountain-type)	1
Ground cloth	1
Ice axe	1
Pack frame (Army plywood)	1
Goggles	1 pair

A pool of extra equipment was also maintained and used.

Porters on the march to Base Camp need goggles, which can be purchased in Pakistan. Food is supplied by porters up to the last village, but thereafter it must be furnished, together with men to carry it, by the expedition. Cigarettes and matches (ten per day per man) are essential. Several large tents, tarpaulins, or blankets (one for each three men) are helpful but not absolutely essential. It is not possible to supply footgear, but each man's shoes and clothing should

289

be checked at time of enlistment. It is necessary to issue numbered metal identification disks to each man against his name on recruitment. Porters must provide their own cooking and eating utensils, and their own food and fuel, but sugar, salt, and tea must come from general stores and be regarded as luxuries for special issue. Beyond the last village, food and fuel bought by the expedition should be carried by extra men. A contractor is neither needed nor desirable, but some member of the expedition who knows the people, the dialects, and the country must be charged with complete management of the caravan and should deal directly with a responsible head of all the porters. Care should be taken to avoid overpayment (porters always want more) or tipping except for outstanding performance.

MISCELLANY: There is no point in listing the hundreds of lesser items familiar to all expeditionaries. The main thing is to have the essentials, to know what you have and where it is, and to avoid excess. It is too easy to "take everything" and end up with a huge, unwieldy and expensive, slow-moving and easily disrupted caravan, carrying tons of equipment, much of which is left unused.

AN AIRDROP might be flown from Skardu to Camp I, thus avoiding the problems of the porter caravan. In favor of the drop would be the simpler approach march, the opportunity to bring more supplies without much added cost, speed of access, and availability of all gear at Camp I (which is beyond reach of the large caravan), instead of at Base Camp. Against the airdrop is the risk of losing items which might have to be replaced from the U.S.A., the uncertainty of precise scheduling because of uncertain radio contact and weather, the complexity of packing, risk of breakage, and the cost, which would probably exceed that of the equivalent in porters. An airdrop, either free or with chutes, to a crevassed glacier at 17,000 feet in a narrow valley with 27,000 foot peaks and turbulent air currents, would have appreciable risks.

RADIOS: Our Raytheon AN PRC-6 walkie-talkies functioned almost perfectly. Though usually limited to line-of-sight communication, we often had good reception and transmission when one camp was hidden behind a ridge. Fresh batteries operated well even when cold, but after a short period of use we found it better to warm the batteries for a half hour or more in a sleeping bag before use. We received broadcasts from Asia, Europe, and occasionally from the U.S.A. on our Zenith portable, which functioned very well at Base Camp. Thanks to the Pakistan Army Meteorological Service and Radio Pakistan we had weather forecasts twice daily which, though seldom favorable, were amazingly accurate. We did not take a long-range transmitter to contact Skardu from Base Camp for several reasons: weight, cost, reluctance to release news we could not control, military and political sensitivity of the region, and uncertainty of reception. To base plans on the belief that a message has been received, and received correctly, under conditions prevailing in the Karakoram, would be a mistake, in my opinion, though good arguments were advanced in favor of such contact. A Travis Tapak tape recorder was used most successfully to record music, conversation, and most effectively of all, a discussion of the climb at Base Camp on the day following our descent. We were slow to realize the possibilities of this equipment, and in the future much greater value could be obtained from it.

CAMERAS: a matter of individual choice. They must be carefully winterized and should be light and simple. High-altitude photography is tricky and difficult, both technically and because of the inertia induced by altitude. The light values are very great and the contrast tremendous. Ultraviolet light tends to make color too blue, but a haze filter seems to make the color too brown. Heat and cold, moisture or drought did not significantly affect our film. An exposure meter is essential.

STATIONERY: Typewriter, paper, air letters, extra pens, pencils, and notebooks should form a common pool at Base. Our Expedition Letter, written daily by several members and mailed home for duplication and mailing to friends of the party, was an excellent arrangement. Weekly mail runners, in pairs, should be planned in advance, but care must also be taken to ensure safe transfer of mail from runner to post office. We had the invaluable assistance of the surgeon, Major Khan, at the Skardu Hospital, who gave us excellent mail service.

PERSONAL EQUIPMENT LIST

(Given to Each Team Member)

This list is intended as a guide only, representing the type and amount of equipment which seems best suited to our needs. Each man's kit, *exclusive* of ice axe, crampons, photographic equipment, but *including* boots, sleeper, and air mattress, must weigh less than 60 pounds packed.

Items marked "X" are provided by expedition; those marked "P" are provided by the individual.

Mountain Equipment

X	Lightweight woolen underwear	3 suits
P	Lightweight woolen sweaters	3
P	Woolen or flannel shirt	1
P	Wool scarf	1
P	Wool helmet (Balaclava type)	1
P	Snow goggles	2 pair
P	Handkerchiefs	3
P	Puttees or gaiters	1 pair
P	Watch, compass, pocket knife, canteen	1 each
P	Ice axe	1
X	Climbing trousers	1 pair
X	Windproof trousers	1 pair
X	Parka	1
X	Woolen socks (two sizes)	6 pair
X	Fine woolen finger gloves	1 pair
X	Woolen mittens	3 pair
X	Windproof gauntlets	2 pair
X	Boots, high-altitude	2 pair
X	Boots, Korean	1 pair

K 2—THE SAVAGE MOUNTAIN

X	Insoles	6 pair
X	Down jacket	1
X	Crampons	1 pair
X	Sleeping bag and air mattress	1 each
	Pack frame (expedition or individual choice)	1
X	Insulated gloves	1 pair
X	Insulated suit	1 suit

Traveling, march in and out, Base Camp

P	Light trousers	1 pair
P	Shorts	1 pair
P	Light short-sleeved shirt	1
P	Socks, lightweight	2 pair
P	Shoes, walking	1 pair
P	Slippers, camp, light but warm	1 pair
P	Pajamas	1 pair
P	Towel	1
P	Toilet set (razor, toothbrush and paste)	1
P	Traveling suit, shirts (2), ties, shoes, hat	
X	Poncho, nylon	1

ROBERT H. BATES

3. Food

Have you ever been away from fruits and salads so long
that you would gladly trade your best hat for an orange or a
green salad? You sometimes feel that way on a mountain
or arctic expedition when for weeks or months at a time you
are living on concentrated foods that are well balanced and
have plenty of nourishment but are not fresh. But despite
occasional cravings for fresh milk, vegetables, or fruits, the
member of a modern mountaineering expedition lives very
well. Modern dehydrated foods and plastic packaging have
greatly reduced the weight and increased the variety of what
can be taken.

On K2 weight of food was, of course, a critical matter, but
so was the ease of preparation. We could not take slow-
cooking foods, because too much gasoline was required to

cook them, and gasoline is heavy. Pressure cookers are heavy, too. At our high camp, both to increase simplicity of preparation and to save weight as well, we took items that required little or no cooking. Hot water was all that was needed to prepare tea, baby-food cereals, soup, meat bars (each a pound of steak dehydrated to 4 ounces), and precooked dehydrated potatoes or rice. Most of our high-camp items, including all our lunches, could be eaten cold.

At Base Camp, of course, lightness of weight and time of cooking was less important, so that more varieties of canned meats and fish, and a few luxury items, could be added to the list. And during the march in to the mountain, an even different list could be used, because local chickens, eggs, sheep, flour, and fruits were frequently available. As a result we planned three types of rations: food for the march in from Skardu to Base Camp and return—25 days; Base Camp food—15 days; and high-camp food—55 days. Total: 95 days' food.

We based our high-camp food especially on Dr. Houston's experience that physiologically a mountain climber does his best work if he has mainly carbohydrates in the daytime for quick energy, and proteins for the evening meal. In practice this plan did not work out so well as had been hoped, for the amount of sugar in the ration for lunches was excessive, and there were requests for meat at breakfast.

Food for K2 in 1953 was vastly superior to food for K2 in 1938 in ease of preparation and packaging. These characteristics went together, for each item of high-camp food (except powdered milk, jam, butter, and biscuits) was heat-sealed into polyethelene bags in quantities sufficient for two men for one meal. These little packets were collected into larger plastic bags, weighing 17 to 20 pounds apiece with the addition of the bulk items listed above, were packed three at a time into cloth bags. These outer bags gave added protection while loads were being carried up the mountain. Results of this system were excellent. Not only did the plastic preserve the food well with a minimum of weight, but the system made preparation simple; and one could always tell at a glance how much food was at a given place at a given time. Prepackaging the high-camp food at Exeter before the expedition's departure was a tremendous advantage later. It would not have been done without Mrs. Houston's invaluable assistance.

A few notes follow. On the route to and from the mountain, flour is available for making local breads (chuppatis and pirattas) which are especially good when eaten hot with butter and jam. Considerable planning is necessary to have all food easily available in a minimum number of boxes for this part of the journey. The fewer porter loads that need be disturbed the better.

Outstanding high-camp foods were the meat bars, pan forte (Italian fruitcake), and date squares with almonds. More hot chocolate drinks and puddings would have been welcome, and a slightly stronger pilot biscuit.

K 2—THE SAVAGE MOUNTAIN

BASE CAMP FOOD LISTS

(8 men—15 days)

Item	Oz. per man per day	No. of days	Total weight (lbs.)
Breakfast			
Prunes (5)	3	6	9
Apricots (20)	3	6	9
Apple flakes	1½	3	2¼
Maltex	4	5	10
Ralston	4	5	10
Corn meal	4	5	10
Canadian bacon	2	7	7
Klim	2	15	15
Tea bags	2 bags	15	240 bags
Borden coffee	$\frac{1}{10}$	15	12 oz.
Sugar	4	15	30
Butter	2	15	15
Kipper	2	7	7
Lunch			
Ham	4	4	8
Tongue	4	4	8
Luncheon meat	4	3	6
Tuna	4	3	6
Triscuit	½ box	8	32 boxes
Pilot biscuit	$\frac{3}{16}$ can	8	12 cans
Raisins	3	5	7½
Date bars (with almonds)	1 bar	7	56 bars
Figs	3	4	4½
Jam	3	15	22½
Chocolate	4	15	30
Candies			
Malted milk tablets			
Dinner			
Roast beef	4	3	6

Item	Oz. per man per day	No. of days	Total weight (lbs.)
Corned beef hash	4	4	8
Corned beef	4	2	4
Chicken	3	4	6
Salmon	4	2	4
Minced clams	4	2	4
Instant potatoes	1½	6	4½
Precooked rice	2	4	4
Carrots	2	3	3
Cabbage	2	2	2
Beets	2	2	2
Onion soup	½	10	2½
Chicken noodle	½	2	½
Beef	½	3	¾
Hemo	½	15	3¾
Pilot bread	⅛ can	15	15 cans
Pudding and Jell-O			5
Additional meats			15

HIGH-CAMP FOOD LISTS

(based on eight men—55 days above Camp I)

Item	Oz. per man per day	No. of days	Total weight (lbs.)
Breakfast			
Apple flakes	1½	30	22½
Orange juice	1½	25	19
Ralston	4	20	40
Oatmeal	2	20	20
Corn cereal	2	15	15
Klim	1½	55	42
Tea bags	3 bags	55	1320 bags
Sugar	4 oz.	55	110
Salt		55	4

Item	Oz. per man per day	No. of days	Total weight (lbs.)
Lunch			
Date bars	1 bar	25	200 bars
Figs	4	10	20
Raisins	3	10	15
Apricots	3	10	15
Triscuit	½ box	20	80 boxes
Pilot biscuit	³⁄₁₆ can	20	30 cans
Ry-Krisp	½ box	20	80 boxes
Chocolate	4	55	110
Cheese	3	20	30
Pan forte	2	20	20
Nuts	2	20	20
Malted milk tablets	1	35	17½
Candy	1	20	17½
Ham			5 lb. extra
Jam			10 lb. extra
Butter			3 lb. extra
Dinner			
Pea soup	½	18	4½
Beef soup	½	22	5½
Chicken noodle	½	6	1½
Tomato soup	½	10	2½
Meat bars	4	30	60
Ham	5	11	27½
Chicken	5	7	17½
Tuna	5	7	17½
Potatoes	1½	30	22½
Rice	2	25	25
Jam	3	55	82½
Ovaltine	2	15	15
Cocomalt	2	15	15
Jell-O	2	15	15
Butter	1	55	27½

300

CHARLES S. HOUSTON, M·D.

4. Medical problems

The medical aspects of the 1953 K2 expedition can be
divided into three sections: problems of the march to and
from Base Camp, problems on the mountain, and certain
aspects of acclimatization. A detailed list of the medical
equipment taken is appended.

All who have traveled in the Himalayas, where sanitation
is primitive and many diseases endemic, have recognized
the need for great care during the approach march to ensure
that all personnel reach the mountain in the best of condition.
A march of 150 to 200 miles through country densely popu-
lated with people whose ideas of cleanliness and health are
those of the Middle Ages exposes Europeans to diseases unknown in our civilized lives, to which, as a consequence, we

have little or no resistance. In the Karakoram such intestinal diseases as amoebic and bacillary dysentery are very prevalent. Tuberculosis, typhoid fever, bronchitis, and dengue fever are common. Intestinal parasites, such as round and flat worms, and certain of the flukes are also seen. A variant of influenza appears sporadically; epidemics of typhus are not rare. Louse and flea infestations are common; plague, though infrequent, does occur. Malaria, on the other hand, is rare, and yellow fever unknown. Trachoma, bacterial and viral conjunctivitis, and a wide variety of skin afflictions are also common.

These are the ailments against which the party must be protected, and for which the natives who flock to "sick call" must be treated. For the sake of good will, as well as for obvious humanitarian reasons, the expedition doctor must do what he can to help the sick in the villages through which the party passes, though little can be accomplished in the brief time available. It was my practice to see as many natives as wished help, but I could not and did not try to give much save symptomatic relief. On the approach march we were accompanied by a medical officer from Skardu who bore the major share of the medical work with the natives.

Obviously we avoided unboiled water or uncooked food on the approach march. A water filter, inadvertently omitted, was sorely missed, and chlorine tablets for disinfecting water were very helpful. On occasions when we had unwittingly used dubious water, it seemed prudent to place the entire

302

party on prophylactic aureomycin for several days. Though we camped in villages, we tried to keep the inhabitants away from our tents, and our cooking was done by our own men. On the homeward march we gorged on fruit and vegetables and ignored most rules, but the resulting diarrhea and intestinal upsets were due to greediness rather than infection, and subsided promptly.

One member of the party developed a mild grippelike illness at the end of the first week; two others subsequently developed the same symptoms of fever, headache, general malaise, and weakness. All recovered in a few days. I considered their illness to be dengue fever, of the type contracted by Petzoldt in 1938 and by Tilman in 1937. Though exposed constantly to the coughs and colds of the natives, none of us developed any upper respiratory infection on the march in and, more surprisingly, we remained free on the return trip also. Nor did we have any of the sore throats which have plagued Everest parties both on the approach and on the climb. The principal problem on the approach march was management of blisters and sore muscles in the climbing party, and stone bruises, cracked calluses, and minor infections in our porters.

Once at Base Camp, after dismissing all save six Hunza porters, we were free from infectious diseases and only the problem of maintaining optimum health prevailed. Our diets were planned to be high in carbohydrate for breakfast and luncheon, thereby gaining a few thousand feet of altitude

303

benefit by the specific "oxygen-conserving" qualities of carbohydrate (a theoretical point actually proved to be true in a few experiments), with protein and fat for the evening meal.

Though this proved sound in principle, we all felt the need for more evenly divided protein. A therapeutic vitamin capsule was taken regularly for part of the time, and some felt better when taking this. On another trip I would place the vitamin capsule in the daily food-ration bag. A combination of iron, B12, liver, and folic acid was also taken intermittently, on the assumption that our diet lacked these essentials. Worthy of mention is the mania for fresh fruit which we all developed during the return trip, suggesting that mild deficiency in Vitamin C may have developed.

Only three medical problems marred our climb: an abscessed tooth, extracted at Camp II, Gilkey's thrombophlebitis, and several cases of frostbite. Thrombophlebitis is almost unknown in mountaineers, a surprising fact in view of the polycythemia (excess red cell formation) developed during acclimatization, since this is a frequent complication of polycythemia at sea level. Undoubtedly the dehydration and inactivity to which we were all exposed at Camp VIII contributed greatly. Dehydration is in itself one of the serious problems at great heights. The air is almost completely dry, so that with each exhalation (and there are very many!) the climber loses a significant amount of water. Melted snow is the only source of liquid above 20,000 feet, and gasoline is

304

an added load to carry for this purpose. Because of the effort to save gas, the time consumed in melting snow, and the frequent difficulties in keeping stoves lighted in high winds, we seldom had enough to drink before returning to Base Camp. A determined effort should be made to see that each climber takes enough fluid every day to provide a urinary output of at least 1 quart, preferably more. This probably requires an intake of 2 to 3 quarts, which should be distributed among fruit juice (concentrates were used), soup, water, milk beverages, and tea, with less emphasis on the latter because of the insomnia so easily induced as well as the irritative effect on the stomach.

Management of frostbite is still a controversial subject, and a wide range of treatments are suggested. After reviewing the available literature before we left I resolved on a conservative approach, using a peripheral vasodilator taken by mouth (Roniacol) as soon as the potential victim reached his sleeping bag, and local cleanliness and antibiotics once frostbite had developed. I elected against the anticoagulant medications (heparin and dicumerol), agents which are said to decrease capillary permeability (rutin), and intra-arterial injections. George Bell had severely frozen toes, three on each foot showing black gangrene; and several of the others had ulcerated heels. But Bell has lost only one small toe and half of one great toe, and all other cases have cleared completely, which would seem to vindicate the conservative approach. Undoubtedly the frostbite and the ulcerated heels

305

were aggravated by the dehydration of Camp VIII, which caused even more clumping of red cells in the greatly thickened blood, and this may also explain the continually cold feet which we all experienced even in our sleeping bags and even in the vapor-barrier Korean boots.

Acclimatization to high altitude, or more precisely to lack of oxygen, is still imperfectly understood despite the wealth of data collected on the subject. This is not the place to discuss the physiology of acclimatization, and I shall comment only on our own experiences. To provide maximum acclimatization at the optimum rate, the body must be supplied with a full, well-balanced diet, an excess of blood-building materials (iron, vitamins, minerals), and adequate fluid (to eliminate waste products); similarly, deterrents such as infection, fatigue, and stress must be minimized. A gradual ascent, or repeated ascents, effect better acclimatization than a rapid or high ascent. Exercising subjects appear to develop better acclimatization than those at rest. Artificial aids (ammonium chloride, methylene blue, cytochrome C) may have a place which is not yet clearly apparent. Oxygen is of great help to unacclimatized men, of less help (at least to 25,000 feet) in well-acclimatized men. Perhaps the greatest benefit from oxygen comes in improvement in sleep when oxygen is breathed during the night.

Our attack on K2 was made over a two-month period: we remained for 68 days at and above 16,500 feet, 45 days at or above 19,200 feet, 18 days at and above 24,000 feet, and for 10 days at 25,500 feet. We "packed high and slept low"; that is, we carried loads up to the next camp, but tried to sleep at the lower camp as long as possible before moving up to continue the attack. We all carried loads, varying the weight between individuals and on different days as desired. I firmly believe that load carrying, if not pushed to severe fatigue, enhances acclimatization, but in any event the nature of the climbing and the dearth of tentsites on K2 forces the climbing party to double as porters. We made no effort to have "vacations" at Base Camp or to descend to recuperate—this policy I believe was a mistake, and on a later trip I should plan rest periods at lower camps at regular intervals. Nor did we spend any additional time on smaller climbs or at Base Camp before the actual attempt on the mountain; this training period might be of some help if time were available.

That our acclimatization was very good is attested by our ability to do difficult rock climbing (several vertical pitches of 40 to 50 feet), and to carry loads of as much as 35 pounds over deep snow and steep slopes at 25,000 feet. We were generally free from headaches (which occurred only during the first few days at Base Camp). Our mental and physical stamina after ten days in camp at 25,500 feet, and after a tragic accident, was great enough to bring us all safely to Base Camp through severe storm. I believe we would have been better acclimatized had we had better food and drink at high camp, and had we taken some rest periods.

My own feelings about the use of oxygen may be put as follows. I believe that 28,250 feet can be reached by well-acclimatized men without added oxygen; I am satisfied that K2 can be climbed without oxygen. Oxygen equipment will always be heavy, delicate to manage, cumbersome to climb with; it presents an added supply problem, requiring added carrying power on a mountain where camping facilities are already strained. Failure of oxygen equipment high on the mountain would be serious, possibly fatal, to a man accustomed to its use.

The following medical lists show the medical supplies I took, mostly for use on the march to and from the mountain. As will be apparent, I was prepared for many eventualities, and a far smaller kit would have sufficed. Aspirin, adhesive, sterile compresses, and Band-aids were short, and probably always will be so long as the natives know they are available. A vermifuge was lacking, and I could have used a good deal on the natives suffering from intestinal worms.

MEDICAL LIST

Penicillin (crystalline)	200,000-unit vials	10
Procaine penicillin	3,000,000-unit vials	20
Bicillin	1,000,000-unit ampules	50
Streptomycin-penicillin	(ampules)	75
Aureomycin	250-milligram capsules	200
Terramycin	250-milligram capsules	200
Triple sulfa	5-grain tablets	200
Penicillin	200,000-unit tablets	200

Procaine penicillin	1,000,000-unit ampules	25
Aspirin	5-grain tablets	300
Phenobarbital	½-grain tablets	100
Nembutal	¾-grain capsules	200
Benadryl	25-milligram capsules	50
Pyribenzamine	50-milligram tablets	50
Aralen	2-grain tablets	50
Quinine	5-grain tablets	100
Carbarsone	0.25-gram tablets	100
Digitoxin	0.1-milligram	100
Quinidine	3-grain tablets	50
Pronestyl	250-milligram capsules	100
Pronestyl	10-cc vials	3
Salyrgan	1-cc ampules	10
Alophen	Tablets	50
Evacugen	Tablets	50
Bismuth subcarbonate	5-grain tablets	200
Gelusil	Tablets	100
Alka-Seltzer	Tablets	200
Roniacol	25-milligram tablets	200
Rubraferrate	Capsules	500
Theragran	Capsules	300
Dibenzyline	10-milligram capsules	100
Morphine sulfate	¼-grain tablets	40
Aspirin and codeine	½-grain capsules	50
Emagrin	5-grain tablets	100
Dexcdrine	5-milligram tablets	100
Cortisone	25-milligram tablets	60
ACTH gel	5-cc vials	2
Adrenaline	1-cc ampules	10
Coramine	2-cc ampules	10
ACE	10-cc vials	5
Plazmoid	500-cc bottle and dispenser	6
Baume Bengué	Tubes	6
Spectrocin ointment	Tubes	4
Obtundia cream	Tubes	4

Desenex ointment	Tubes	3
Butyn and metaphen ophthalmic ointment	Tubes	12
Neosone ophthalmic ointment	Tubes	12
Metaphen	4-ounce bottles	2
Vinethene	Vials	4
Procaine crystals	200-milligram vials	1
Novocaine solution	25-cc vials	1
Sterile water	40-cc vials	1
Zinc oxide	Tubes	12
Catgut and needles	Sterile ampules	6
Needle holder		1
Fine forceps		1
Rat's-tooth forceps		1
Scissors	Small	1 pair
Scissors	Large	1 pair
Hemostats		3
Scalpel and small blades		1
Scalpel and large blades		1
Sterile gauze pads		100
Bandage	2-inch and 1-inch	8 rolls
Ace bandage	2-inch and 4-inch	8 rolls
Band-aids		200
Syringes and needles	10-cc	2
Syringes and needles	5-cc	2
Thermometer		2
Stethoscope		1
Blood-pressure machine		1
Catheter		1
Dental forceps		1
Eye spud		1
Adhesive tape	2-inch	3
DDT bomb		1
Phenyl cellusolve	Bottles	2

CHARLES S. HOUSTON

5. Finances

The 1953 K2 expedition left New York on May 25 with the pious hope of operating well within its budget of $25,350 to cover all expenses from New York to New York. Our final expenditures, from inception of the expedition to return on September 5, 1953, were $30,958.32—an excess of approximately 20 per cent. A detailed breakdown of costs is not particularly helpful, but the following outline is presented here as an indication—for 1953 at least—of the cost of equipping eight men and sending them halfway around the world to attempt to climb a great mountain.

Unforeseen expenses included a porter cost closer to six times that in 1938 than to the threefold increase budgeted. Air travel from Karachi to Skardu was more expensive than anticipated, and return fares somewhat greater, since several men elected a different route. Thanks to the hospitality of the Ata-Ullah family, our living expenses in Rawalpindi were considerably less than planned, and in fact our entire stay in Pakistan was marked by the most gracious hospitality from all sides. Cost of porter food was less than we expected; the category "miscellaneous" was a smaller scrap basket than expected.

Raising funds for an expedition of even this modest size is a serious problem. Our money came primarily from members of the party and friends of the American Alpine Club. Both the National Broadcasting Company and *The Saturday Evening Post* gave substantial advances, and their payment for film and first magazine rights respectively was most helpful. We received little in the way of free food and merchandise, but what was received was most appreciated. We operated on a slender shoestring, so slender that upon our return to Skardu we were forced to borrow money from the subtreasury there. It is one of the fondest memories of the trip that the Political Agent, Skardu, should have been willing to loan the expedition nearly $3,000 on a note of hand signed by me, without security, asking only for repayment "as soon as convenient."

The financial affairs of such an expedition are complicated and must be carefully handled by one individual. We owe a great debt to Bill House, who took over our finances after Dick Burdsall's tragic death. He has handled them in an exemplary fashion ever since. He has been patient with the weird jugglings indulged in by some of us, has loaned us personal funds in time of greatest need, and generally has given the type of support which cannot be described in words.

Item Expense	Budget (February, 1953)	Actual 1953 Expedition	1938 Expedition
Equipment	$2,750.00	$4,273.66	$2,620.73
Food (climbers)	1,500.00	1,205.81	364.24
Photographic supplies	500.00	482.16	430.63
Tel., tel., postage, etc.	500.00	427.49	58.28
Travel– in U.S.A.	500.00	341.29	— —
Travel—N.Y. to Skardu and back	11,200.00	14,182.01	3,803.80
Freight—U.S.A. to Skardu and back	900.00	2,542.60	387.07
Porters	2,000.00	6,195.45	1,441.33
Porter food	500.00	769.15	80.44
Expedition Letter	— —	139.93	— —
Miscellaneous	5,000.00	398.77	247.51
Total	$25,350.00	$30,958.32	$9,434.03

6. Transport

There has not been the same amount of travel in the Karakoram as there has in the southern Himalaya, so there is no established system for arranging transport to that region. There are no Himalayan club representatives who can be asked to enroll porters. There are no fixed rates of pay. Nor is it possible to fall back on the many travel agents in Srinagar. Access from there to the Karakoram is no longer possible, for this would mean crossing the "cease-fire" line from Indian-held Kashmir into Pakistan.

When asked to act as transport officer to the Third American Karakoram Expedition, I was faced with three problems:

(1) How to get the expedition from the plains of Pakistan

into the foothills of the Karakoram. This would be about a two-week journey on foot

(2) How to get to Base Camp and what coolies to employ for this journey

(3) Whom to employ as porters to work on the mountain

The first problem was easily settled, for since the partition of the subcontinent in 1947, two airfields have been constructed in the area: one in Gilgit and one in Skardu. Regular flights are made to both these places and these airports have become the main means of supply to this remote region. We were able to arrange, through the Ministry of Kashmir Affairs, for Orient Airlines to fly the entire party, with all our baggage, from Rawalpindi to Skardu. This saved a great deal of time and, although the cost was considerable, it was undoubtedly less costly than to make the long journey on foot.

From Skardu, for the approach march to Base Camp, the local Balti coolies were enlisted from Skardu and the villages round about, and others were collected from the villages as we went along. For the mountain porters we eventually decided to employ men from the small state of Hunza, north of Gilgit. The people of Hunza are well known for their good health and hardihood and, living as they do in a high and mountainous valley, it was hoped that they would prove as useful as porters as the world-famous Sherpas. They had had little opportunity until now of proving their worth as mountain porters, but they had been spoken of highly by previous

315

travelers in the Karakoram. Two of them climbed high on Tirich Mir with me in 1950, when I was with the Norwegian expedition, and these came again to work with us on K2. This would be the first time that Hunzawals had been entirely relied upon as mountain porters on a major expedition. They were to prove themselves more than worthy of our confidence.

After landing in Skardu after a flight there from Rawalpindi, we spent a few days repacking our gear into the 60-pound loads which each coolie would carry, and in enlisting the coolies, who would be working for us on the approach route to Base Camp. Many of these came from the village of Satpura, a few miles from Skardu, and this party, under their village headman, proved to be the most reliable and faithful of all the coolies who worked with us. Because of their reliability, we arranged for them to come up from Satpura and carry out the remainder of our stores on the return journey.

In Skardu the rates which we would pay were settled in consultation with the Political Agent. They would be as follows:

Rs 3/– per day Skardu–Koshumal—2 stages
Rs 4/– per day Koshumal–Askole—4 stages
Rs 4/– per day (plus rations) Askole–Base Camp—8 stages

This was many times more than previous expeditions had paid, but no expeditions had been to the Karakoram since 1939, and since then there had been many changes in condi-

316

tions of employment. The coolies would not work for less, for there was plenty of other work available: for instance, carrying stores to the troops in their positions on the cease-fire line or working on the new roads which were being constructed.

At Skardu I arranged for a contractor to be responsible for enlisting and paying the coolies. This turned out to be a grave error, for little of the money reached the pockets of the coolies. There was serious unrest and it seemed that we should not be able to keep to our planned program. After the first few stages we sacked the contractor, and from then on all went well. The coolies were happy to receive their pay from me, but they were not prepared to work for us as long as a contractor had his cut of their earnings. Never again will I attempt to employ coolies through a contractor, although the lack of one makes more work for the transport officer.

After the first three stages, the coolies were not prepared to follow the south bank of the Braldu River to Askole, for they said that the path was too dangerous for them to traverse with heavy loads. This meant our having to cross to the north bank a little above Bahar. The only way of doing this is by using locally constructed goatskin rafts or zahks. If we had known that this crossing would be necessary, we could have sent one man ahead to arrange for a zahk to be prepared and ready at the planned place of crossing. We should have saved time if more than one zahk could have been available, but this would have meant having rafts sent up from lower down the Shigar Valley. As it was, ferrying our loads across

317

to the north bank took two days. On the return journey we were able to float down from just below Bahar to Skardu on a zahk in one long day.

Before reaching Askole, we had to cross two rope bridges. It would have been well worthwhile sending a man ahead to warn the villagers to put these in good repair, ready for the large number of laden coolies who would be crossing them. We were able to have such repairs made before our return journey.

As far as Askole, the coolies were responsible for obtaining and purchasing their own rations from the villages through which we passed. There are no villages above Askole, and the expedition had agreed to be responsible for their porter rations for the eight stages from there to Base Camp and for their return to Askole. This meant enlisting fifty additional coolies from Askole to carry rations for the original party. Since about four coolie loads of rations were consumed each day, this number of coolies were paid off and sent back. To avoid increasing the size of our transport column too considerably and for the more speedy return of the unladen coolies, sufficient rations were taken only for the actual number of stages to Base. It was therefore essential that we should move strictly according to our program once we had left Askole. A day's delay would mean that our transport column would run short of rations and that the coolies would need to be paid off and sent back before we reached the planned site of our Base Camp.

The going, once we climbed up over the crest of the Baltoro Glacier on the fourth day above Askole, was very hard for the heavily laden coolies, particularly as they use only a very primitive type of footwear. But primitive though these people are, they seem to have learned the modern technique of striking, and this they did on two occasions between Askole and Base Camp. The cry was for shorter stages, and on one occasion they set down their loads long before noon and reckoned that they had already done a full day's work, although we could hardly have covered 2 miles. Only with the help of our hard core of men from Satpura were we able to persuade them to move on to our planned campsite. We could not afford to miss a stage because of the limited amount of rations, which I have already mentioned.

Some of the rations had been carried from Skardu, such as tea, sugar, and rice, but the main bulk, in the form of "atta," locally ground flour, had been purchased in Askole. There it is readily obtainable at Rs 12/– per maund (80 pounds), and when made into chuppatis forms the staple diet of the local coolies. In addition to this food, we had taken some spare blankets and sufficient dark goggles for all of the coolies we expected to employ, but no other equipment was issued to them below Base Camp. The goggles were necessary only during the last two stages, when the boulder-strewn surface gave way to ice and snow.

The hardihood of these Balti coolies is unbelievable. At night they are quite contented to huddle together in groups

319

of ten or twelve, and squat in the small enclosures which they construct with rocks, each man throwing a single blanket, which he always carries, over his shoulders. With such limited protection for the porters, our last stage to Base Camp was a critical one, for the weather was uncertain. We reached there too late to send the coolies back the same evening, as we had planned, and so they had to spend the night on the glacier. There they consumed the small reserve of atta which we had with us.

For the last three stages to Base Camp, the coolies who became spare as their loads were consumed were used to carry firewood, collected from the last meadow at Urdukas, to enable them to cook their chuppatis. On reaching Base Camp, we paid off the coolies, and the men from Satpura, who had worked with us all the way from Skardu and had proved most reliable, were told to come back and collect us on the tenth of August. We had reached Base Camp on the nineteenth of June.

During the course of our approach march we had selected the six most enthusiastic and fittest of the party of Hunzawals. These six remained with us and later did excellent work carrying to the lower camps. The remainder were sent back. Our six quickly picked up the basic essentials of mountain craft and before long they were making good use of the rope and their ice axes. Their rates of pay had been settled with the Political Agent at Gilgit, who had kindly arranged with the Mir of Hunza to send these men to Skardu to join us. We

320

provided food, climbing clothes and equipment, and paid at the following rates:

> Rs 4/– per day to Base Camp
> Rs 5/– per day above Base Camp
> Rs 6/– per day high camps
> Rs 7/– per day maximum

We became very much attached to these Hunza porters during the weeks we were working together on the mountain. Their continued help and particularly their loyal support when the emergency arose showed the essential spirit of the expedition. Without them and without the services of the many Baltis who carried us to Base Camp, we could have done little.

7. Acknowledgments

Many individuals and many groups helped to make this expedition possible; some with funds, some with equipment, and others with encouragement—which was often the most needed. To those members of the American Alpine Club who gave the expedition approximately $8,000, we owe our greatest thanks.

By his continued interest, constant encouragement, and tireless help on innumerable occasions, Henry S. Hall, Jr., has been throughout the godfather of the expedition. Our debt to Bill House, our companion in 1938, who seemed to be with us all the time, and who has counseled and aided us in innumerable ways, has already been mentioned. William H. White of Time-Life, Inc., provided a wealth of advice in

322

material things; he accompanied us to Pakistan and we parted regretfully soon after leaving Skardu. He has continued to be of great help in many ways, and I consider him a member of the party. Bradley Gilman, president of the American Alpine Club, also lent valuable help and advice at crucial times. Of the U. S. Diplomatic Service, the Honorable Avra Warren, then Ambassador to Pakistan, obtained for us permission in the first place and helped us through many political tangles. We shall never forget the hospitality and help of Ambassador Horace Hildreth, his assistant William Crockett, and members of his staff, who endured much from us. Bob Dodson designed and produced the aluminum boxes kindly given us by the Aluminum Company of India. Mr. Curran, of S. S. Pierce Co., was indefatigable in supplying food lists, boxes, short items and, as he has to so many mountain expeditions in the past, gave us his invaluable support.

To Bob Graff, Herbert Swope, and Dave Taylor of the National Broadcasting Company we owe particular thanks for their interest and sympathetic handling of our moving pictures, as well as for use of the title "K 2—The Savage Mountain." Our gratitude also to *The Saturday Evening Post* for permission to reprint the color photographs used in this volume.

Most of our food and equipment was purchased from many companies around the world. The following firms generously donated supplies and we wish to thank them here:

Abbott Laboratories

Asfar and Co. Ltd.

Eddie Bauer, Outfitters

Becton-Dickinson & Co.

The Borden Co.

Chunky Chocolate Co.

Commercial Solvents Corporation

Empress Manufacturing Co. Ltd.

R. T. French Co.

General Foods, Inc.

Junket Brand Foods

Lederle Laboratories

Megowen Educator Food Co.

Paillard Products Inc.

Jean Protiaux Co.

Raytheon Mfg. Co.

The Saturday Evening Post

E. R. Squibb & Sons

The Upjohn Co.

Wyeth Inc.

Zenith Radio Corporation

Index

325

Gloves, 282
Gilman, Bradley, 324
Godwin-Austen, H. H., 33, 34
Godwin-Austen, K2 designated
    as, 33
Godwin-Austen Glacier, 87, 250,
    251
Goggles, 284

Hall, Henry S., Jr., 323
Health (*see* Medical problems)
Hidden Peak, 38–39
Hildreth, Horace, 324
House, William P., member of
    First American Expedi-
    tion, 39, 40
refusal to participate in
    Third American Expedi-
    tion, 48
management of financial af-
    fairs, 52, 312–313
House's Chimney, first ascent
    by House, 41
description and climb of,
    121–122
moving loads up through,
    129, 133
descent, 231–232
Houston, Charles S., leader of
    First American Expedi-
    tion, 39
permission obtained by, to
    lead Third American
    Expedition, 48
selection of medical supplies,
    58

extraction of Bates's tooth,
    124–125
in accident, 194, 198–199,
    203–204
injuries and gradual recov-
    ery, 198–199, 212, 219,
    226, 228, 229
return to Base Camp, 253
daily sick call, 264–265
chronology, 277–279
Houston, Mrs., 54–56
Hunza porters, employment and
    arrival of, 50, 78
at Base Camp, 93
use of, as mountain porters
    beyond Base Camp, 97,
    288–289, 315–316, 320
training and brilliant per-
    formance of, 101, 110,
    114, 127–128
welcome to party descending
    to Camp II, 236–237
rates for, 321

Indus River, crossing of, 78–79
Italian expeditions, 36–38

K2, naming of, 32–33
controversy on height of, 33–
    34
description of, 95–96, 112
Karakoram Range, geographi-
    cal description of, 31–32
Kitchen equipment, 287–288
Korean boots, 283

329

Dr. Charles S. Houston has long been known as one of America's foremost mountain climbers. Born in New York City in 1913, he was graduated from Harvard with an A.B. degree in 1935 and from the College of Physicians and Surgeons of Columbia University, where he received his M.D. degree in 1939. He interned in medicine at the Presbyterian Hospital in New York from 1939 to 1941. Entering the Navy as a lieutenant, junior grade, in the fall of 1941, he obtained his flight surgeon's wings just prior to Pearl Harbor.

In February of 1942 he opened an altitude training unit at the Naval Air Station in Jacksonville, Florida, and later in that year opened a similar unit at the Naval Air Station in Miami. From 1942 until 1946 he was engaged in training flying personnel in the effects of high altitude, and during that period somewhere between 35,000 and 45,000 pilots passed through his units. During the last year of his naval service he was transferred to Pensacola, where he undertook a long-range study of the effects of acclimatization to high altitude, which was called "Operation Everest." The account of this study was published in booklet form by the Navy.

After leaving the Navy in 1946, he spent a brief period at the Bellevue Hospital in New York and came to Exeter, where he and others opened the Exeter Clinic in April, 1947. He obtained his specialty boards in internal medicine in 1948.

Dr. Houston was introduced to mountain climbing in the Alps by his father at the age of eleven. Since that time, he has been twice to Alaska, the first time to climb Mount Crillon with Bradford Washburn in 1933, and the second to make the first ascent of Mount Foraker in 1934. He has been three times to the Alps and climbed a number of the more difficult Alpine peaks. He went to India in 1936 and was part organizer of the successful Anglo-American expedition which climbed Nanda Devi, a 25,660-foot peak and the highest summit then climbed. In 1938 he led the first American Expedition to K2, and in 1950 he went with his father on his expedition to the south side of Everest, an area they were the first Europeans to visit. Although the expedition was extremely brief, they obtained many photographs and may in a sense be said to have pointed the way for the successful climb in 1953.

333

K 2—THE SAVAGE MOUNTAIN

Dr. Houston has a wife, Dorcas, and three children: Penny, aged 9, Robin, aged 6, and David, aged 2.

Dr. Houston was the leader of the Third American Karakoram Expedition in 1953.

Robert H. Bates was born in Philadelphia in 1911. He, too, developed an early interest in mountain climbing. His family spent their summers in New Hampshire, and by the time he was eight he had climbed all the major peaks of the White Mountains. During his freshman year in Harvard in 1929, he began to climb seriously with Bradford Washburn and other classmates. He joined Washburn on expeditions to the Fairweather Range in Alaska in 1932 and 1933. In 1935 he spent the winter with Washburn on a National Geographic Society expedition mapping 10,000 square miles in the southeast corner of the Yukon. In 1937 he and Washburn climbed what had been the highest unclimbed mountain in North America, Mount Lucania (17,150 feet). With Charles S. Houston he planned the first American expedition to K2 in 1938. The party reached 26,000 feet, an American altitude record. Out of this expedition came the book *Five Miles High*, which was edited by Mr. Bates.

In October, 1941, Mr. Bates became a consultant at the War Department and was commissioned shortly after the outbreak of World War II. He had charge of developing Arctic equipment in the Quartermaster General's Office. In 1942 he was executive officer for the Alaska Test Expedition, which climbed Mount McKinley (20,300 feet) and helped develop many lightweight items used by all troops. He went to Italy as special observer for the Quartermaster General. He served at Anzio with the Third Division and ended the war a lieutenant colonel in Italy, where he received the Legion of Merit. In 1951 he was a member of the Arctic Institute of North America party that made the first ascents of two big border peaks in the Yukon (Hubbard and Alverstone). In 1953 he was a member of the Third American Karakoram Expedition to K2.

Mr. Bates has taught English at the University of Pennsylvania (1935–1939) and at Phillips Exeter Academy (from 1939 to the present). In 1947 he received his Ph.D. degree from the University of Pennsylvania.

334

Brotherhood! No word said can make you brothers!
Brotherhood only the brave earn and by danger or
Harm or by bearing hurt and by no other.

Archibald MacLeish
From "Speech to Those Who Say Comrade"

The Tapes

DEE MOLENAAR thoughtfully brought along to our reunion in the Wind Rivers the tape recordings we had made at Base Camp on August 16, the night we were all down safely off the mountain — all except Art Gilkey, that is. One evening around the campfire we played the tapes on Dee's portable recorder and talked about them, first hesitantly, and then with a rush. Though we each had a copy and had probably listened to them now and then, this was the first time we had listened together and had a chance to compare notes and clear up hazy memories. Although the emotion in our weary voices against a background of gusting winds and buzzing Coleman lantern is missing from the written word, the words are also powerful. Reproduced here, unedited save for a rare grammatical correction, is the tape we made that night, way back in 1953.

HOUSTON: It's August sixteenth, and our badly battered expedition is down here again, and we're going to talk over the events of the last three weeks, which have consisted almost entirely of storm. We left Camp III after a two-day storm, optimistically, and worked our way up to Camp IV, which we established. We climbed the famous House's Chimney and established Camp V, where we were again battered by another two-day storm. From then on, life seems to have been a continual series of winds, storms, snows, and other disasters. Bob Bates, you and Pete reconnoitered from Camp V to VI. What did you think about that route and the weather? And what do you think about the circumstances that accompanied us from then on?

BATES: Well, from V to VI we noticed that it was snowing, snowing lightly, and it took us quite a little while to find a good route. As a matter of fact, we would try first one side of the ridge and then another in an attempt to find something easy we could pack over. It was not a terribly long route, but it was one that caused us considerable anxiety because of the snow on the rocks. But we finally saw two tent poles sticking out against a black rock buttress above us. We were very pleased, we thought we'd be there in a few minutes, but it took us quite a while to huff up to it, and there we found something I will never forget. We found the remains of two camps with three sleeping bags and a primus stove, three packs all made up, all ready to go. These were the packs that the Sherpas had used 15 years ago when they had attempted to bring Dudley Wolfe down from the Camp VII of the Wiessner Expedition. The three men went up, attempting to bring him down, and never returned. What happened to them, we don't know. There was evidence that they were all set to return, and that they had expected to be gone not very long. Pete, was there anything else on the reconnaissance that you remember?

SCHOENING: No.

BATES: Nothing special. Well, from then on the plan was to pack up from Camp V to Camp VI, and that was done in fairly bad weather. Camp VI was established, and from Camp VI on the reconnaissance was made by Charlie, Bob Craig, and George. George, you remember that reconnaissance?

BELL: I remember it. We went up to Camp VI in the morning and got tents set up. That was a noteworthy afternoon; there was no wind; it was warm. The route-finding was a little tricky and we were certainly grateful for the good weather conditions. And if I recall, that was about the best afternoon for the next three weeks, or something like that. We really couldn't call it very good, because it was overcast and there was no blue sky.

337

HOUSTON: What day was that?

BELL: Beats me.

HOUSTON: Anybody remember the day? Twenty-sixth? Twenty-seventh? Or twenty-eighth of July. That could be said to be our last good weather, right?

BELL: It was just one afternoon. After some storms, and high winds, and so forth, and before more. I guess, Charlie, you remember the next day rather vividly.

HOUSTON: We came back about six that afternoon, fairly bushed, and the next day we made a full-scale reconnaissance up to what we were going to call Camp VII. Do you remember how you hated that gully from VI to VII? Well, it certainly was as bad as anything you remember. Slabby, very steep, lots of ice and snow. The weather was bad; it got windy, cold, snowy, and that was the day that I came to grief and got thoroughly chilled, frosted my feet quite badly, but not too badly, and came back to camp to find the entire party assembled at Camp VI. That, I think, could be said to be the beginning of the bad weather that we had. July twenty-seventh. What do you think about the reconnaissance, Bob?

CRAIG: Well, I was struck by the difficulty of carrying loads up over the terrain. I think even in good weather it would be the sort

338

of terrain that would require good porters, not average porters or persons who had little experience. It requires a lot of judgment, and unfortunately we didn't have as much fixed rope as we probably needed. But I think the biggest thrill of the reconnaissance team for George and me came when we went up and saw the ice slope that we had seen in pictures before and heard so much about, and we were very much impressed. It's a very smooth, hard stretch of ice and it's quite a formidable obstacle. But I think above all we were terribly worried about Charlie's frostbiting his feet that day; that's the thing that stands out in my mind. It was a cold, biting day when we went all the way up to Camp VII.

HOUSTON: Now, the next day was the twenty-eighth of July. What happened then?

MOLENAAR: Well, I have it in my journal that the next day Craig started to pack to Camp VII, and we only got as far as what we called the cache, the lower cache. It was a very cold day, and the wind was blowing quite hard, and a lot of us were fearful of frostbite, and I think two or three did get pretty badly chilled, and by the time they got back to Camp IV, they were very cold. Do you remember that day, remember when we were trying to get up that little section of fixed rope, and it was ice over rock?

CRAIG: I remember it was very, very cold there, and windy, and there was danger of rockfall, especially with eight men on one steep pitch of cliff with loose rock. It's very difficult to keep the top man from kicking off rocks that would hit the bottom man. As I recall, Tony was hit on the head that particular day.

STREATHER: Yes, I got hit quite hard on the head once.

CRAIG: It was snowing hard, wasn't it. Yes, as I recall, a very mean day.

HOUSTON: As I recall a big rock came off and very nearly missed four or five of you. Just went right between you.

STREATHER: It exploded up between us, it hit hard, between Bob Bates and me, and went off with a hell of a bang.

HOUSTON: Well, anyway, we dumped our loads at the camp that day, and came back to VI, a little discouraged because we hadn't found a place for VII, right? The next day we took a party up determined to establish Camp VII, right? Pete and I, correct? Pete, do you remember that day?

SCHOENING: Yes, I think the idea was that Art and I were going to pack very light, just taking our personal gear — pack light, go fast, establish Camp VII, and then the remainder of the party would come up later in the day and back us up and help us to establish a very solid Camp VII. We got up to the ice slope in something like three or four hours, which is quite fast. From the ice slope, the old Camp VII from the previous attempt on the mountain, there was a traverse of the ice slope. We hoped to establish Camp VII over to a serac field where we'd get protection from avalanches and so forth. From information we got from Bob Craig, we decided it might be better to go up the ice slope and then over to the seracs. We did work up this ice slope, probably about 200 or 300 feet high, cutting steps and using ice pitons. Above the top of the ice slope we ran into a snowfield. We placed a piton anchor at the top of the ice slope and then continued on up to about 150 feet or 200 feet higher. The weather was cloudy, or semi-cloudy, and so we couldn't see too much, but we did see the remainder of the party coming from below, so we decided to descend and get together with the rest of the party and see what would be the best thing to do. Up to this time, we had not been able to find the site of the old Camp VII, which was among the seracs. Charlie, you can tell what happened after we came back down and met the rest of the party. I remember this day was also very cold, very windy; there might have been some snow falling, I'm not too sure about that.

HOUSTON: I'll never forget that day. We got up there through driving clouds. I think it was snowing lightly, it was very cold and very windy. We saw you coming down what looked like a vertical cliff, and we saw no place for Camp VII at all. I remember feeling, personally, extremely desperate about what we were going to do. We had you-all pretty well committed to stay there. We didn't want to go back to VI, and I remember searching desperately for any place that was flat enough to put a tent, and when I say flat enough to put a tent I mean anything that might be three feet wide and six feet long. We were just about to give up, as I remember — isn't that correct? — and go back to the cache, when Bob Craig dug his axe into the snow in one particular place and found what amounted to a cave, and we were able to dig a shelf there, which was just about three feet wide and six feet long, where we pitched your tent. And I remember leaving you with a sinking heart because it was so bloody up there; cold, snowy, your tent platform negligible. The slope fell away very steeply below you, and we all knew that above you was a very steep slope such that if new snow fell it would be an avalanche slope, and might very well overcome you. Anyway, we went back to VI that night, and the next day planned to come back and rescue you, or at least to move up to help you. And the next day, as I remember, it was very stormy at Camp VI. Fortunately, we had radio contact with you and found that it wasn't quite as bad up where you were as it was at Camp VI. At VI we spent a quiet day in the tents. The wind was terrific. Six of us got into one tent, talking off and on, and while we were sitting in the tent together, Pete, you and Art were really doing Trojan work, and I'm particularly interested in what you found when you crossed the famous ice traverse of 1938 and looked for Camp VII on the other side.

SCHOENING: Well, a little while ago, Charlie, you mentioned that the storm wasn't raging up where we were, which might be called our Camp VII. It was blowing pretty hard, but we were in a position where if it did start to snow we were in a potentially bad avalanche spot, so we had to move. I remember that morning it

341

was quite windy in camp, but the tent was protected by a slight ridge. Our plan now was to find a safer Camp VII, and consequently we decided to make the traverse and find the old Camp VII of the 1938-1939 expedition. By going about 100 feet or 200 feet from where our tent was pitched, we went around more or less to the east, and very luckily got away from the wind. We sort of got behind this little ridge or around a buttress, and consequently in making the traverse we were in no wind, although it was quite cold. I remember the climbing was not too tough. We could kick steps in some of the places, had to chop them in others. At any rate, the belays were quite lengthy; I remember one belay I sat for about an hour, which if you're in very much of a wind can chill down the body regardless of how much clothing you have on. Incidentally, we had on every bit of clothing we had up there at the camp at the time. We did make this traverse and got over to what looked like some seracs. However, it was more or less of an ice wall. Beyond and below the ice wall was nothing but a snow slope. It looked or seemed almost like a wind slab slope. It was quite steep, I suppose maybe about 35 degrees, which isn't really steep as far as snow slopes go, but too steep to pitch a tent on, and it was also an avalanche slope. This day was sort of spottedly cloudy; we could see maybe 100 yards and then the clouds would blow away. We saw nothing that would resemble a campsite. We concluded from this that there'd been quite a change from 1938 and 1939, and that the previous campsite had been obliterated by either a large avalanche or just a slow change in snow conditions in that area.

During this time we had radio contact with Colonel Ata-Ullah down in Base Camp, but not with you at Camp VI because your radio was not transmitting, although it was receiving. After finding this development we returned to our precariously pitched little tent and decided that we'd better follow the steps we'd made the day before and go up the ice slope and see what we could find up on top. We thought maybe we'd be able to dig into a ridge someplace. A ridge would be safe from avalanches anyway. We did work up the ice slope, using the anchor we'd made the day before, for two rope lengths and continued on up this snow slope, which again we analyzed as an avalanche slope. It was ankle- to knee-deep snow. After running out two rope lengths we continued on, leaving our piton anchor, of course, and worked on up the slope for possibly seven or eight rope lengths. In elevation it'd be about 400 feet, I suppose. All this time we couldn't see much of the mountain; the clouds were quite thick, except when wind blowing by would just give us enough leeway to keep on going and know that we weren't getting ourselves in a very precarious position. After a while, we did reach the top of what you might call a ridge — it would actually be the shoulder of K2 — and found a very good campsite protected from avalanches, and a nice level spot, plenty of room for tents. This was definitely right on the shoulder. We dumped our loads, light loads, probably about 20 pounds, and returned to our previous Camp VII, the one that's sort of pitched on a little ledge chopped in the snow right at the edge of the rocks, and reported our findings to you on the radio with the idea that on the following day we would continue up and establish this higher camp, which was eventually called Camp VIII. You want to add anything to that, Charlie?

HOUSTON: I've got nothing to say, except that it was a wonderful job you did that day. We were all filled with admiration for you, because the weather was such that we didn't want to go out of Camp VI. Now, the next day the weather was just about as bad, blowing, snowing, correct? Everybody remember that? We decided that we would try to go up anyway, because we felt we had to help Pete and Art move camp in order to get them established, and we wanted to get on up the mountain ourselves. By this time, as I remember, we were beginning to feel that if you didn't move in bad weather on this mountain, or at least in dubious weather, you wouldn't move at all. So, we went on up, reaching Camp VII — that miserable ledge camp — as I remember it, about noon, after a rather unpleasant trip, and we found Pete and Art just about ready to move up to Camp VIII. So we all packed up loads and in about three hours we arrived at Camp VIII. I for one was pretty bushed. There was very little wind, as I remember it, but big clouds and snow. We pitched the tents and climbed in about four o'clock in the afternoon of July thirty-first, or August first?

CRAIG: August first.

HOUSTON: We considered ourselves pretty happy and successful

343

at getting to Camp VIII, which we reckoned as being between 25,500 and 25,300. The wind blew all that night.

CRAIG: Early in the evening it looked very nice, and then it started blowing.

HOUSTON: Then it started to blow, and it blew hard. The next day we had a beautiful sunrise, crystal-clear, warm, sunny. We thought, oh boy, this is the beginning of the good weather. We had good radio contact with Camp VI, with Bob and you, Tony, and the arrangement was that you were going to come up and meet us at Camp VII, or at the cache, provided the weather continued good. Tell us about your trip up.

STREATHER: Well, that morning, Charlie, was one of the best we'd had for quite a few days. The sun dawned quite bright and Bob and I were full of cheer. We'd stayed down, you remember, the day before, and we were still in Camp VI, and we'd decided that we would come on up and join you that day. We arranged to meet you at the cache and then all join there and go on up to Camp VIII together. We got up early and soon after we started the weather started to go back to its normal miserable self, it started clouding over. However, we were quite determined then that we would come up, we'd already gotten ourselves ready. I think we both realized that if we didn't come up then, we'd probably never get any higher. We eventually left camp at about eight o'clock. The weather continued to deteriorate, and we very soon found that we were in for quite a difficult time, under pretty bad conditions. We continued to climb the rest of the morning and at about twelve o'clock, it must have been, we heard you up at the cache at VII and you were shouting something at us. It was very windy.

HOUSTON: We heard you shouting first.

STREATHER: You heard us shouting, did you? Well, we thought we heard you say that you were going back, going back to Camp VIII. But it might well have been, as it turned out later, that you were telling us to go back, because you thought the climb would be too long. But having gone all that distance, particularly having climbed over the difficult slabs, the steep slab rock between VI and the so-called VII, we thought that it would be easier to go on than it would to go back over these difficult slabs.

HOUSTON: The only reason we shouted was that the storm was

Route up Abruzzi Ridge

so bad that we were afraid you'd get up above the cache and find no place to camp, and be unable to get on to VIII, so I thought it was safer for you to go back, so that's why we were so insistent on you going home, going down to VI.

CRAIG: I might say one thing: that is the coldest day that I remember working on the mountain outside of the tenth of August when we had our retreat from the mountain. It was a terribly cold day, and I know that Dee and I got back into Camp VIII with very, very cold feet and hands and I think a nip of frostbite.

STREATHER: Well, anyhow, I think once we got going we were determined to get up to Camp VIII. I remember we stopped and ate a little lunch and we both climbed into my bivouac sack to keep the wind off us and rested; that helped us quite a bit. We climbed and got to the cache campsite, so-called Camp VII, and we squatted there for a bit to put on our crampons, and then we set about following the route up the last part of the snow slope.

345

HOUSTON: I think that was the part that scared me, I didn't think you'd be able to find your way up that ice slope. Terribly steep slope, deep snow at the top, we knew it would be blowing, and I was afraid that, number one, if we waited for you, we'd get frosted, and number two, if we didn't wait for you that day you'd never find your way to Camp VIII in spite of those willow wands that we put into the snow.

STREATHER: Well, the first steep part of the ice slope, we were able to see the route; you put in the willow wands and the fixed ropes. Art and Pete did a wonderful job on the fixed ropes and the step cutting, and we just followed up there. Then once we got above the fixed rope, you'd been very thoughtful in putting willow wands and we could just see from one to the other, and as we went slowly forward up the snow slope we could see one willow wand and then the next. Bob was leading and he did a really wonderful job. We went very, very slowly but eventually Bob turned around to me and said, "We're there," and in a few more steps we were up over the shoulder and into the camp in front of us. It had been a pretty hard day, and as far as I can remember we'd been climbing for nearly 10 hours in a fairly consistent storm.

BATES: The first part of the route up from Camp VI was so covered with snow that it took us about three times as long as it normally would, and after two hours of climbing we'd been over slopes that we just didn't want to go back over, and we were just determined that if we possibly could we were going to make it up to VIII. I can't add anything else except that the wind never stopped all day and that the snow storming in one's face made it difficult to keep one's sense of direction, and use the holds that one should. We were very glad to be there at Camp VIII.

HOUSTON: Boy, were we glad to see you. I think we were all pretty surprised. Well, we were surprised in a way, but I had a feeling all afternoon that you were going to turn up. I was frankly a little upset that you had done it. Now this was on the second of August.

CRAIG: Surprised or not, we were all tremendously delighted to see you. All of us at 25,500 feet and in good condition, ready for the top.

BATES: And less than 3,000 feet to get to the summit.

346

HOUSTON: Well then, going to the next day — all of us were there. It blew like hell that night; it was furious. We were glad to be together, but we needed a break. The next morning was about as stormy as any day we'd had, I think. Nothing happened that day, except we lay in bed . . . [The tape is unintelligible here.]

HOUSTON: And you lie there in your sleeping bag, warm, with snow blowing in on you, the tent buffeting over your head, unable to cook, can't light the stove, can't melt snow for water, can't cook. It seems impossible to endure it, and it goes on and on and on and on. Now I'd say that one of the really bright spots of that week of storm was the fact that we communicated with you, Ata, over and over again morning and night, and could talk to you and get cheer from Base Camp. It just seemed as though we couldn't stand it otherwise. The only other thing I want to say about the storm is that George and I were in this impervious tent which isn't too bad, but during the night of August third the fabric of the tent split. It didn't actually tear, but the split grew wider and wider and we could see the light through the crack and finally about seven o'clock that morning the tent gave. We had a feeling all that night that should the tent go down we wouldn't stand a chance of surviving. We made up our minds to stay in the tent, even though it blew down, right? We couldn't get out. Because we decided if we did go out and put our boots and gloves on and go the ten feet to the other tent — six feet I guess it was — we thought we'd freeze to death before we got there. Well, it was a pretty bad night as I recall it, and in the morning when the tent finally gave, we had stayed in it for long enough to get our things on in the daylight and then we went over each to another tent. I went in with you and Bob Bates, Tony. And George went in with Art and Pete. Three men in those little tents in a storm is no fun. Now what do you remember about the next day, Tony?

STREATHER: Well, Charlie, before you came into our tent, Bob and I had had on the first day of the storm quite a job trying to keep the thing down and from dragging away with both of us in it. When the storm was really at its strongest, the first day, we both huddled in one end with our shoulders against the end of the tent, so it would neither float a bit or fly away with both of us in it. We eventually had a chance to get out in a slight lull to make the tent a little more secure with the ice axes we could find, and then on the day that your tent went, you came on in with us. Well, we were in the Swiss tent that had a liner, and the first night was terrible with three of us in the minute space under the silk liner. We very soon realized that the only good thing we could say about it was that it was dry, so the next day we took the liner off and just had the outer part of the tent, which made it much larger, but not as dry, and certainly not as warm. Well, the days just went on. Each evening we'd say, "Well, perhaps tomorrow will be better, and we'll get a break," but we never did. The wind just kept on and on and on and on blowing. The tent sides flapping against our heads and shoulders driving us crazy. But what was probably most important of all, the tent flapped so much that we couldn't cook because we couldn't keep a stove lighted. We could eat dried food, but we didn't have anything to drink, and at that altitude drink is absolutely essential to not becoming rapidly dehydrated. I think as a doctor you'll tell us that our blood gets thicker and we feel the cold more.

HOUSTON: Now wait a minute, there's something very important that we forgot. About that day, somewhere near the day that George and I came in to you, we decided to select the summit team. Our hopes were really getting pretty high then. We thought, "Since we've had five days of storm we can't possibly have any more storm." So, we did something which I think is unique to this expedition, something which I think we ought to be very proud of: we balloted for the summit team and we selected a first team and a second team. By choice of the entire expedition of those who were fittest and most likely to get to the top, we selected two teams. The first team was George and Pete. No, the first team was George and Bob Craig. The second team was Pete and Art. We had our plans made to move up to Camp IX. All of us would carry up to Camp IX. The first two would move up to Camp IX first, and then the next day the next team would do the same thing. I think for a Himalayan expedition that's an unusual way to choose a summit party — to have eight men at 25,000 feet in such good condition that we could — that we were not forced to, but found it desirable to — ballot to see who could go to the summit. I think that was very exciting. I remember Art Gilkey particularly was determined that all eight of us would get to the top if we had good weather. The rest of us were not quite so optimistic. Well, anyway, every night we went to bed thinking tomorrow's going to be the day, tomorrow we'll send the first team up, and tomorrow maybe they'll make a bid for the summit. And we were in a position to do that. And then all of a sudden the real blow came. What day was it that Art first complained about his leg? Do you remember, Bob? The seventh? The first day that Art complained about his leg was a real blow. The first indication that anything was wrong.

MOLENAAR: I think that Bob Craig and I were going up with Art to Camp VIII. Art was at the bottom end of the rope and he wanted to untie the rope because he couldn't keep up with us even at the slow pace we were going through the deep snow. That was probably the first indication that he had something wrong with his leg.

CRAIG: But we first knew about it really on the seventh when Art got up and he was walking over from the tent to Tony, and walking over in the snow there he had a fainting spell and fell in the snow momentarily, and Charlie went over and examined him. Isn't that the case, Charlie?

HOUSTON: It was a fairly warm morning. I wouldn't say it was a nice morning; it was cloudy and it was snowing, but it wasn't blowing. He fainted, and when he came to he said that he had a charley horse in his leg, and I examined him and found that he had blood clots in his left leg — thrombophlebitis — without any question at all. And I put him back into bed with a bandage on it, and then I came and told you-all that he was probably going to be unable to walk for some time. That was the first thing that showed us that we were coming close to disaster.

STREATHER: That was on the seventh wasn't it, Charlie?

HOUSTON: The seventh. Now my memory gets a little hazy after that, but it seems to me that we had no choice, because the weather deteriorated again, and we had so much storm that we couldn't do much.

CRAIG: Didn't we make an attempt to haul him down by the main way? We tried to haul him down that day, but ran into extremely dangerous avalanche conditions.

HOUSTON: That was the first day without real storm and we

tried to haul him down. We broke camp fairly completely, packed him up in a sleeping bag and tent, started down the slope, and got about 300 feet, or 200 feet, snow sometimes hip deep, sometimes knee deep, and very obviously it was an avalanche slope, and decided that we had to go back. So we brought him back — taking about an hour and a half to cover 200 feet. I know it was one of the most frightful skirmishes that we had. He tried hopping on one leg, then we'd jerk him up. He'd hop, and we'd jerk. And then the only thing bright about that day was when Bob Craig and Pete decided to go down another route to see whether there was a way around this avalanche slope. Pete, tell us about that trip down, because that was really the thing that saved our lives. If you hadn't done that I don't think we'd be here.

SCHOENING: On the way up we'd come up the ice slope, and then up this potential avalanche slope. Our new route, which Art and I had noticed on a reconnoiter trip, was along the ridge. There was a rocky ridge that extended down and eventually ran into Camp VII. Bob and I followed this ridge down approximately 300 feet, whereupon it went off sort of an abrupt cliff, but at this cliff point it was possible for climbing members — or members that could climb — to climb down the rock, more or less down the cliff. It would be possible to evacuate a person by sliding him down the col, or snow groove, between the rocks and the snow slope, which was off to our left as we faced down. At the base of this cliff was an ice traverse of possibly 100 feet or 200 feet that ended up on the rock near where Camp VII was situated. Bob and I were just able to look over this route through the clouds which whisked by, and see that it was feasible, and then return back to Camp VIII. The fact that we did have a route that would get us down to Camp VII was quite a relief in our minds, and to that extent it was quite valuable.

HOUSTON: It was life-saving. It was the only thing that gave us an out. If we hadn't had that route that you and Bob found, we would have been absolutely licked there. We couldn't have come down that avalanche slope safely. That's an understatement, Pete. Then we took Art back and settled down in the tent — that would be the seventh still. On the eighth and the ninth we just sat there.

More storm. Terrific storm. I don't think any of us have ever experienced a storm like that.

CRAIG: On the eighth it did calm down enough so that in the afternoon you sent two of us to go up, to see how far we could go up and look around and see where we were on the plateau. We did go up three or four hundred feet above Camp VIII, but we were in fog. We couldn't see more than a rope length ahead, climbing up the side of a broken-up part of the glacier — this plateau glacier, more or less an ice fall — climbing on the right side of it, and I suppose we got to 26,000 feet, 25,800 feet, somewhere in there. Well, we couldn't see a thing, and we waited for 20 minutes in the fog. We were very apprehensive about Art by this time; we talked about the need for getting down, the fear of being stuck up there, the fact that people were getting tired, deteriorating, and then we came back to camp. We talked to Charlie and everyone seemed to have crystallized this feeling in his own mind at the same time.

HOUSTON: As you said, we decided that [inaudible] ... and let him get well, and then all of a sudden, bang, the other leg became involved, and his lungs were involved. At that point it became obvious that if we were going to get him down alive, he had to go then. We were getting to the point then, ourselves, of being so weak, so dehydrated, and so undernourished, that if we didn't go down, we might not survive. Beginning about the seventh of August I felt that we were fighting for our own lives, as well as Art's, and that if we didn't start down pretty soon, none of us would survive. What did you think about that, Bob?

BATES: Well, for several days I'd been very concerned about the

351

condition we were in, the amount of food, the fact that we were having so much difficulty cooking, that we couldn't get enough water, that we were all having cold feet, mainly because of dehydration, the fact that it took practically all night to warm up one's feet in a sleeping bag even though we were inside a tent. I was tremendously relieved when you announced that the best thing was to have two people stay up and wait until Art improved enough so that he could walk down. I was very concerned about the idea of trying to lower him down, we had such great difficulty on the seventh when we first tried it. The only thing that worried me was — if you and someone else stayed there — whether a support party would be able to come back with enough food and gas so that you would be absolutely safe. When you made the decision that we ought to take Art down, again I was worried because of the weather. It was a helluva day. It was blowing and storming. And yet when you told us that there was one chance of saving his life, there was absolutely no question but that it was the thing to do. What did you think yourself about that trip down on that day?

HOUSTON: Well, I'm no rescue expert. The rescue experts told me that we could get him down. As far as I was concerned it seemed to me about as desperate a thing to do as we could try. Pete, you were pretty optimistic about getting him down. How come?

SCHOENING: I'm optimistic about getting a person off a mountain, even a mountain with the terrain that we had to go over. I think Tony and Bob will back me up about the morning we had to leave — the tenth. The weather was frightful and making an evacuation in bad weather is really something terrific, and I expressed to both of them that I was really worried about that day because of the bad weather. Bob, you've done a little rescue work; what did you think of the situation that morning?

CRAIG: I shared your optimism when I started, except for the weather, and another thing that I don't think you or I realized, though it was in the back of Charlie and Bob's minds because they had been here before: that's a terrible thing called altitude and wind. I know, having reached you after bringing Art down through this snow and ice gully, myself being belayed by the others above, that I was finished, at least for an hour. I could hardly lift my arms

352

I was so tired, so completely worn out, and so completely cold. I think that's where the danger to the men in the party lay. Seven men's lives were in the balance, along with the one life they were trying to save.

HOUSTON: Art was wrapped up in a sleeping bag and a tent, with gloves, socks, boots, and a little pillow under his head. I think he was fairly warm, he seemed comfortable, with a rope around his waist and under his arms, a double rope as I remember. We let him down that gully and held him there for a long time, and that's when the avalanche went over Bob Craig.

STREATHER: I remember that bit quite well, Charlie. You and Bates belayed very strongly on a rope, and Bob Craig went down with Art and I remember I was a little way down so I could shout to you and shout to them, because the wind was so strong that they couldn't hear, even though they were only a rope's length away. I remember the rope suddenly cut through the snow and started off quite a large avalanche. I shouted down to Bob Craig, but he didn't hear. Fortunately, he hung on tight just below us, and I remember very clearly seeing the two of them just disappear as the snow went down through this very narrow gully, over their heads. As the snow cleared I was very relieved and a little surprised to see them both still there. From then on Bob Craig was pretty well waxed; that was about the last thing which really sapped the strength out of him. I remember shouting up from the bottom, "Hold him! He's on the edge of a cliff."

HOUSTON: Oh my God, I'll never forget that: "Hold him! He's on the edge of a cliff."

STREATHER: You were just holding on, freezing up at the top there. Pete and Dee had gone on ahead, and then I think I saw Pete come up to Bob and secure him — no, I think it was Dee — to eventually pull him across the ice slope.

CRAIG: One thing I think we shouldn't forget here is that — at least while I was going down with Art — George Bell, who had frostbitten feet to begin with, was in a belay position up above all the time and gave one of the soundest belays that you could possibly want to both Art and me, and I think that George jeopardized his feet a tremendous amount, both in this particular operation and later on.

353

HOUSTON: Well, from there on my memory is gone.

BATES: Well, after that you and I both climbed down, and George — down the rocky cliff — and Tony — I guess the four of us — and reached Pete, who was belaying Art, who was just below a short but very steep cliff. Tony at that point climbed down to Art to see if he could help him, and anchor him, and see if he could help work him across to Camp VII.

STREATHER: Yes, as far as I can remember after we got down through that narrow gully, Pete and you and Charlie belayed Art down a very steep cliff, and George Bell belayed me and I went down with Art. I remember it was so steep that the ropes which were around him kept catching on little bits of rock. I remember once he got completely caught, and I shouted up to you to try to pull him up a bit. I kicked off the ropes and eventually he slipped down. You lowered him down the cliff, and George lowered me down, and we got just onto the ice slope below the cliff. Well, that was the last ice slope and it leads across to Camp VII. As we looked down we were on the right of it, and we had to pull Art and get ourselves across about 150 feet to the left to where the ledge from Camp VII would be. Well, it was just about here that the accident really happened. I remember there was a double white rope to Art, and having gone down with him, I made sure this was secure, had a last word with him, and then got across the ice slope to where you and Charlie had come down. We then had a double white rope to pull Art across the ice slope, and Pete was belaying him still from the original rope above the cliff. George, at that stage, was still up top; he stopped belaying me and started to climb over to join us. Well, George had been having a very bad time; he'd already been frozen fairly badly, and the extra time waiting at the top there seemed to have frozen him even more, and I remember looking up and seeing him climb across, but his hands seemed more like clubs; they didn't seem to be very effective. I remember seeing him appear to take a handhold and then begin to slip; I can't remember who it was that shouted, but suddenly he was sliding and going very fast down this very steep ice slope. I could see that he was trying very hard to arrest himself, but his hands didn't seem to be effective, and he just didn't stop himself. He was still tied to me, and we weren't tied to anyone else. George

354

went past me going fast and I tried hard to get my belay firmer, but we were on a pretty steep slope and all we had was an ice axe driven partly into the ice, and our crampons. Well, as soon as the rope tightened I was whipped off the slope like a fly. I remember quite clearly everything that happened from then on. I went off and I fell quite a ways trying to arrest myself, but it seemed to have no effect at all. After a few seconds of falling there was a very sudden jerk and I stopped just momentarily, and that must have been when George's and my rope crossed the double white rope from Art. And you, Bob Bates, and Charlie were both onto that, and so was Dee. I can't remember how everyone was tied. That second jerk meant the rest of you three were falling. I fell again, possibly another 50 feet, quite helpless, there was nothing I could do about it. Suddenly there was another jerk and I stopped. There seemed to have been three successive tugs around my stomach and miraculously we had all stopped. I think what happened is that George's rope and my rope must have crossed the rope to which Art was anchored: that stopped George and me. At the same time I crossed your ropes and pulled the three of you off at the same time. When I finally finished falling there were about a hundred ropes around my stomach, and yours had somehow caught around me, and somehow miraculously we all held; we were all held by Pete, who had a very, very good belay on Art, who was way, way above us by then, about 200 feet above us. I think it was really remarkable that Pete was able to hold all five of us. I think we ought to mention that if Pete hadn't done that remarkable job he would have been pulled off himself, and Art would have gone, and we would have all gone, except for Bob Craig, who was unroped. I remember then trying to look around, and I saw George just appearing out of a little gully. He slowly started to climb again after the fall. I didn't see you other three. You'd all disappeared over a rocky cliff, and I didn't know who was there. I remember standing to my feet and moving slightly forward, and then eventually after the chaos, Charlie, you and Bob and Dee climbed up from the rocky ice cliff down behind me on the right, and George started climbing up from the very bottom. He must have fallen 250, 300 feet, a full rope length above and a full length below me. I think

25,200

24,500 VII

23,300 VI

22,000 V

21,500 IV

20,700 III

19,300 II

17,700

Abruzzi Ridge profile

Bob Bates was then probably in a better position to see what went on after that.

BATES: I saw Tony swept off the slope as if by a giant hand, and Charlie a fraction of a second later, and the next thing I knew I was flipped over backwards, and went bump, bump over rock ledges, sure that this was the end, there wasn't a chance that anything could hold us, and by a miracle, just when I thought the next big bump was going to be 150 feet or more, it stopped. I stopped with my hand tied up in the rope, head-first, backward, down the slope, apparently right on the edge of something, and just by a

356

miracle I heard a voice above me, and somebody said, "Who's there?" and I said, "It's Bob," and it was Dee, and he released me. When I started to my feet I saw George coming up from below — George, who had been 100 feet above us before, was now 75 feet below me, with his hands white, saying, "My hands are freezing." Down below me was a figure which I figured out was Charlie, unconscious. Dee was beside me, and above me I could see Tony struggling to his feet and moving around. As soon as George got a little closer, I went down and gave him a spare pair of Indian mittens which I happened to have in my pocket, and then unroped and went down to Charlie Houston, who was unconscious. I shook him; he came to, but he didn't know where he was. He kept asking what had happened, and where he was, and what he was doing there, and I got him to climb up a very steep 15 feet or more to Dee, who was belaying him. I climbed up after him and went over to the tiny tent platform of Camp VII, to see if we could get some kind of shelter from the raging blizzard where Bob Craig had been working. Bob took Charlie over to the tent platform, and the couple worked on the tent there and finally got it up. George came over, and pretty soon the whole group of us was there, either working on the tent, or working on another platform for a bivouac tent which would be able to shelter the whole party from the elements. We were all terribly weak, and almost everyone had some trouble. Dee had a cracked rib, Charlie had a concussion and a bad rib. Bob had been pretty well exhausted from the previous effort, and Pete had trouble with his chest; also for a while he had terribly cold hands. By the time we had the two tents up, we'd probably been away from Art for 45 minutes, or possibly an hour. Before Craig had come down to help us, we had gone over and anchored Art very securely; Tony had also put a belay on Art, so that there were two very strong ice axe belays on him. Bob had also told Art a little of what had happened, and he had told Art that he would come back as soon as the injured from the fall had been taken care of. About an hour elapsed between the time that Bob had told him this and the time when three of us went back to see if we could move him. When we came back to the slope, which is only about 200 feet from where we were working — about 150 feet — to our amazement, the slope was bare! We don't know what happened, but probably an avalanche had come down and swept Art and the ice axes and everything off the slope. We never heard it, we never saw it, but when we came back, 150 feet from where we were working, the slope was bare and Art was gone. It was just as if the hand of God had swept him away.

HOUSTON: Didn't Tony see something there?

STREATHER: Well, we went back to do something with Art. What we had in mind was making a little ledge in the slope and resting him there for the night, covering him up and resting him. We realized that the three of us, all very weak, would be unable to drag him over to VII, and the rest of the party at that time were in even worse state than ourselves. We got to the slope, and Bob said, "There." Now most of the day we'd been working without goggles because the goggles just fogged up. And I know that I and Bob Bates were both going a little blind. Bob I remember went first and said, "Art's gone," and I went right on past Bob, he gave me a belay, and I went right out onto the slope where Art had been. The whole thing to me looked different. My eyes were hazy, but I'm sure that through the haze I saw a peculiar groove right down the middle of the slope and somehow the rest of the snow looked different. It was a different texture. I remember seeing a rock at the top of the groove, and the first thought that went through my head is that there'd been an avalanche and Art had been swept clean with the slope. That was the impression I got through a very hazy, exhausted look at the slope. We came back to Camp VII, where we bivouacked for the night.

BATES: When we got back there, four of us got into a very, very small tent which we'd had on the main slope, and three of us got into the bivouac tent, on the other little ledge. There was just room to sit shoulder-to-shoulder and try not to let our feet go over the side. The tent billowed dangerously because the ledge was so narrow that the tent overhung the ledge, and we couldn't nail the tent onto the slope very well because of the nature of the ice. There was a great danger all night long that if we leaned a little bit forward the whole tent with everybody in it would go down. It was a long, very, very tedious night. Charlie was out of his head and kept wanting oxygen and to cut a hole in the top of the tent. The three in the bivouac tent were miraculously able to get a stove going and cook some tea and hand out cups to the other tent. All seven managed to get through the night. Thank God it was a windless night, the first windless night we'd had in weeks, and the first break that the weather had given us in a long, long time. Next morning we got up and were able to eat a little food and get started down to Camp VI. We knew we had to get down, we had very little gas and food and we had to get down to a real camp. Bob, would you like to talk a bit about that trip down? It was a helluva morning as I remember it.

CRAIG: Charlie was beginning to come around again, so Charlie, Pete, and myself climbed on one rope, and I remember Bob Bates, Tony, George, and Dee climbed on the other rope. I must say that Charlie, having had a very severe concussion and a very painful injury to his chest, climbed down very nicely and gave really strong belays, although most of our climbing didn't depend so much on belays as on just staying on our feet, and not falling. It was icy, snowy, and very, very bitterly cold climbing down. When we finally arrived down at VI in mid-afternoon and started digging out the tents there which had been collapsed after this continuous snowfall of the last four weeks of storm and wind, some of the guy ropes were down. We got things ready and the second rope finally came in. When they got in, everyone was bitterly cold, chilled right through to the bone, and we had quite a problem warming up. Then began, I think, one of the most desperate parts of the trip. We were by no means out of danger. The trip from VII to VI was a most important one, but from VI on down we began quite a fight. I think George Bell is one of the most important people in that fight because he showed remarkable courage in coming down with frostbitten feet, badly frostbitten, climbing beautifully down over ice-covered rock all the way. The mountain fought us all the way down to Camp II, where we finally began to feel that we were safe. George, what do you think about the trip below?

BELL: Well, it was a pretty hideous descent. The weather never let up and the route was entirely different from the first ascent, but we knew we had to get down because there were no great reserves of food or fuel above, and we were getting weaker by the day. So it was just a job that had to be done, and was done.

HOUSTON: The thing I remember best about the descent — the

thing I remember *worst* about the descent — is that we just never had any surcease from the wind and the snow, we never had enough strength, we never had anything to drink. Remember mixing up that jam with snow? You lived in a tent with a hole in it, you were covered with snow, you were all cold, our sleeping bags were wet, we had insufficient everything, two sleeping bags had been lost, we'd lost our cooking pots, we'd lost one radio, we'd lost our stove, and we had to get down because, first of all, we were short on fuel and food, and secondly because of the condition of George's feet, and the fact that the rest of our feet were getting pretty bad. The one thing I remember bright at Camp VIII was the contact that we had had with Ata at Base Camp. It was cheery for us at night and in the morning, and it was enough to give us a lot of courage — then 36 hours without radio contact with us, at which he was as desperate for news of us as we were for getting down to Base Camp. That was after the radio had been lost, and before we got down to Camp VI. I don't know how we got from VI to V. That was really in some way the worst day of all, but we did get there. And when we did get to V somehow we managed to get down House's Chimney, the last part of it in the dark. Then we got down to IV, and through IV. The next day we went down to III, and the weather was very much the same. The route from IV to III, I remember as being particularly unpleasant. When we got down to III we tried to decide whether to go down to II that afternoon, for we'd been climbing about six hours already. We had to decide whether to go down in our weakened condition or make a bivouac there. I think we decided correctly in going down. And then came one of the great experiences of the whole trip. Remember when we got close down to Camp II — we heard the Hunzas shouting and we shouted to them. We arrived at Camp II just at dark — we must have been climbing about ten hours — close to exhaustion. And we were greeted by our Hunzas, who came rushing up, tied together with little quarter-inch ropes, and threw their arms around us, burst into tears. They had prayers, sobbing, shouting. Go on from there, Bob.

CRAIG: Well, I can't describe it except to say that it's the deepest experience I've ever had with a human being. The Hunzas came up to meet us in groups as we came in by ropes. The first rope included Charlie, who did this marvelous job of leading us down from Camp III through very difficult ice-covered rock. They took our packs off our backs on traverses that were slopes of 40 degrees, in the one case. Just took our packs off our backs, and embraced us and cried on us, and then when we got into camp we were so overcome by this display of emotion and feeling and warmth that we just didn't know what to say or what to do, we were all in. They brought us hot rice and milk and tea and hot parattas, the national biscuit of Pakistan, and they completely surrounded us, rubbing our legs and giving us the most thoughtful care, taking care of every possible need. That night it was just something. They gathered together, we told them about Art, Tony explained to them in Urdu what had happened above, how we just barely got down, and then a very spontaneous and I think a very touching prayer was led by Kairal Hidayat. It was the first time we really had a chance to express our feelings all together. Then to bed; we were completely exhausted. The next morning we were waked up finally and had breakfast, more feelings were expressed, and then on down to Base Camp we started. By this time George's feet were very bad, pretty severe frostbite, so carefully roped we started down.

[Here the 1953 tape ends.]

361

Here the tape ran out and our thoughts turned to those no longer with us. Art Gilkey, our friend whose death we had tried so hard to prevent but in vain. Ata-Ullah, who had strengthened us in so many ways during times of desperation. We talked about them almost as if they had been with us, and we talked too about Bill House, who had been such a strong member of the 1938 party and had patiently served as our treasurer in 1953, but was unable to share the reunion with us. We talked about many adventures in many places, but we came back again and again to the days of trial at Camp VIII and during the nightmare descent, trying to fill in gaps in our sometimes varying memories. So much of the expedition was as fresh as yesterday, and so much was clouded by the pain and sorrow that climaxed all.

HOUSTON: Listening to our voices on those tapes makes me realize how close to complete exhaustion we were when we got down. The nightmare at Camp VIII was still blurred, at least for me. For example, I've thought for years that Art's phlebitis began about the third rather than the seventh of August, and that we had many days of worry and uncertainty. I remember talking with Ata many, many times — not that he could do much except send us courage. I knew, but could not tell the rest of you, that Art's chances of survival were almost zero under those rugged conditions. We had very few options: we could all stay at VIII until Art got better, or died, or until we all died. Or we could leave Art and save ourselves while we still had strength, but no one even considered this. Or one or two people could stay with him while the others went down, recovered, and came back for us. Obviously, as the doctor in the party, I would stay with him, and all the others offered to stay with me, but should anyone else? Or we could try to haul and carry him down that rocky, almost unknown ridge that ended in the cliff above Camp VII — difficult enough in good weather, but I thought impossible in storm. None of these choices was very appetizing. Ever since then it has seemed to me that we agonized for many, many days, not just for three. I can't listen to that recording without great feeling — there's so much in it and so much we didn't say. Meeting Ata-Ullah on the glacier, the loving welcome at Camp II and again at Base where there was space to move about, and water — all the water we could drink. Unforgettable memories. I was still very shaky at Base and had trouble moving my head. I couldn't read the service for Art, near that splendid cairn the porters built a day or two later. Do you remember that, Bob?

BATES: I certainly do. We were still so tired that climbing the short slope to the cairn was a major effort. Our battered group

363

stood there with bowed heads, perhaps each of us thinking, "Why Art and not me?" It was a moving though simple service.

HOUSTON: Our Hunza porters were very moved. The whole little party had grown very close. Then the Balti porters came in, on schedule, on August sixteenth and we packed up and left next day, carrying George on an improvised stretcher. How much of that do you remember, George?

BELL: Riding on the stretcher wasn't very memorable, especially since the weather continued foul and there weren't even any good views. But I will never forget being carried on the back of Mohammed Hussein and the other Satpura porters for all the toughest miles. I particularly remember peering over Mohammed Hussein's shoulders and watching his great bare feet carrying both of us from one sharp boulder to the next, with no hesitation and perfect balance. Also, the first fruit and fresh vegetables in Askole and beyond seemed the best in the world.

HOUSTON: And finally, on the twenty-sixth, we reached Skardu and two days later flew to Rawalpindi. There we were taken into the home of friends, and gradually the immensity of our experience made itself felt. Dorky had come out to Pakistan to meet us and we stayed with Tahirah and Shahid Hamid and I'll never, never forget their kindness. Others stayed with Ata's family, and arrangements were quickly made for George to fly directly home for further hospital care. George, your toes had really done remarkably well, thanks to antibiotics and being dressed as gently and carefully as I could twice each day. Of course, your guts made a huge difference, but you certainly had some awful hours being carried over the rough paths.

BATES: Listening to the tapes with all of us together has made me think of things that were never entirely clear: For instance, what do you remember of the day of the accident, George?

BELL: First of all, I remember sitting up on the ridge in the wind for an eternity, belaying somebody (must have been Craig since Charlie and Bates were belaying Art), getting colder with every gust. Also, I could never get my windproof parka on over the down jacket since the arms had been cut too slim. This didn't help. Eventually Craig must have reached the end of the rope and untied for I recall then going up to Charlie and Bates to see how they were doing.

Just before the accident I had belayed Tony across the ice slope and Pete was preparing to lower Art, with the rest of you to pull. I thought the rope between Tony and me was fouled on Art or on the ropes across the slope to him, and that I had better hurry down the gully so as not to delay the lowering operation, or I might get pulled off. At the bottom of the gully it was necessary to start traversing the ice slope, and it appeared to me that a long step would take me to the first of some steps which Pete and Dee had cut across the slope. So I took the long step, the crampons didn't hold, and I was off.

I don't recall making any effort at all to stop; it seemed hopeless. I also felt I was falling many hundreds or thousands of feet. When I finally came to a stop I was hanging more or less freely in space and I assumed that the rope between Tony and me had snagged on a pinnacle and that perhaps we were not far from Camp VI. I am also pretty sure that I still had on my pack, mittens, and my glasses, but I couldn't see because they were packed with snow. Not wanting to spend the rest of my life — which seemed likely to be a very short time indeed — dangling at the end of the rope, the first priority was to try to get my weight off the rope by climbing the cliff. To that end I threw off my pack, thus losing glasses and mittens, which probably fell most of the way down the mountain — except for the small bag containing toilet kit, spare glasses, and expedition financial records, which lodged near Camp VI. Anyhow, I could then climb the cliff, which ended not far above me, and you know the rest.

CRAIG: If it hadn't been for the avalanche earlier, I would have been on the slope with you and been pulled down the mountain with you. About halfway down that wretched ice gully I had unroped so my rope could be used to lower Art down a bit further, and I was holding onto the rope which led to Art, and without any belay, when the avalanche came down over us. I certainly hung on for dear life. Then Dee roped me up and belayed me partway across the steep slope toward where Camp VII had been. I went on alone, but I had to rest about 20 minutes before my strength came back and I could work on the tent platform. I was almost all in. During that time, you all fell.

MOLENAAR: I remember, Bob, that after you came out from under that little avalanche I gave you a belay toward the site of Camp VII. You were really all in. Your crampons were coming off and you were having a helluva time getting them back on because they never really fitted those huge Mickey Mouse boots. I knew the avalanche had been a near thing and that you were nearly exhausted. When you were safely over the slope I went back to rejoin the party then working Art along the ice slope to a better place. I remember wandering about with all kinds of pitons and stuff hanging off my belt, stuff that Pete and I had gathered when we cleared the slopes above. It seemed like many hours that some of you had been sitting in the bitter wind up on the ridge belaying Art down. Pete and I had come down earlier and didn't fully realize how much was involved. After you unroped from me, Bob, I went back to lend a hand and tied onto Art's rope to Pete. Art had just been lowered over a small steep bit and we were getting ready to pendulum him over toward where we put up Camp VII. Tony was next to me while I took in the slack around my axe, driven into the ice. About 10 to 15 feet above us Charlie and Bob Bates were doing the same thing. I was looking up the slope at the time and suddenly saw George going down the ice on his back, feet first. I remember yelling, "Goddamn, there goes George!" A couple of seconds later everything else happened. I was quickly jerked off and slid on my stomach, face downward, so the slope was coming up at me. My only sensation was exhilaration, and thinking that I would be knocked out when I reached the rocks. Then suddenly I was brought to a stop a little way below the top of the rock. Another person was on top of me. It was Bob Bates. Charlie was about 25 feet below, lying among the rocks; Bell was starting to climb out of the ice gully and trying to protect his hands, because he had lost his gloves. Tony was a short distance above, on the lower part of the ice slope. Bob Bates then climbed down to Charlie and tied him to the end of a rope so I could belay him. He talked to Charlie, urging him to climb up to me. After Bell came up, Bates gave him some extra gloves, and we all traversed over to where Bob Craig was scraping out the ledge at VII. I didn't lose any gear in the fall; my pack was at VII, where I had dumped it a short time before.

Northeast Ridge 1978

© 1978 DMOLENAAR

HOUSTON: I have only the dimmest fragmented memories of that day. Bob, you've often described what happened when you painfully made your way down to where I was lying. What did you actually say and do?

BATES: Just what it says in the book, Charlie. You didn't know where you were and were very confused. We couldn't carry you or pull you up the rocks to Camp VII. At that point only you could do it — and fortunately you did!

HOUSTON: Well, I don't remember any of that. The rest of you were almost exhausted, I guess, and desperately trying to get some kind of shelter ready for all of us. It's lucky we were so close to the narrow ledge where we had put Camp VII some 10 days earlier. Bob Craig was over there chopping out a platform, and I guess all of us tottered over to help put up tents, leaving Pete to anchor Art to the two ice axes. Does anyone have anything more to add to the taped description of that awful afternoon and night?

MOLENAAR: It certainly was a night to remember! You were in a nightmare of your own, Charlie. We worried about your being able to climb down, and also about George Bell. George had been frostbitten badly before, in South America, and besides he was a lot bigger than the rest of us; the blood had to travel a lot farther to reach his extremities and he was probably a lot more susceptible to frostbite. I remember that Craig and I had frostbitten heels and were hobbling on the balls of our feet. But George was in the worst shape and the condition of his feet was the main concern in our hurrying down to Base. I remember the trip from Camp VII back to Camp VI. I had a slightly cracked rib that made breathing a little difficult, and when I was in the tent at VII, I had to lie on my back to breathe comfortably, half in and half out of the tent. It wasn't too bad a night, not too cold, and I was getting fresh air outside the tent. Next morning, after we started down, my leg began giving the most trouble. I finally found I had a cut about half an inch deep, but it didn't bleed because of the cold or the thickness of my blood at the altitude.

BATES: That morning we had trouble getting Charlie's crampons on and we didn't know how he would climb, but instinctively he climbed beautifully.

HOUSTON: I don't remember anything about the start. But I re-

368

member one terrible thing very clearly, all too clearly. Very soon after leaving Camp VII — I was leading down — I saw splotches of color on the rocks. They looked yellowish and it took a little time for me to realize that these were bloodstains where Art had fallen. For what seemed an eternity we had to climb down alongside these bloodstains, and fragments of the tent and the sleeping bag he had been wrapped in. No one mentioned this, and I guess I assumed that I was hallucinating. Anyway, I don't think we have ever discussed this until now. It was a terrible time.

MOLENAAR: Yes, we found the remains of Art's litter — a tangle of ropes along the track where the avalanche had taken him. The evidence was that Art had died almost immediately after the fall started. As a matter of fact he was almost unconscious when we ourselves fell. When we got into VI, I recall getting into the ripped, snow-filled tents. For lack of anything to do, I got out my thread and needle and did a little sewing in the tent while the others were trying to get the snow out. That was a rough trip for Charlie.

BATES: As belay man coming down from Camp VII, I didn't want to be distracted by the stains. I focused my whole attention on belaying and watching where I put my feet. Nobody wanted to talk about what had happened. Charlie, do you remember that night at VI and how you kept waking up and putting your hands on cans of food and thinking you were in a warehouse? Next morning you seemed yourself and you did a great job of hacking away the ice so we could take the tent down. You were climbing well and seemed perfectly normal. George's feet were bad, though, and we were all worried about him.

BELL: I knew my feet were in bad shape, and we made no attempt to thaw them out since I still had a long way to walk to safety. Certainly no one in the party was strong enough to carry me! I had to get myself to Base. My hands were bad too, but after Bob Craig found the little bag with my glasses I was sure I could get down. Everybody was climbing safely, and the rope was a real spiritual bond between us.

BATES: Charlie, how much do you remember of the day we went from Camp VI to IV? You climbed well all day and you talked about George's feet, and frostbite that Bob and Dee seemed to

On Northeast Ridge
near Camp III

IV

V

Polish
1972

American
1978

VI

have, too. You seemed mentally and physically completely normal except that you were slow. Do you remember how we worked together with George to chop out the good tent at VI? We were the last to get to Camp V, and at the top of the Chimney we helped the others lower their loads and then we belayed them down. It was slow work and Pete kept calling to everybody to hurry. Your pack caught on a snag as we were lowering it, and when the others pulled from below and we pulled from above it slipped loose and clattered down off the mountain.

HOUSTON: I don't remember anything of the part from Camp VI to Camp V. But then my memory clears completely and I remember, just as vividly as if it were yesterday, standing at the top of House's Chimney. You know, we were always apprehensive, at least I was, about getting down in bad weather. It's not a terribly hard section but hard enough, and here we were, the weather not exactly good, all of us hurt and weak.

CRAIG: What I remember best about the trip from Camp VI to the Chimney is how well everyone was doing. We were climbing carefully, slowly, but not too slowly, each one looking after the others. It was a good demonstration of how experience and guts can help. We were climbing almost instinctively, and that's what got us down.

HOUSTON: I don't remember who went down the Chimney first. It doesn't matter, because each person went down so well. But I do recall being determined to go last. I was the leader; I was responsible. I didn't feel at all handicapped even though my left eye was partly blind and I couldn't move my head very well. I must have made quite a scene by insisting that I go last.

BATES: After your load was lost, there wasn't much daylight left. I could see that if we took the time to lower my load, it would be dark before we could get down. I wanted to belay you down but you wanted to be last. There was no time to argue. Then it came to me that if I roped down quickly—for I was moving faster than you—and *carried my pack,* that would give you a little extra time before it got too dark to see at all; there was a low ceiling of storm clouds and the light was fading very fast. I remembered too from our Alaska days together that your vision in bad light is better than mine. The sudden idea seemed brilliant at the time but it didn't turn out that way. It was a serious mistake.

After I started down, you threw me a rope and insisted on my tying on. Then you held the rope and said that you had been the first one up the Chimney and wanted to be the last one down. That was true but I was interested in speed, in our both getting down fast. When I got down the Chimney I could still see fairly well, so I unroped and walked over to camp, where Tony asked me to help him guy the second tent, which he had been digging out. It didn't occur to me that you would have trouble in the Chimney because you didn't have a pack and because Pete was holding a rope to you from below. It was only after Tony and I had been at the tent for 5 or 10 minutes and heard Pete shouting that we realized you hadn't even started down yet. Then we did worry, plenty! Finally you did start and managed to get down nicely. It wasn't until this reunion that I realized how badly disoriented you were at the top of the Chimney. Thank God you did all the right things.

SCHOENING: Well, I was off in the group to one side of the bottom of the Chimney and I remember shouting to you to get started. It was getting dark and visibility was pretty bad when you finally did start, but once you began you came steadily and quite fast.

HOUSTON: After Bob left I remember, ever so clearly, thinking I couldn't possibly do it. There were three ropes in the Chimney— one from 1938, one from 1939 (both hemp and too rotten to trust) and our good one. I couldn't tell them apart in the dark. I knew I couldn't use them but I would have to climb down, with Pete's rope from below keeping me from the big fall if I slipped. I thought, "I can't do it. I'll fall down on the others and knock them off. Better jump off to one side and get it over with." Well, it was a deeply emotional moment. I knelt in the snow and said the Lord's Prayer. Next thing I remember is being grasped by strong arms and helped into Camp IV.

BATES: You must have had a hideous time, a horrible experience, Charlie. It never occurred to me that you were mentally confused again, but I know nothing about head injuries and relapses. If you had done something crazy up there, I don't know how I could have stood it.

CRAIG: The rest of the descent was unremarkable, though I don't think anyone has commented on how we got down that overhanging tower just below Camp IV. That was always a tough one, but we made it, and down through the terribly deep soft snow to III, where we ate and rested for a long time before going on to II and our meeting with the porters.

STREATHER: As I have been listening to these tape and thinking about the climb, I realize again how remarkable this party was. None of us were what one might call expert, at least by today's standards, and I was the least experienced of any. We had been through quite a bad ordeal, and we held together through a grueling descent. Without the strong bonds between us I don't believe we could have done it. There is quite a contrast between this descent and one or two of the famous tragedies, for instance Nanga Parbat in 1934. I imagine that some of the K2 experience helped get me through the Haramosh accident several years later. But I would rather not talk about that now. In our crisis we were physically and emotionally together.

BATES: Well, that's the story, and what more is there to say? Perhaps that something from those storm-swept days has been fused into our bones and will never leave us. It has made a brotherhood, a special kind of friendship that is very rare and very precious.

Members of the Expedition

Colonel M. Ata-Ullah

[Written by his daughter]

When he was invited to join the American Expedition to K2 in 1953, Colonel Ata-Ullah was 50 years old. A few years earlier he had been forced to give up tennis because of arthritis in his knees, but he prepared vigorously for the expedition, going on a crash diet and exercising in the enthusiastic company of his children. As a result he did very well, climbing to Camp III and making several journeys throughout the region during the long wait at Base Camp. The following year he accompanied the Italian expedition, led by Ardito Desio, that was the first to climb the savage mountain, though not without loss. Ata-Ullah helped to bury Puchoz, who died of altitude illness, close to the monument raised for Art Gilkey's memory.

Both of these expeditions came when he was going through a career crisis. The Ayub government had cashiered him from the Army because of his religious beliefs and he was at loose ends, not wanting to start private practice (ophthalmology), for which he was so eminently qualified, because the notion of accepting money for what is a humane duty to the sick did not appeal to him. Premature retirement would mean too heavy a financial burden since all five children were still going to school. But let him speak for himself:

"Our future was indeed to be fuller than our past.... [It] would bring more leisure and from unexpected sources more money than we had ever wanted or hoped for. I would go on journeys to Europe and America, make new friends and meet old ones of whom we had many around the world, receive warm hospitality from complete strangers who recognized me [from] a film or book about the much publicized K2 expeditions, and climb in the Alps, Dolomites and elsewhere with famous mountaineers who behaved as if I were doing them a favor. I would stumble into a short and fascinating association with a Texas millionaire in an oil prospecting venture. There would be an unsought but exciting interlude with American movies as an actor in Lowell Thomas' Cinerama production *The Search for Paradise*. I would fulfill a childhood ambition—to learn to fly in spite of my defective eyesight, and discover a new dimension of physical thrills in fast aerobatics. I would write a book for a well-known publisher. There would be many other joys never dreamed of before.... I was at the threshold of a great new world, not at the untimely end of a cherished career."

Ata-Ullah's autobiography *Citizen of Two Worlds* was published by Harper in 1960 and subsequently translated into Urdu and reprinted in English in Pakistan. Then his wide-ranging intellectual interests led him to mathematics and engineering, subjects in which he saw great potential for Pakistan. He not only read engineering seriously but led two of his four sons to the subject. In 1961 a Yugoslav engineering firm working on a project in Pakistan invited him to join as a partner. Through the next decade he developed and expanded his own company, the Indus Valley Construction Company, and worked on some of his nation's largest projects.

All through this period he kept in touch with mountaineers and every summer went with his family to the Karakoram foothills. To the steadily increasing number of grandchildren who went along, camping at 14,000 feet was considered routine — though the knowledge that some of the equipment was "vintage K2" was always thrilling. Ata-Ullah became a permanent advisor to the Pakistan Alpine Club, playing host to numerous expeditions on their way to the Karakoram. He was actively engaged in Red Cross programs to improve hospitals and blood banks.

Like his love for mountains, Ata-Ullah's interest in the piano came late in life. When he was well over 60 he taught himself to play for two reasons: "Because it's there" and because he hoped it would help the arthritis developing in his fingers.

In 1969 Ata-Ullah was asked by Government to head a study group to plan reorganization of his nation's health services. The document that resulted, written by him, is still consulted, and in 1972 one of his proposals was accepted — establishment of an Armed Forces Medical College in Rawalpindi. He was decorated for his work.

At 70 he became restless. He was in excellent health and very active. His company had reached a size beyond which it could not grow without major changes, and he felt that Pakistan did not offer a large enough market for his efforts. Two of his sons joined the concern, thus giving Ata-Ullah time to travel; he spent all of 1974 visiting many places around the world and in 1975 set up operations in Nigeria. Work there was hampered by a variety of unforeseen events, chief of which was overthrow of the government.

In 1976 Ata-Ullah returned to Pakistan; the family enterprise was flourishing and he felt it was time to hand over to his sons. He wished to complete the book he had started while in Nigeria. If his first book was an account of his life's efforts, his second would present the wisdom he had extracted from this life. While he worked on this project, he maintained his passion for Bach. And every day he did a hundred push-ups! Unfortunately he could finish only the first draft of early chapters. In 1977 while visiting a friend in Peshawar, Ata-Ullah died in his sleep from carbon monoxide poisoning traced to a faulty heater in his room. He was in wonderful physical and mental health, one might say at his prime.

One of the mourners came from deep in the Karakoram ranges: Vilyati, leader of the 1953 high-altitude porters. He found Ata-Ullah's death unbelievable because a month before the man whom Lowell Thomas had called "Wise and witty citizen of two worlds" had, along with his wife Qamar and two grandchildren, spent an energetic three weeks in Vilyati's native village, tramping and climbing among the spectacular mountains he loved.

Robert H. Bates

The major change in the quarter century since K2—indeed, in my entire life—was my marriage in June 1954 to Gail Oberlin of Cleveland, Ohio. Our home is in Exeter, New Hampshire, where I taught for many years at the Phillips Exeter Academy before mandatory retirement at age 65. Gail loves mountains and the outdoors, and together we have traveled far.

Among our experiences is a visit to Nepal in 1954 and a leave of absence in 1962-63, when I directed the first Peace Corps program there. Looking out for volunteers in various villages was absorbing and delightful, for it required frequent treks through beautiful mountain terrain. We have continued our interest in Nepal and still have many friends there, including her able monarch.

Another outstanding memory is our visit to the huge, bone-dry Atacama Desert in Chile to determine whether the Ojos del Salado is the highest peak in the Western Hemisphere. At that time Chileans claimed it was and Argentines that it wasn't. Our small party was organized by Adams Carter, an old climbing friend, at the request of the American Geographical Society. Surveying showed the Ojos to be the second highest peak in the Americas, less than 100 feet lower than Aconcagua.

In 1966 I returned to Alaska with a small team, including Eric Shipton, whom I had met in Zermatt the preceding summer when we were guests at the 100th anniversary of Whymper's ascent of the Matterhorn. Shipton, one of the great expedition climbers and mountain travelers of our time, was a delightful companion there, and later—even after 12 stormy days together in a crowded two-man tent that constantly seemed about to be buried. Our climbing objective was a new route up Mt. Russell in the Alaska Range, but the storm was too much for us; it smashed one tent and forced a retreat to base camp, where everything except the top of an antenna was buried.

That was my last climbing expedition except for a brief visit to the Ruwenzori in Uganda, but in 1974 I was able to satisfy a yearning to return to K2—this time not to climb but to see it with Gail. We reciprocated for the Ojos del Salado experience by asking Ad and Ann Carter to join us. At Skardu, where there is now almost daily air service from Rawalpindi in good weather, we met our former porter Tashi, who greeted us warmly. He arranged for us to get seven porters from Satpura, with Mohammed Hussein, who had carried George Bell so many miles, as sirdar. Mohammed promptly christened us the Memsahib Expedition, and when Gail and Ann bravely crossed the swaying rope bridge over the Punmah River, the porters cheered.

The region had obviously changed since 1954. The bridge had recently been rebuilt for a Japanese expedition that was ahead of us, hoping to force a new route on Broad Peak. When I came over a rise on the Baltoro Glacier near Concordia I saw a red tent with a head protruding from it; and a Japanese voice asked in perfect English, "Will you have tea or coffee?" Not all changes were so pleasant, however, for we had already noticed litter along the way, and particularly that some expedition (German, I think) had chiseled the names of all its members in big letters on one of the prominent rocks overlooking beautiful Ur-dokas, the only pleasant stopping place along the Baltoro.

But K2 had not changed. It looked as high and imposing as ever, and clouds moved in as Carter and I pushed slowly up the Savoia Glacier to look at possible routes on the west side. As I stared up at the great ridges disappearing in the mist, I felt deep pleasure at seeing once more this magnificent monarch of the Karakoram. There was naturally a twinge of regret that our group had not been able to reach its summit, especially Charlie, who had done so much more than anyone else. But Italian climbers had a long claim too, and our route-finding had at least given us a share in their success. As I thought back over our past endeavors, what struck me most was my great good fortune in being able to twice challenge the great peak. What an adversary, and what grand companions!

George I. Bell

When I first arrived at Massachusetts General Hospital from K2 after all that time at altitude, my blood was so thick they used me as a blood donor. After several weeks in the hospital, I lost only one small toe and half of a big toe, thanks to the long wait-and-watch period that is so essential in allowing a clean demarcation to form between the dead and healthy tissues. "Freeze in January, amputate in July" is an old saying that in my case paid off.

In the summer of 1954 I undertook an expedition in the Cordillera Blanca of Peru, but my feet were still sensitive to cold and battery-heated socks were not helpful enough. Though I did make the summit of Chopicalqui (21,000 feet) I had to turn back from Huascaran and Huandoy because my feet were so cold.

The following year I was invited to join Norman Dhyrenfurth's international expedition to attempt a post-monsoon ascent of 27,800-foot Lhotse, Everest's southern neighbor. Lhotse is the fourth highest summit in the world and at that time the highest unclimbed, since Streather and others had just climbed Kangchenjunga.

There were many contrasts with our K2 expedition. For one thing, the approach march through the rice paddies and monsoon-soaked jungles was quite different from our march through the clear, arid Braldu Valley. For another, the technical difficulties of the route, which ran up via Everest's West Cwm, were minor compared to those we had faced on K2, and it was possible to get down in almost any weather without fear of falling off the mountain. On this trip my feet gave me no trouble whatever, thanks to the superb high-altitude boots. These were traditional Swiss-made Vibram-soled boots, but made of reindeer hide with the fur outside. Reindeer hairs in the soup are a minor vexation when the feet are warm!

But the most striking contrast with our 1953 K2 expedition

was that the several nationalities on Lhotse did not function as a team, united toward a single goal, but rather as a collection of individuals, each with his own goals, which while often similar, were sometimes in conflict. The problem was not simply a diversity of national backgrounds, but also that team members had been selected for their mountaineering talents without regard to compatibility and the good expedition philosophy that Charlie Houston had emphasized so strongly in choosing our K2 team. This experience convinced me of the overwhelming importance of these considerations for a difficult expedition. We were defeated on Lhotse by high winds that, above about 23,000 feet, were furious and relentless even by K2 standards.

In 1960 I joined Nick Clinch as climbing leader of his Pakistan-American expedition to Masherbrum. We flew to Skardu again but approached the mountain from the south — the side away from the Baltoro Glacier. We had a strong and compatible team and after the usual problems with bad weather, first Willi Unsoeld and I and then Nick Clinch and Jawad Akhtar reached the summit, from which we had a magnificent view of K2. One of the men who had carried me out from Base Camp in 1953 — Mohammed Hussein — was an effective high-altitude porter on this trip, and I was sorry not to be able to converse with him more effectively and to recall those closely shared days.

In addition to these expeditions I have, since K2, spent many happy days in the Andes, the Alps, the Canadian Rockies and Selkirks, and most of the ranges of the United States. Sadly, I have lost more friends to climbing accidents than I care to remember. But I suppose that even when we were young we knew that skill and prudence were not always enough and that a little luck or an immovable Pete Schoening at the end of the rope is sometimes required.

Professionally, I have spent most of my life at the Los Alamos Scientific Laboratory solving theoretical problems; this happens to be a fine place from which to climb, ski, hike, and run rivers. My main research interest is the application of mathematical methods to problems in biology and medicine, especially immunology, and I have a splendid group of colleagues. I also have administrative chores helping to run the Theoretical Division, an organization of some 150 scientists who are working on an enormous variety of challenging problems.

I was married in 1956 and now have two children in college. Our finest family project has been the construction of a log cabin, starting with the standing Douglas firs, on land near some great cliffs in northern New Mexico. It is especially pleasant to ski to in winter, when the snow is four feet deep and the nearest neighbor several miles away.

In looking back on it all, there have been many good times and fine adventures, but never another K2.

Robert W. Craig

I returned from the 1953 K2 expedition with feet that were frostbitten just enough to permit me to assume a slightly heroic stance, and within three months I wound up a brief career as civilian consultant to the Mountain and Cold Weather Command of the U.S. Army and began a speaking tour of the western states. With the help of electric socks I was able to teach skiing within the year as my frostbite recovered.

Early in 1954 Walter Paepcke, the Chicago businessman whose vision and energy was responsible for the Aspen Idea, invited me to work as his assistant in the newly founded Aspen Institute of Humanistic Studies. For the next 11 years I worked in the Aspen Institute, first as assistant to the president, then as executive director. I worked for almost seven of those years under the inspired leadership of Paepcke, until his untimely death. Working with him was a rare privilege: he was generous, unfailingly creative, a hard and demanding leader; but he cared about civilization more than most men do. His rather awesome presence only poorly concealed a whimsical spirit and great kindness.

The basic dream with which Walter started the Institute was to bring leaders from business, government, labor, science, and academe to share in trying to understand fundamental problems of contemporary society. It was a grand vision, perhaps 10 years ahead of its time, and it grew slowly into today's Institute.

Then in 1965, after seaching for a ranch throughout the north-

381

ern Rocky Mountain region, my wife and I bought a ranch on Woody Creek and began running cattle in a beautiful area only 10 miles from Aspen. At the same time I became partner with a group of old friends in a large design firm, with which I worked for the next 10 years, based in Aspen but traveling a great deal.

After years of abstinence, I returned to serious climbing around 1970 and rejoined old friends in many happy ventures in the West and Canada. I was elected a director of the American Alpine Club, and later vice president, an activity that proved in some ways more strenuous (and certainly more frustrating) than mountaineering, or business for that matter. But it was rewarding to help guide the AAC through a period of considerable change and turmoil.

In 1972, with the generous help of Jerry Hart (then president of the AAC), who was instrumental in the success of the Soviet-American climbing exchanges, I began communicating with the Soviet Federation of Mountaineering with the aim of mounting an American expedition to the Pamirs in the southwest of the USSR. Our first efforts failed, but in the fall of 1973 the AAC received an invitation to participate in a Soviet mountaineering camp. Pete Schoening and I were reunited in this venture and helped to select a group of outstanding American climbers who set out to climb several major routes and summits in that remote range, as part of an international gathering of outstanding mountaineers from 14 nations. It was an intense, complex, and tragic experience, during which I was nearly killed by the avalanche that took the life of my tentmate, Gary Ullin; and in the course of the summer many other mountaineers were lost. The story of that experience is told in my book, *Storm and Sorrow in the High Pamirs*, published in 1977.

Since 1975 I have been serving as president of the Keystone Center for Continuing Education in Colorado to develop a program of lifelong continuing education. We have programs of environmental education for school-age youths, exchanges of views between leading industrialists and government officials, and high-level meetings in various fields of science. Like the Aspen Institute, the Keystone Center has been intensely exciting and frustrating, for one sees how much could be done if only one could find out how to do it best.

As for climbing, I have always considered myself a devotee of the more whimsical aspects of mountaineering, and I have found little to change my view of the meaning of the sport: organized quixotism that in its lighter moments takes men and women beyond the folly of everyday life, and in its rarest (though not infrequent) moments exposes them to much that is secret and perhaps even sacred. I have been enormously impressed with the style and attitudes of many young climbers and I believe, despite the fussing and fuming of many old climbers, that American mountaineering is in good hands.

Arthur K. Gilkey

[Largely excerpted from the April-May 1961 issue of *The Iowan* magazine.]

After Art Gilkey died, his family received nearly 500 letters, many from eminent geologists who were shocked by the loss of one of the most promising scholars in the field.

Art achieved much in his 27 years. He grew up in Ames, Iowa, where his father headed the Department of Theoretical and Applied Mechanics at Iowa State College. After three years of high school he entered Iowa State but enlisted in the Navy after his freshman year and served 22 months as a radio technician. Vacations were spent in the Tetons or Sierras, and in 1947 after his return to college, he made the sixth official ascent of Devil's Tower in Wyoming. The following summer Art held an assistantship in the Tetons, as he did again in 1949.

Following graduation, Art was offered assistantships at Harvard, Johns Hopkins, and Columbia. He chose Columbia, where he majored in structural geology. In 1950 he was with the Juneau Icefield Project in Alaska and the next summer in an Atomic Energy Commission program in New Mexico. In 1952 he led the American Geographical Society program in the Juneau Icefield. At the time of his departure for K2 he had completed his thesis but had not put it in final form. Columbia University awarded the Ph.D. posthumously and also established a book collection in his memory.

Among many tributes to our lost friend are these: the Gilkey

383

Fund, established by the American Alpine Club to help scientists who are working in mountain areas; the Gilkey Glacier, 16 miles long, named in recognition of his work in Alaska; Cerro Gilkey in the Chilean Andes, named for him by Polish and Argentine climbers, who wrote:

"When we read about the American attempt on K2, we were profoundly impressed by the magnificent spirit that prevailed in that expedition. But what impressed us more, was the great comradeship: the fact that all climbers stood by Arthur Gilkey when his life was in danger, is what inspired us most, for that spirit is one of the most sacred values of mountaineering. Therefore, although we weren't acquainted with Arthur, we felt we had to honor in some way such splendid comradeship. And that's how we came to naming one of the beautiful Patagonian summits with the name of Art Gilkey."

In *Of Men and Marshes*, a book dedicated to Arthur Karr Gilkey, Paul Errington wrote:

"To a man of civilized ethics, manners, and scholarship, yet one who loved wilderness, too.

To a man of self-direction and discipline who loved freedom, too.

To a man of strong friendships who loved solitude, too.

To a man who loved the natural out-of-doors, whether of marshes or of mountains, for itself and for its own values, for its drama of the living and the non-living, and for the peace that it gave him.

To an admirable man and a beloved friend."

We will always miss him.

Charles S. Houston

The events of the first two weeks in August 1953 affected me more deeply than I realized for many years. After we were safely home and the reality of everyday work was faced and the huge task of tidying up unfinished odds and ends was done, I turned back toward my family, much as Bates had urged when he roused me from unconsciousness after our fall on August 10. I gave up climbing almost completely, though I had never been as avid an addict as many; and instead Dorcas and I and the children happily took up less adventurous sports. Despite some excellent "firsts" when I was early in the Alps, my heart had really been in exploring huge unknown mountains and regions — like Nanda Devi in 1936 or K2 in 1938, and of course our first approach to the unvisited south side of Everest in 1950. After these wonderful experiences, where could one go?

For a few years K2 absorbed a lot of time. Lectures, writing, and editing film on top of a busy family practice in a rural area left little time except for the family. Then in 1956, Bob Craig persuaded us to visit Aspen, where Walter Paepcke (a great influence on my life) invited me to work in the Aspen Institute. Though we were settled in Exeter, the lure of Colorado was too great. We moved there in 1957 and spent five happy years in what was then a charming small town in unspoiled mountainous country where we camped and fished and walked extensively.

In 1959 I was called to help rescue a young skier who had become sick far in the mountains, and what I expected to be a simple pneumonia turned out to be a mysterious accumulation of fluid in his lungs. Paul Dudley White, the great cardiologist, was visiting us and I showed him the patient; he felt the problem was due to high altitude, urged that I publish a report and thus started another great change in my life by setting me off on research in high altitude, which I had first tasted 20 years earlier while a flight surgeon in the Navy. That interest was interrupted from 1962 to

385

1965, when Bob Bates and Sargent Shriver persuaded me to take over direction of the Peace Corps in India.

This became one of the richest periods for all of my family. As director for India, my mandate was very large and free. I traveled everywhere, often taking some of my family with me, visiting almost every part of India, Nepal, and even into Afghanistan. Today one tends to forget what a hopeful, shining, and idealistic period that was in world history — the dawn of a new type of internationalism. The Peace Corps Volunteers were an inspiring group; the Washington bureaucracy, not yet stale, was equally exciting.

But like so many others, the dream died during the terrible Vietnam years and the disillusion of the late sixties generation. We were all torn between loyalty to leadership and growing doubts. The worldwide doctor Peace Corps program that Shriver asked me to develop in Washington was stopped by the doctor draft for Vietnam and we left Washington for Burlington, where I became chairman of the department of Community Medicine at the University of Vermont. Feeling as strongly as I do about the role of medicine in society, it is not surprising that the advent of a new and conservative dean put an end to the intense, active community involvement of the department and my position. We decided to stay on at the University, for I love teaching; during the last six years I have taught environmental health, delivery of health care, and clinical medicine, and it has been most rewarding. For a hectic six months I served on the Governor's Commission that wrote Vermont's environmental legislation — a fascinating and worthwhile experience.

In fall 1966 Walter Wood, a pioneer in the St. Elias Mountains in the Yukon Territory, invited me to help develop a physiological research program to add to the earth science research conducted for several years by the Arctic Institute. After some preliminary years I became director of the High Altitude Physiology Study, now (as of 1979) in its eleventh year. So successful and productive has this Canadian-American multi-university program become that much of my time and energy goes to altitude research, and more relevantly, perhaps, to comparisons between mountain sickness and the problems that affect people whose illness causes lack of oxygen at sea level. I have written many papers and am still working on a book about high altitude, an interest that has taken me to the USSR, Britain, and Mongolia, as well as each summer to Mt. Logan in the Yukon Territory.

What the reunion did for me was to focus my mind on the events of August 1953, clarifying many details that had been obscured by my concussion or perhaps because of my terrible sense of failure concerning our effort and the death of our friend. At our reunion I recognized the reality of what I had often said, without being sure I really meant it: ours was an immensely successful effort, not only because we survived, but more because we grew together, because we gained affection and respect for the great mountains and for one another, and perhaps most of all, because we were able to share these feelings with so many people. Since then I have shown the K2 slides many hundred times to groups ranging from 20 to 2,000 persons, always with a lump in my throat when I describe the first two weeks of August 1953. People seem to hear without being told what a tremendous feeling for each other and for mountains we developed.

Undoubtedly I was disappointed when the Italians climbed the mountain in 1954, along our route, because I already had permission to return in 1955. It was nonetheless a thrill to be invited to welcome Ardito Desio and his successful team back to Genoa in October 1954, and to give a brief speech to some 50,000 persons! To my astonishment I was presented with the red, white, and blue umbrella I had abandoned at 22,000 feet. It had been given to our team when we left New York, and it was a joy to bring it to our reunion.

The impact of our expedition on me was immense and prolonged. I remember thinking during the long march out, "After this, nothing will ever bother me again." Alas, this has been far from true, but K2 1953, and our gathering 25 years later, has changed my life, I hope for the better.

Dee Molenaar

For days after our 25th anniversary reunion I continued to feel a contemplative afterglow. To be together again after so many years was an experience of the spirit probably enjoyed by few adventurers who have shared a common struggle.

Upon my return from K2 to my job as civilian advisor in the Army's Mountain and Cold Weather training Command at Camp Carson, Colorado, I found that my frostbitten toes and heels made it impossible for me to resume my work, and I resigned a short time later. In early 1954 I joined the Phillips Petroleum Company's Exploration Division and spent that summer at Katalla in Southeast Alaska, mapping geologic structures in the mountains between Cordova and Yakutat.

At Katalla I learned of the success of the Italian party on K2. Although I felt that I would never have another crack at the mountain, I felt especially sorry for Charlie Houston, who was anxious to try again. However, I was glad that if Americans hadn't made the top first, an Italian party had, for they too had spent much time exploring the peak.

Following the summer's field work in Alaska, I married Colleen Haag of Portland, Oregon. Our honeymoon — the drive back to the Phillips office in Grand Junction, Colorado — was the beginning of a happy partnership and in less than a year we were back in the Northwest, where I had been offered a job with the Washington State Division of Water Resources in Olympia. We designed and built our first home near Olympia, and in the next four years Karen, Peter, and David came along to join Erin, my daughter by a previous marriage.

In 1966 I accepted a job with the U.S. Geological Survey's Water Resources Division in Tacoma. There I served as district reports specialist and also continued to make studies of the geology and groundwater resources of various parts of the state.

Living near Mt. Rainier again provided an opportunity for me to resume ascents of the peak with climbers of a younger generation, doing new routes both winter and summer. I also continued my private project of documenting the climbing history of this Northwest landmark, which led in 1971 to my first book, *The Challenge of Rainier.* The book is now going into its third edition with updating of the peak's climbing history.

In March 1965 I joined with the late Senator Robert F. Kennedy and several others in the first ascent of 13,900-foot Mt. Kennedy in the Yukon Territory, and also climbed nearby 15,300-foot Mt. Hubbard as part of the mapping survey planned for later in the spring. Since then my climbing has been mainly in Washington, plus a few trips to the Canadian Rockies and in 1973 a journey to the Alps in fulfillment of a long-held dream to do some of the classic ascents.

During many of my climbing trips I have carried a small box of watercolors, and my work has gradually been accepted in prestigious Northwest exhibits. I have also done many sketches and maps for tourist and climbers' guidebooks and artwork for exhibits of the U.S. Forest Service and National Park Service. Since 1965 I have become involved at home in producing and publishing a number of large pictorial landform maps of various mountain areas of the Northwest.

My love of the mountains comes from several sources, including the satisfaction of physical activity in the outdoors (enjoyment of simply "putting one foot above another") and studying — from a high point or from a plane — the geologic makeup of the peaks and valleys and interpreting these experiences through writing and painting. Also, there is the rewarding companionship of mountain friends; as one grows older he enjoys even more the get-togethers with those with whom he has shared a rope on a glacier or rock face. At age 60 I still enjoy climbing on Mt. Rainier, or working on a painting or map in my studio. To paraphrase John Muir, whether in the mountains or thinking mountains, I'm "at home." Doubtless, K2 was the high point in my mountaineering life, and memories of the climb — and the close friendships resulting from it — have continued to "charge my batteries" in the years since.

Pete Schoening

Upon returning from K2, I married Mary Lou Deuter and we have three sons and three daughters. In 1960, I left a job with American Marietta Company and took over Chemical Proof Company near Seattle, a specialty firm that makes industrial fiberglass fabrications and products.

For several years I taught mountaineering at the University of Washington, and I have taken part in many search and rescue operations. In 1958, Nick Clinch invited me to lead an attempt on Gasherbrum I (Hidden Peak), 26,470 feet, located in the Karakoram Range. Andy Kauffman and I made the summit — the first time Americans had reached the top of an 8,000-meter peak and the only American oct-thousander first ascent. As on K2, the party was strong and congenial and we had a happy time together. I had a chance then to revisit our base camp near K2 and the cairn built in memory of Art Gilkey and enlarged in memory of Mario Puchoz.

In 1967 I managed to get away, again with Nick Clinch, to the Sentinel Range of Antarctica, where our team made first ascents of five peaks, including 16,800-foot Mt. Vinson, highest in the continent. Many logistic and political problems had to be solved.

Afterward I stayed close to North American peaks until 1974, when the American Alpine Club invited me to lead a group of American climbers to join the Soviet International Mountaineering Camp in the Pamirs. This remote and magnificent range had been off-limits to Americans. A tragic succession of earthquakes, hot weather, and heavy snow brought death to one of our party, Gary Ullin, and almost killed several others, including Bob Craig. Our group did make a first ascent on the north face of Peak 19, and we reached the top of Peak Lenin by two different routes. Further we started a continuing mountaineering exchange with Soviet climbers.

Mountains are a very important part of my life, and I especially enjoy being with young people. Our house on the shore of Lake Washington is a frequent gathering point and I manage to get away climbing or skiing as often as possible. The company takes an unfortunate amount of time and energy, but I like the work and enjoy forging bonds between our people's capabilities and our customers, much as one does on a really good expedition.

Tony Streather

I have never really considered myself a dedicated mountaineer but mountaineering is one of my hobbies, and through an accident of circumstances it has had a considerable influence on my life. I like instead to think of myself as a mountain traveler, and it is the mountainous areas and the people who live there that hold more interest for me than the actual climbing.

The accident of circumstances was the last World War, which had me joining the Indian Army straight from school and then serving among the mountains in the North of India and later in Pakistan. Our duties took us daily through the mountains and often over snow-covered passes, but we did not think of this as mountaineering.

It was while serving as the last British Officer north of the passes in Chitral in 1950 that I was invited by the Norwegians to join their expedition to Tirich Mir, one of the first peaks of over 25,000 feet to be attempted since the war, when major expeditions had not been possible. I was to help look after their porters and make general good use of my local knowledge. The first attempt at the summit failed as one of the team had to be evacuated from high on the mountain with what was thought to be pneumonia, but which today would be recognized as pulmonary edema. This gave me my break, and I went to the summit in the second attempt.

Looking back, we were lucky to get away with it. The Norwegians were fine climbers, but our equipment was basic by today's standards and our knowledge of high-altitude mountaineering was scanty.

When I returned to the United Kingdom some months later, after six years of service out East, I was very surprised to find that I was something of a name in mountaineering circles and was the only British climber to have reached the summit of a major peak since before the war. I was even considered for possible membership on the British team that was to attempt Everest in 1953 but was rejected through lack of technical climbing experience — one mountain was hardly enough. I was, however, elected to the elite Alpine Club.

Within days of hearing that I had not been selected for Everest, I received my second mountaineering break: a letter from a Doctor Houston in the United States inviting me to join a team he was leading to attempt the world's second highest mountain, K2. He had had the confidence to invite me before we had even met, and I had no hesitation in accepting. Little did I know what impact this acceptance would have on my future life. It was to be the start of many expeditions to the highest mountains in the world, but more important, it was to lead to a close-knit team who would remain a band of brothers for years to come.

What if the weather had been kind to us? Would our small, skilled, and extremely fit team have reached the summit during the same year that Everest was first climbed? We can but speculate, but one thing is certain: none of us would have returned from the mountain had we not been such a close team.

After K2 came the invitation to join the British team to attempt Kangchenjunga in 1955. This time we were successful: the weather was kind to us. Under the unassuming but brilliant leadership of Doctor Charles Evans, four of us reached a point only a few easy feet below the summit. Out of respect for the people of Sikkim, who believe their gods live there, the summit was left untrodden. We had gone to the mountain as a reconnaissance party, had found a route, and had pushed it through to the summit. The mountain wasn't to be climbed again for more than 20 years.

I will always count myself lucky to have been privileged to be a member of those two expeditions. There has been nothing like them since.

Two years after Kangchenjunga came the invitation to lead the Oxford University team to Haramosh. Here was an opportunity to return to the part of the world that had always fascinated me, and once I had met the likable team of young enthusiasts, I needed little persuading. I could never have guessed what trials and tragedy were to follow. I still often ask myself whether the accident was just bad luck or whether there was more we could have done to prevent it. That story has been told in *The Last Blue Mountain.*

Soon after this the Army Mountaineering Association was formed and by 1959 they were ready to send their first party to the Himalayas or the Karakoram. I was asked for advice about possible goals and said quite firmly that I did not believe they should attempt a really high mountain but rather should establish a base camp from which many peaks of about 20,000 feet would be readily accessible. Small parties would then have far more opportunity for climbing than they would packing loads to establish high camps on a single high peak. This idea met with approval and I was asked to lead.

I was reluctant to do this so soon after the Haramosh accident and I wasn't too sure that my frostbite was fully recovered, but it seemed that I was then the only serving soldier with knowledge of the area so I was persuaded to go. Anyway, it would give me a chance to make sure I hadn't lost my nerve on Haramosh. We had a grand expedition, visited a lot of new passes, and climbed numerous peaks on the flanks of the Hispar Glacier. Some of the team were to go on to greater things in later years.

I had now had my fill of the high mountain regions and besides, expeditions there were becoming impossibly costly and complicated. The pioneering days were rapidly coming to an end and the great national enterprises were taking over.

Next followed a period as chief instructor at the Army Outward Bound School and the satisfaction of being able to pass on experience and knowledge of the mountains to the young. This interest in introducing the young to the thrills of exploration has continued and has included expeditions to Greenland, Greece, and the mountains of Kenya and Ethiopia. Now, 25 years after Everest was first climbed, I shall have a last look at the mountain when I take a party of young people to Base Camp this year.

Unexpectedly, I saw all too much of the mountain in 1976. Just as an accident of circumstances had sent me to my first great mountain 25 years previously, so another, this time tragic, sent me as leader of the Army Mountaineering Association Expedition to Everest in 1976. The previous year four of the Army's leading climbers had been killed in the Himalayas and they were now short of experience for their long-planned attempt on Everest. I was asked if I would get my boots out just once more, and it was made clear that if I did not go the expedition would probably founder. Seventeen years had passed since I had been to the Himalayas and I would be 50 by the time we reached Base Camp, but my long-suffering wife gave her support yet again and the children were keen that I should go. It was their "you're not *that* old, Daddy," that finally persuaded me! As I completed my trio of expeditions to the world's three highest mountains, I was able to play my part in the team that put the first soldiers on the summit of Everest.

What of the future? Our expedition to Everest was organized on conventional lines with plenty of backup at all the camps and a route made as safe as possible with ladders and fixed ropes. It was only this that enabled us to get the summit pair safely off the mountain after they had been forced by bad weather to bivouac at around 28,000 feet. But this type of expedition requires manpower and money, which is no longer readily available.

We are sure to be forced to have smaller parties and attempt to climb the highest peaks by so-called alpine methods. There will then be no backup if things go wrong and more loss of life is inevitable. But the real danger is the increasing tendency to look for gimmicks in order to attract publicity and sponsorship.

Sadly the days of genuine mountain exploration are over, but perhaps now we can enjoy once again just walking in the mountains.

Camp VIII, 25,200 feet
August 5, 1953

Dee Molenaar had a small box of watercolors with him on K2 and
painted scenes during the climb. Besides lassitude, his only problem was having ice instead of water come off the brush when he
painted outside the tent. Dee recalls painting this scene during the
storm at Camp VIII while sitting up inside his sleeping bag with
the wind slapping the tent against his head and shoulders. His
tentmate Bob Craig also tried a small painting, but Dee says he
still holds the record for high-altitude artistic endeavor because he
was on the high side of the tent.

Have you seen these books from The Mountaineers?

Storm and Sorrow in the High Pamirs. Robert W. Craig describes a tragic summer where climbing, the primary objective, became secondary to survival.

The Challenge of Rainier. Dee Molenaar documents every significant event in the climbing history of Mt. Rainier. Sketches by the author and more than a hundred photos give the climber's perspective.

Challenge of the North Cascades. Fred Beckey chronicles three decades of adventures among these rugged peaks, including numerous first ascents. Photos, maps, and a list of more than 500 ascents by the author.

Mountains of the World. Handy, compact guide to climbing routes on every continent, on islands large and small, in regions seldom thought of as even having mountains, let alone climbing.

The Ascent of Denali. Original account of the first complete climb of Mt. McKinley together with the previously unpublished diary of Walter Harper, the first man to stand on the highest point in North America.

The Unknown Mountain. Discovery and exploration of Mt. Waddington, the "Mystery Mountain" that turned out to be the highest peak in Canada's Coast Range.

Tales of a Western Mountaineer. Fascinating first-hand accounts of early climbs on Mt. Adams, Rainier, Baker, Glacier Peak, Hood, Stuart, and Shasta, combined with recently uncovered details of the author's eventful career.

The Mountaineers, 719 Pike Street, Seattle, Washington 98101